MORE PRAISE FOR *FAMILY WARS*

"One of the most interesting and unusual books on family businesses I have ever read... profound, rich and reflective."

Konstantin von Unger, fifth generation family member and member of the Supervisory Board of the Henkel Group

"Lessons of failure can be as instructive as lessons of success. Devoted business-owning families study both. Two long-committed students of family business have collaborated on this interesting and valuable book."

John L Ward, Principal, The Family Business Consulting Group, Intl and Clinical Professor of Family Enterprises, Kellogg School of Management

"Where would insurance, engineering and aviation be without the thorough examination of disasters? Where would medicine be without the postmortem analysis of pathology? Grant Gordon and Nigel Nicholson have made a tremendous contribution to our understanding of family dysfunction and conflict. Family Wars is conceptually thorough with many real-world case examples from which the authors draw important practical lessons. The book is essential reading for anyone interested in both the discontinuity and continuity of family enterprise."

Ivan Lansberg, PhD, Senior Partner, Lansberg, Gersick & Associates

D0217602

FAMILY WARS

STORIES AND INSIGHTS FROM
FAMOUS FAMILY BUSINESS FEUDS

GRANT GORDON & NIGEL NICHOLSON

LONDON PHILADELPHIA NEW DELHI

Publisher's note
Every possible effort has been made to ensure that the information contained in this book is accurate at the time of going to press, and the publishers and authors cannot accept responsibility for any errors or omissions, however caused. No responsibility for loss or damage occasioned to any person acting, or refraining from action, as a result of the material in this publication can be accepted by the editor, the publisher or any of the authors.

First published in Great Britain and the United States in 2008 by Kogan Page Limited
First published in paperback in 2010

120 Pentonville Road	525 South 4th Street, #241	4737/23 Ansari Road
London N1 9JN	Philadelphia PA 19147	Daryaganj
United Kingdom	USA	New Delhi 110002
www.koganpage.com		India

© Grant Gordon and Nigel Nicholson, 2008

The right of Grant Gordon and Nigel Nicholson to be identified as the authors of this work has been asserted by them in accordance with the Copyright, Designs and Patents Act 1988.

ISBN 978 0 7494 6055 6

British Library Cataloguing-in-Publication Data

A CIP record for this book is available from the British Library.

Library of Congress Cataloging-in-Publication Data

Gordon, Grant, 1956-
    Family wars : stories and insights from famous family business feuds / Grant Gordon, Nigel Nicholson.
        p. cm.
    Originally published in 2008 as: Family wars : classic conflicts in family business and how to deal with them.
    Includes bibliographical references and index.
    ISBN 978-0-7494-6055-6
    1. Family-owned business enterprises--Management. 2. Family-owned business enterprises--Succession. 3. Family-owned business enterprises--Case studies. I. Nicholson, Nigel. II. Title.
    HD62.25.G67 2010
    658.4'053--dc22
                                    2009045671

Typeset by Saxon Graphics Ltd, Derby
Printed and bound in India by Replika Press Pvt Ltd

To our families

Contents

List of figures

Acknowledgements

We would like to thank the people who have helped us at various points in the preparation of this book. Katrina Collinson helped us in the early stages of the case study research, and subsequently Akhila Venkitachalam was invaluable in helping to locate, assemble and integrate the large mass of information that has gone into the recounting of these stories. We also have very much appreciated Mark Skeen's research, especially to generate the genograms and check the accuracy of our data. We would also like to thank our publishers Kogan Page, first in the person of Pauline Goodwin as the first enthusiast and committed supporter of this project, and subsequently Helen Kogan for her encouragement, advice, and energy in helping bring this to fruition.

We would like to express our appreciation of our long-suffering assistants, Sharan Sandhu and Yvonne Szuca, for helping make sure the book did not turn our diaries upside down. Profound gratitude is owed to our wives, Brigitte and Adèle, and our children, for tolerating our endless phone conversations, general absorption and absent-mindedness, and occasional abuse of weekends and evenings during the periods of maximum flow during this project.

Finally, we want to thank all the inspiring families in business we have met and worked with through the Institute for Family Business and the London Business School. It is their learning and wisdom that have made this book possible.

Grant Gordon
Nigel Nicholson

1

Family wars

The chief executive officer (CEO), James, is speaking. 'I've been thinking. Are we being too loyal to Smiths [a main supplier of the family business's raw materials]? I was at a lunch the other day where I met an old college pal who told me we could source at maybe 15 per cent better terms from overseas.'

The chief financial officer (CFO), Susan, replies. 'Really James, you do talk rubbish sometimes. You spend too much time listening to gossip at these boozy lunches you have with your buddies. Smiths have been our partners for three generations, and you want to think about dumping them for some here-today-gone-tomorrow outfit who are operating in a place where we have no influence.'

'I'm doing your job for you Susan. You spend too much time in the past. You should get out more!'

The marketing director, David, intervenes. 'Stop squabbling. Let's be rational about this. We owe Smiths a lot for their partnership with us, so if we think they're becoming uncompetitive we should talk to them as friends. You agree?'

Susan and James smile broadly. 'Agreed' they say, almost simultaneously.

Several things are striking about this interaction. One is the informality. Second, the emotions are somewhat raw in these exchanges – downright rude, one might say. Third, quite big decisions are being considered that can be made quite speedily by this small group. Fourth, at the centre of their deliberations lie matters of loyalty and responsibility in their stakeholder relations. Fifth, even though the air crackles with sharp feeling, they are remarkably able to recover quickly without rancour to a good-natured consensus. Oh yes, and a sixth point – you have a woman in a senior executive position, and quite unabashed by the idea of challenging her boss in forthright terms.

Is this just a fantasy? No, it's just another day in the boardroom of an ordinary family firm. For James, Susan and David are cousins with executive roles in the 80-year-old business of two families.

Is this kind of scene unusual, and what does it tell us about family firms, or any kind of firms for that matter? Does this scene stand as evidence of a profound weakness or a unique strength of family business? The answer to the first question is no, it is not unusual, and yes, family firms do have an edge of danger and a promise of performance. For the fact is that family firms have the capacity to outperform non-family comparators, but at the same time they are at risk to family hazards that can overspill and engulf them.

Why should people outside the secretive world of family business care about them? For three reasons. One is that family businesses are the backbone of the economy of just about every country on earth, and the wealth of nations depends on them.[1] The second is that many – most even – of the major corporations on the planet had family business origins. Third, understanding family businesses can unlock one of the greatest and most elusive challenges in the business world – what it takes to make a large company feel like a small one, or more precisely, what the secret is to building a truly admirable culture. Non-family businesses have a lot to learn from family firms, because all organizations retain elements of 'familiness' in every layer of their operations, and capitalizing on their better qualities, while avoiding the worst, can be the key to building competitive advantage through culture.

Here's some of the evidence:

- A recent study of S&P 500 firms found those with family ownership outperformed those without it. Other studies in European research have confirmed the trend.[2]
- Some of the world's oldest companies are those that have stayed in family ownership. They include a 40th-generation Japanese business that repairs temples (founded 578), an Italian vintner (founded 1141), and a French paper maker (founded 1326). There is a big clutch of businesses in the New and Old World that have

survived intact the entire 20th century and that are still turning in world-beating performances in the 21st century.[3]

- Many of the world's largest and most successful companies retain a strong family identity: Cargill in the United States, Samsung in Korea, LVMH in France, BMW in Germany, Clarks Shoes in the United Kingdom, H&M in Sweden and so on.

So why should we write a book about family wars? Because family businesses have a dark side that time and again erupts onto the business pages – often the front pages – of our newspapers.[4] The world of family business has much to learn through such cases as we document here. We could have written about stories of greatness – a book about firms holding a steady course, as they sail the seas of their markets, avoiding the storms and reefs. But as the history of art, science and politics tells us, there is more to be learnt from failure than success. Frankly, it is also more interesting. We could also have written a recipe book for good governance and best practice. There are plenty of these already on the shelves of business bookstores.[5] Few books systematically explore the nature of conflict, its origins and conditions, hence the journey we have taken in this book. We believe a number of important new insights as well as familiar truths can come from our dissection of family wars.

Yet we also wish to avoid compounding the error, fostered by movies and soap operas in the Dallas-Dynasty mould – that family firms are in the main seething hotbeds of melodrama. Let us clear the air on this point.

First, yes, it is true that the elements that make family businesses spontaneous, informal and passionate can easily tip over into something much more unpleasant and chaotic. Feistiness turns into fearfulness. Love turns into possession. The family dynamic is a potent force – it needs control and constraint to achieve its best, and those controls have to come from within the hearts and minds of the members.

Second, we all need help in self-control, and there are good and bad ways of organizing a family business and making decisions. These can be lumped together under the heading of 'governance', but it is more than that – it is about patterns of communication and interaction that drive decision making, and the systems and processes that people submit to.

Third, warfare is not unique to family firms. Any business can dissolve into conflict if free play is given to the dark side of human motives and wants. Enron fostered a tooth-and-claw culture, to the point where it fell apart in a mêlée of acrimony and wrongdoing. Many a merger or acquisition is marred by warfare, and there is systematic guerrilla fighting going on in the undergrowth of many widely owned public companies.

A lot of the observations we shall be making here could apply to non-family firms. For example, battles for succession are not unique to family businesses – it is common for there to be protracted and painful leadership battles over favoured 'sons' in many corporations, and sibling-like squabbles between wannabe leaders infect many a boardroom.

But our primary focus is on family firms, and this book is for the people who run them, are born into them, advise them, and for the legions who just find them important and fascinating. For so they are. We are not just going to dig up the historical facts in the cases we set out before you, but to try to unravel the barbed wire that binds them and identify the poisoned wells from which their protagonists are drinking.

In the next chapter we shall set the frame for the real-life stories that we shall be telling about family firms, exploring the causes in general, and the frameworks that can help us to understand and analyse them. The remainder of this book comprises the compelling dramas of family wars from around the world of business. One can enjoy the *schadenfreude* (a wonderful German word meaning pleasure in another's misfortune) of these tales, but we want more than that. We want to diagnose, analyse and prescribe – to point out how things could have turned out differently, for there, but for the grace of fortune, we go also. Many people reading this book we hope will come to understand the symptoms and warnings, and perhaps see how they can play a part in resolving the conflicts they come into contact with in family businesses. Indeed conflict is endemic to human existence. The winners are those who can recognize the warning signs early, deal upfront with the issues and do so in a manner that the parties affected consider to be fair. Our hope and intent is that this analysis of family wars will help more firms and their owners find peaceful paths to success.

2

The ideas: The roots of family warfare

> The most successful executives are often men who have built their own companies. Ironically their very success frequently brings to them and members of their families personal problems of an intensity rarely encountered by professional managers. And these problems make family businesses probably the most difficult to operate.
>
> (Harry Levinson)

To get to the bottom of any particular instance of family warfare and extract lessons in search of peace and wisdom, we need a broad array of tools. These are ideas that we can draw on to understand the underlying dynamic and infer how conflict could have been avoided or neutralized. In this chapter we shall outline ideas under five headings:

1. What is the nature of warfare, and how does it come to afflict family firms?
2. How does conflict arise and grow in many of life's situations, and how susceptible are family firms?
3. What has blood got to do with it? What are the special sources of conflict and cohesion in families as a function of how people are related? This is what we shall call 'gene politics'.
4. What are the key dynamics of families, and what impacts do these have when translated into a business environment?

5   How does culture affect the key themes we have identified?
    What role does personality play in the inception and control of
    conflict?

FAMILIES AT WAR

THE NATURE OF WAR

What makes war break out in a family? We need to watch our language
– war is a strong word. But feelings run high enough in families to
merit it. The causes of war in society can be readily listed:[1]

- One group invades another for spoils – space, resources.
- One group seeks to subordinate another politically and
  economically.
- A dispute between parties escalates in a tit-for-tat vicious cycle of
  attack and retaliation.
- A bystander group becomes drawn into an ongoing conflict
  as a third party by virtue of its alliance with one of the main
  protagonists.

Sure enough all these things happen in family wars. Siblings try
to outmanoeuvre each other. Sons fight fathers to seize the crown.
One family branch engages in a turf war to control or marginalize
another. Differences of opinion about an aspect of running the business escalate into major schism. Complex triangular situations arise
when family members become drawn into family conflagrations not
of their making.

In wars many of these elements occur simultaneously. Moreover,
the origins of a conflict do not always foretell its later development –
look at the First World War. An obscure assassination in the steamy
cauldron of Balkans politics drew the great powers into a war of
unimagined severity, extended duration and lasting consequences.
The wasteful scything down of a generation would not have happened
had not the great powers been in a state of armed readiness, nursing
resentments and territorial ambitions. In family wars we also see
tragedies on an epic scale – where a once-mighty business empire
is reduced to rubble through successive failures to arrest the causes,
block the triggers and get off the escalator. Several of the stories we

shall be telling in this book have this character. Once ignited the spark of conflict turns into conflagration, and cool reflection is overtaken by heated confrontation.

FAMILY WARS

Of course in family wars the big difference from 'real' wars is the presence of emotion. It is not that emotion is absent in political and economic conflicts, rather that they use emotions as a tool of manipulation – it is the mood music played to mobilize public opinion and stiffen the resolve of combatants. Raw emotion is rarely a prime cause of warfare in the modern era, though it continues to motivate many sectarian disputes. It was different in former times when the battles of princes and barons were genuinely 'personal'. They not only resembled family wars – they *were* family wars.[2] They were dynasties vying for succession and family branches seeking to promote their interests through conflict, steered by feeling as much as cool reason.[3] For when families fall into conflict, feelings fuel it at all its stages and in all its forms. We shall see several instances of these hot-blooded conflicts, especially among families where close relatives are locked together inside the walls of the family and their business.

Some family wars are cold-blooded and mercenary. These are typically fought out by families at a mature state of development where the relatives may be distantly related. Armies of lawyers acting for dispersed family interests have the effect of amplifying and sustaining the conflict. We shall see a few cases where this becomes the final act of a family drama, but most of the stories we shall be telling are more akin to bare-knuckle fights between protagonists, split asunder by the family feelings and emotions that should in normal circumstances be drawing them together.

THE TWO FACES OF FAMILY BUSINESS

So what is it about families that cooks up such a bewildering bubbling cauldron of emotions? Family-firm scholars are divided into two broad camps. In one are those who extol the virtues of the family business model as an engine that creates wealth and well-being. In the other are those who see hazards and liabilities when bloodlines run businesses.

Let us briefly consider the two arguments. The pro-camp claims that 'familiness' is a tangible resource that can be a unique and inimitable source of competitive advantage to a business.[4] At its core are the love, commitment, trust and confidence of people who know each other intimately – almost telepathically sometimes. It is what makes people go the extra mile for each other, and enables them to voice problems and solve them with great directness. It is the capacity of positive relationships to flow around the family and beyond, streaming outward to embrace all the major stakeholders, creating a special sense of solidarity and community.[5] It is the unique quirks of character embodied in the family leaders that enable them to give the firm a distinctive cultural feel. It is the vision of the intermingling of bloodline and business that makes people able to take a long-term multigenerational view of the firm, not just as a bundle of assets but as a heritage and a legacy. There is plentiful evidence, both anecdotal and academic, that family firms can outperform their non-family counterparts at all points of the spectrum, from the small or newly formed to the mature privately owned or publicly listed business.[6]

But there is also plentiful evidence of family failure, where incompetent leaders and bad judgment rule. For on the other face of the Janus double profile of familiness is the ever-present risk of negative spillover from the personal sphere into the public and professional.[7] Here one finds the risks of family members making bad decisions guided by sentiment rather than reason, or just devoid of the skills that are required to carry out the job successfully.[8] Here is the everpresent hazard of family members paying more attention to their personal interests and needs than to those of the business. Here lies the danger of bad appointments made on the basis of blood and family connections rather than competence – in a word, nepotism.[9] Ever present is the danger of jealousies and animosities poisoning the well from which everyone draws their water. And time after time one sees the tragi-comic road crash of mismanaged succession. This is where family firms act out truly Shakespearean battles – King Lears who won't let go, Richard the Thirds who try to choke off bloodline that threatens them, Prince Hamlets who boil with suspicious resentment at a senior relative taking power, and in many, many places, jealous princes fighting for the crown.

Which side are we on – the optimists or the pessimists? You might think that the contents of this book would put us firmly in the negative camp, but that is not the case. On the contrary we believe strongly in the positive magic of family firms, but recognize that this comes at a price of increased vulnerability. Family firms have to be smarter and more alert than other kinds of firm to regulate the flow of positive emotional energy and avoid the dark side. They need to practise constant vigilance to manage the risks that are germane to this form of business. Indeed, we have written this book precisely because we can see how quite simple measures and good risk management would have saved many of the great firms we are looking at here from the anguish that awaited them.

ANALYSING FAMILIES

The classic novels and dramas of world literature contain depictions of the dynamics of family life that encompass just about every danger and pitfall one can imagine. The Bible is not short of stories in this vein. Given the diversity of family sagas we might wonder what could possibly be added to these stories. But there is more to family wars than mere storytelling. There is a science of family relations.[10] We shall not trouble readers with any lengthy and tedious theorizing – and for sure there is a lot of that about! But in order to see the patterns, extract a deeper understanding and derive lessons, it will help to have a toolkit of ideas and concepts about the key principles and processes that underlie family conflicts. These we shall set out in the remainder of this chapter.

Our aim is not only to provide a means for unpicking the origins of conflict, but also to point the way to resolving family wars. A key idea underlying this book is that wars are not so much problems to be solved as risks to be prevented. The aftermath of war is a sad business of cleaning up, swallowing regrets, and trying to build new aspirations on a firm footing. It is much better to have sound policies, principles and practices that make war unlikely. This can be mundane and somewhat unrewarding labour. It is a shame that in life we scarcely take time out to celebrate our successes in avoiding trouble in life – the accidents we didn't have and the quarrels we avoided. Prudence is an undervalued virtue, as is boring reliability and the absence of strife. Here we celebrate these qualities, and seek to help organizations enjoy them. As we shall show, actually we are in favour of some sorts of conflict. There are some varieties of opposition and conflict that are engines of creativity and change.[11] But creative tension is a tricky tightrope to walk, and as often as not in family wars it passes a tipping point, leaving commentators like us to sift through the trail of destruction and learn the lessons.

THE ROOTS OF CONFLICT

There are two aspects to conflict: issues of content and issues of process, which are, respectively, what a conflict is about, and how it is created. These two dimensions are often intertwined, but it is useful to separate them – to ask what any conflict is really about.

THE INGREDIENTS OF CONFLICT

Content issues are basically people wanting incompatible things, or people competing for the same thing – that is, where one person's loss is another's gain. Most of the time we don't come into conflict because we are able to accept trade-offs, find alternatives, and do side deals that keep us safe and happy enough. But this depends on what actually is the bone of contention. What interests are at stake?[12] Matters of materiality are the most easily resolved. Money and resources can be replenished. Many family firms buy their way out of conflict – paying off dissenters and malcontents, separating the financial interests of warring relatives. But it is much less easy to avoid conflicts around matters of ethics, values and principle. People will go to extraordinary and irrational lengths to pursue what they believe is right. They will go even further where this is tied in with relationships – with personal attachment, envy, desire and self-esteem. Conflicts over love, loyalty, the threat of personal loss have a capacity to keep returning to the same emotional source to recharge their animosity. This is a chief source of family firms' vulnerability – the liability of any conflict to become bound in with the personal.

CONFLICT IS PERSONAL

From a psychological perspective, at the root of the most poison-ous conflicts is **identity** – the idea that one is being diminished or damaged; that one is wounded or threatened in some essential way.[13] We rarely recognize the degree to which this is a central part of the problem. But think about it. A conflict over money can be resolved by simple compromise or resigned acceptance if 'it's just money'. But emotion heats up when the resources somehow symbolize a person's intrinsic worth. In families, money often represents all kinds of psychological elements, and most powerfully when it stands for how much one is valued or loved. Personal identity and self-esteem are involved in all close relationships – the more so the closer the relationship.[14] It is especially hard to be philosophical about relation-ship problems when they seem to reflect on how we are perceived by others, or how we see ourselves. Just as the loss of a loved one feels like we have lost part of ourselves, so does conflict with a loved one seem to tear apart our sense of ourselves. That's the nature of human attachment. Family wars generate a lot of their heat from the heavy interlacing of ethics, emotions and identity at all levels. In several of our cases, including for example Koch Industries (Chapter 3), child-hood animosities reverberate over the years into the adult world.

CONFLICT AS PROCESS

The **process** of conflict is the doing of it. One of the simplest ways of igniting conflict is to set up incompatible goals for people and then force them to share the resources necessary for achieving them. Think of a football game – two different goals, one at each end, and just one ball for the two sides to share. Now think of families. They fit the model – family members have different goals and a shared resource base. Conflict is avoided in families by resource allocation that sepa-rates interests, but some resources are less easily divided than others.[15] Think of love and attention, for a start. Generally speaking conflict within the family decreases the more independent and self-resourcing individuals become.

Family businesses add a twist to this. They keep orienting people to the same central pool of resources, and the business binds them into shared fate longer than they would have done without it. Interdependence tends to persist, even through to mature adulthood. Some family firms seek to avoid the problem by spinning off business divisions for family members to run – a common device in the extended families of South Asian firms.[16] However, this creates separation. Contested claims can persist, along with deeper sources of enmity. A classic case we recount is the story of Reliance, the mighty Indian corporation, where the empire was split down the middle after the founding father died intestate (without a will) leaving his warring sons battling fruitlessly for supremacy. Eventually a resource separation was reached that has led to continuing business success, but only after a lot of bad blood.

CONFLICT AS RELATIONSHIP

People often think that the most pernicious source of conflict is 'personality'. Personality certainly is a key element, but it is more a condition than a cause.[17] It often adds more colour than heat to a dispute, as we shall see. But the real killer is trust – or lack of it. Extreme incompatibilities of personality can make it more difficult to get on the same wavelength, but we don't always mistrust people we know we are different from in character. Lack of trust comes from whatever leads one person to see another as unreliable, inconsistent, devious or duplicitous.[18] Any of us can appear like this to anyone else. It all depends on actions and attributions. Think of the last time someone mistrusted you and how it felt. When others attribute untrustworthiness to us we are upset, and protest that they have misread our actions or intentions.

Generally we have excellent explanations for our own behaviour, though they may look like excuses to someone else. With a little conversation, more often than not we will forgive and be forgiven when there has been a breakdown of relations. If it happens more than once we may find that we are indulged as eccentric or even difficult, or that we've earned a reputation for unreliability or inconsistency. But none of these judgments is sufficient to trigger full-blown warfare in everyday life, unless there is an attribution of malice – that is, we stand accused of being deliberately difficult. From here it is a short step to engaging in character assassination, tit-for-tat aggression and stirring up general mayhem.[19]

It seems unnatural that this kind of behaviour should erupt so frequently in families, but it does. You'd think people knew each other well enough to forgive and forget. Where does this negative energy come from? More often than not it is based upon assumptions about another's intentions – that they bear us malice. One of the most spectacular examples in family business is to be found in the Gucci saga (Chapter 8), where the entrepreneurial instincts of the second-generation leader Aldo were met with suspicion and then hostility by his youngest brother Rodolfo.

FAIRNESS AND CHEATING

In our regular day-to-day interactions we mostly have no reason to expect others wish to do us harm. Compete, yes. The car that cuts us up at a busy intersection is competing for precedence, not trying to harm us. Road rage comes less from the assumption of malice, since the other driver is a complete stranger, than the perception of **unfairness** and cheating.[20] This is one of the most persistent causes of conflict. People will go to extraordinary lengths to restore equity after someone has created an 'unfair' imbalance. Social scientists draw an important distinction between what they call 'distributive' and 'procedural' justice; that is, between the perceived inequality of shares in some valued commodity, and the perceived fairness of the procedure by which the shares are allocated.[21] People are often enraged more and for longer by the latter than the former: that is, a distribution of resources that has been arrived at by means of some unfair procedure is more upsetting than the mere fact of inequality. In business, people will accept wage differentials if they have been arrived at by a legitimate or fair practice, but will fight furiously over a fractional inequality that is seen as unfair or illegitimate.[22]

In family conflicts, the focus is often over inequality – for reasons we shall explore in the next section – but more often than not it is over what is seen as bad faith. The underlying cause of our hot reaction to unfairness is the persistent idea in all our minds that social life is governed by a social compact – that in our communities we should all be subject to the same framework of rules and constraints.[23]

Exceptions enrage us. Road rage is an extreme example. The offence of the driver who steals the parking place we have been waiting for patiently reflects our strong conviction that the other driver should be bound by the same invisible web of conventions that we accept. The person who breaches them to our disadvantage incenses us, sometimes to extreme proportions. Families are like mini-societies – each has its accepted patterns and implicit rules governing conduct.[24] Yet in families the conventions are constantly changing and being rewritten. Typically, the parents set the rules and then revise them under pressure from each other and the children. Parental governance may be contested continually. Some families are constantly at war about rights and obligations – about what is acceptable and what is unacceptable.[25]

INEQUITABLE REWARDS

Some kinds of process conflict tend to recur. One is the **free–rider problem** – one of the most persistent kinds of process conflict in society, combining various aspects we have considered.[26] A typical example is where one member of a group is seen as not 'pulling their weight'. Work teams can disintegrate if this occurs and is not resolved.[27] The cause may be that members have a different idea about what is a valid contribution to group effort. Unless members find a way of achieving a common perspective, the group may well fall apart. In families, a reason for the persistence of open conflict, more than in many other groups, is that the ties that bind are too strong to dissolve under this kind of pressure – so what you often get is malcontent members continually complaining about each other's contribution, until eventually they are able to fly the nest and escape.

Queue jumpers and people who get unearned benefits are varieties of the same problem. In family business this is a recurring issue – the family member who gets financial rewards without making any kind of contribution to the family or firm; the person who is appointed over the heads of more fit candidates; the one who is given a sinecure in the firm because they are family.[28] Again there is the problem of perception. Free-riding can be perpetrated in a knowing and cynical manner, leading to negative perceptions. As the philosopher said: 'If something is perceived as real it is real in its consequences.'[29]

Perception is reality. The accused free-rider may proclaim their innocence, assert their rights under convention or law, and justify their
behaviour by pointing to how undervalued their contributions are. In
families these sensitivities are often acute.[30] Claims and counterclaims
can be traded to the point of extraordinary triviality and bloody-
mindedness. Irritations that 'normal' people would brush aside are
seized upon and escalated to a high level of extravagance.

What drives this, and all the other passion that inflates family
conflicts to such high drama? The answer lies in 'gene politics'.

GENE POLITICS AND THE FAMILY FIRM[31]

'Gene politics' is shorthand for the root logic of conflict and cooperation among kinfolk. The content and the process aspects to conflict
have a common source in families – biological forces that bind and
separate.

THE EVOLVED FAMILY

The deepest underlying force of the family is biological.[32] Families exist
throughout the animal world for a single purpose – to nurture their
young and continue the existence of the bloodline. Charles Darwin
proposed the compelling theory that since has been confirmed and
elaborated by genetics – the genes we carry perpetuate themselves
through benefiting us, their hosts.[33] It is through reproduction that we
pass them on, so they can work their best to help the next generation
and so on. 'Bad' genes are eliminated by destroying their host or their
host's capacity for reproduction. The simple and compelling logic of
this process is what has driven the evolution of all species, including
humans. In the jargon of modern Darwinism it is called 'reproductive
fitness'.[34]

For many species the formula is straightforward. Find a mate
with 'good genes', reproduce and then die – you've done your work.
Generally, the pattern is that males advertise and females choose.
Advertising good genes is achieved by forms of display and signal-
ling – bird song, prowess, preening and other kinds of showiness.[35] In
more sophisticated species – especially the mammals and birds – it

takes more than one party to rear the young and see them (and their genes) safely to maturity. Parental investment is needed.[36] This means a family.

In the case of humans, one of the penalties for walking on two legs is that the pelvis has to be small enough and rotated to a vertical plane for effective striding, running and jumping. At the same time we have big bony heads to protect our precious and prodigious brains. Put these together and you have the necessity of premature child-birth – the human child has to do a lot of its most critical growing outside the womb, in a state of extreme vulnerability and depend-ence. So it follows that the stable structures of family life are needed to sustain this development, and hence the survival of the species. The family is the school for life, in which our children grow, are educated and acquire the skills they will need to survive and reproduce in the human community.

THE SELFISH FAMILY

So within the family the force that binds us together is our shared biological inheritance. We share our genes and hence our destiny. We love our children and seek to advance their interests in a competitive world because they bear our genes, and we carry genes that make us want to support them – a virtuous cycle serving what biologist Richard Dawkins memorably called T*he Selfish Gene.*[37] Our shared genes make us love each other and fight for each other, especially against the competing claims of unrelated people and other families. This is one of the sources of potency in family business – the love, solidarity and determination to support each other and to perpetu-ate the family's existence. This explains the vituperative energy that families can generate to repel hostile outsiders. It also energizes the conflicts that can be roused between family branches that are basi-cally unrelated, except via the one non-genetic link in a family, marriage.

What about adoption? Humans find it easier to adopt non-kin than many other species, and often do so very successfully, if the newcomer accepts and adapts to the host family.[38] Nonetheless, step-relationships are often fragile and fraught with difficulty, as we shall see in several cases here, most notably the Shoens in the U-Haul story (Chapter 8).

THE MARRIAGE BOND

Likewise **marriage**, or any pair bonding between genetically unrelated individuals, is the weakest link and one of the frequent break points in family dynamics.[39] Our biology programmes us to fall in love and desire to make a family, but romantic love sadly doesn't always last forever.[40] With time it is replaced with a more mature bond between couples, sustained by deep affection, shared passions and more besides. But the most compelling tie is our shared stake in our biggest investment, the children. The divorce statistics in the Western world testify that even this is not terribly compelling. Husbands and wives abandon each other much more readily than they abandon their children, or even their siblings.

This is an area of risk for family businesses in several ways. The most obvious is the break-up of a family firm through the breakdown of a marriage – dividing assets, loyalties and the integrity of the business in the process.[41] In none of our cases is this a direct cause of conflict, mostly because we are talking about mature family firms, and this hazard is especially commonplace among young or nascent businesses, where both spouses are intimately tied in with the business.[42] In the more mature firms we are considering, the breakdown of a marriage is absorbed, though the consequences may still be negative – leaving a residue. Here many of our cases illustrate how corrosive this can be – especially where ownership rights are unequally distributed.

Another consequence of the fragility of marriage is the consequence of remarriage following divorce. In many of the cases we shall review, the marriage bond comes into conflict with the family bond – with individual loyalties being pulled away from the family centre of gravity. In other instances we find spouses acting as amplifiers of conflict between other parties, such as in the war between the rival sport shoe empires of the Dassler family (see Chapter 3).

It has also been observed that people change character as a result of whom they marry.[43] At least, this is how it looks to the outsider. Actually, what happens is that partnership of any kind brings out different aspects of our personalities. Indeed, we choose the partners we do partly to become the people we want to be. But this is also true of the people we partner with. Either party may be mistaken in their judgment of the other. It is also the case that new aspects of character become revealed as a relationship progresses. This can be a joyful voyage of discovery, but often it is the reverse. People have been known to regress to more primitive and ugly behaviours under the pull of the relationship – Shakespeare's Macbeth tells the story eloquently. In the U-Haul case the death of the patriarch's first wife produced a profound change on the style and behaviour of the boss, triggering a chain of events that was to tear the family apart. Others blossom after remarriage – people whose edges were roughened in an earlier union can find them smoothed in a subsequent one. The reverse can also happen!

PARENTS AND CHILDREN

Now let us move into the gene pool, starting with **parenting**. The neo-Darwinian perspective tells us that ambivalence, conflict indeed, is endemic to the relationship.[44] This increases as the child ages. Parents have a strong interest in nurturing, aiding and guiding their offspring onto pathways of success – for their children are bearing the precious cargo of the family genes. The children love their parents in return; it is their instinctive impulse to solidify the bond between them and those on whom they depend so totally.

So far, so good. But here comes the conflict. The parents' desire to manage the destiny of their children is increasingly unacceptable to the children. Parents have to learn to let go, which often proves difficult. How often have you hear parents plaintively cry, 'It's for your own good', while the children retort, 'How do you know what's best for me?' Successful child-rearing is punctuated by skirmishes of this kind, but the cause of them is part of our biogenetic programming. The children are motivated to extract as much value as they can from their parents, and therefore they keep faith with the bargains that parents strike with them, conforming to their parents' wishes. But the children have a growing sense of their own autonomy and the legitimacy of their goals – they are potentially moving into a mirror position to the parents – seeking to control their own destiny, and the future of their own offspring, when they come. Thus the pattern repeats from generation to generation.

The battle between parents and children is played out in every culture. Parents fail to let out the leash fast enough or far enough because they are locked into a less mature model of the child than the child entertains for themself. From the other side the children are perpetually straining at the leash and seeking to move out of the sphere of parental control. Some cultures, such as the Latin and South Asian, weigh in heavily on the parents' side, giving them the right to arrange the marriages and careers of their children. Differences in the character of family businesses across cultures owe a lot to how this conflict is regulated by social norms.[45]

In our case histories we shall see numerous examples of battles for control between parents and children, for when this drama is extended in to the sphere of a business, it takes on extra weight. One of the most poignant examples is at IBM, where Tom Watson Jr fought tooth and nail with his father before in the end Tom Sr let go the reins (Chapter 4). For at stake are not just the choices of the individual: the conflict also carries the full weight of the family and the firm's resources. The most common arena in which this conflict is acted out is succession. Instances are legion of aged patriarchs refusing to hand over control to their middle-aged children.[46] They never stop believing that they know best – sometimes even beyond the grave. They can cast a shadow of control in the way they write their wills and construct their family trusts.

BROTHERS AND SISTERS

Now we come to one of the most potent areas of biogenetic conflict – **siblings**.[47] In the animal world it is common to find species where siblings do not just compete with each other, they kill each other if they can.[48] The egret – a rather attractive stork-like bird, common in many temperate and tropical climates – has a family system that is bloody in beak and claw. The parents sit by as disinterested observers while the firstborn pecks his younger, smaller and weaker sibling to death. Why do the parents tolerate this? It is because the second was conceived as a genetic insurance plan should the firstborn fail to survive for any reason. Once the firstborn is strong enough to be an assured bearer of the family genes, then the parents' genetic mission is fulfilled, and the chances of their offspring's survival can only be diminished by the competing claims of the younger on their limited resources. This enshrines the essence of the politics of sibling conflict – the competition for limited resources.

In the human family siblicide is not unknown – Cain and Abel stand as an early warning for humankind – but sibling conflict to this extreme is thankfully rare, though not unknown. However, enormous bitterness and enmity between brothers and sisters is not uncommon.[49] But then so is a great bond of love, loyalty and companionship. For many of us, our brothers and sisters become and remain our best life-time friends. Many family businesses are founded and run successfully by siblings. Joint leadership between siblings is even quite common. So what is it that turns the bond into something poisonous? The parents play a critical part,[50] as does personality, which we shall discuss shortly.

In the human family the sibling drama is played out on the same genetic model, but with a different set of inputs in each case. Let us explain. The first-born child is the recipient of all the parent's care and attention. That attention becomes divided with the advent of the second-born. The age gap matters, as many parents know.[51] The wider the gap, the easier it is for the first-born to be able to deal with this intrusion – through superior understanding and power. Yet it still is an intrusion, and first-borns deploy strategies that keep themselves in parental favour – often by conforming to parental wishes or and by conspicuous achievement.[52] It is common to find first-borns and only children in the ranks of leadership.

The primogeniture rule, which applies in many societies and in the past has often been practised in family businesses, trades on this relationship.[53] Of course the problem is that the first-born might have the will to succeed but not the ability to do so. Against this supremacy, all is not lost for later-borns. They have a different adjustment strategy in the family system. The realization dawns on them that the cosy arrangement that has been established by their parents and the first-born must be overthrown for them to compete on even terms. At first they are the recipients of all the love and care that a new-born attracts, but in time they begin to see their disadvantage relative to their older siblings who are securely in place. For each successive sibling, as the family size grows, this potential for oppression and diminished share of resources becomes more and more apparent.

What can they do? Rebel.[54] This takes many different forms. It can involve attempts to usurp or undermine the senior siblings. It can be achieved by acting out a different model of relationships and values that will set them apart from their senior siblings. The later-born seeks a ground of their choosing to compete and perhaps excel. Humour, for example, has always been the weapon and defence of those who lack power by other means. Creativity is another. Among the world's radicals, later-borns have been found to predominate.[55] This kind of differentiation is visible in several of our cases.

None of this is sufficient to engender warfare between siblings. Many a bemused parent has witnessed near-fratricidal conflict between young brothers and then seen it transform over time into a mature bond of loyalty and friendship. The reason, of course, is that the resource they contested – parental attention – becomes increasingly irrelevant. They have more to learn and gain from each other as friends than as rivals. Again, family business enters the equation with potentially destructive force. It potentially extends the contested domain into adulthood because it ties people together – family wealth and ownership of the business come to symbolize all that they have been striving for throughout their childhood.

GENDER AND OTHER FACTORS

So what other factors make a difference to the likelihood of conflict? One is the **gender** of the children.[56] Girls and boys compete on different territory – the sharpest conflicts will always be between same-sex siblings, and more for boys than girls. The urge to dominate is generally greater for males than for females. Another factor, mentioned earlier, is **age spacing**. Large age gaps reduce the likelihood of conflict, but do not eliminate it. **Family size** also diffuses conflict. In large families, everyone's share of resources and attention is diminished, and therefore there is less to fight about. Rather, siblings see the futility of the contest and find their own path. Family businesses often work better in large families for these reasons – siblings are more likely to seek a variety of niches, inside and outside the firm.

The role of parents is critical, especially in how they distribute resources. Because all their children are equal bearers of their genes, they are disposed instinctively to divide equally among them. Islamic family businesses have this division of inheritance required of them by the injunctions of Sharia law (though they give a fraction to daughters of what is shared among sons). Of course equality is not always either just or best, especially where it means dividing assets in the name of family 'fairness'.[57] And of course, children don't see it like that – each may be inclined to see themself as uniquely deserving, especially those who occupy positions of leadership in the family business.

Gene politics is thus the interplay of genetic interests through families of different shape and size. This analysis helps to makes sense of many general patterns we see in families. But it does not help us too much when it comes to the specifics of family wars, where all kinds of quite particular games are played out. This is the area we can call family dynamics.

FAMILY DYNAMICS

PARENTING STYLES

Let us start with parents. There are many different ways of being a parent. The most obvious variations are around love and authority. Parents differ in how nurturing they are of their children – the amount of care and attention they give to support them. They also differ in how much they exercise top-down power. Put these together and you get four parenting styles as shown in Figure 2.1.[58]

Attention and support for the children	Top-down power	
	High	*Low*
High	Authoritative	Indulgent
Low	Authoritarian	Neglectful

Figure 2.1   Parenting styles

The controlling authoritarian parent is low in emotional support and high on power distance – typical of the family business patriarch who is obsessed with the business, expecting background support from his family, and managing by edict, such as we shall see in Chapter 5, where Sumner Redstone expects his children to fall in line with his command. The neglectful parent is low on both. This is a feature of family firms where there is no direction or support for children to take an interest in the business. The indulgent parent is high on support and low on power. Parents nurture their children and give them freedom to engage with the business as they wish. This is visible in the Gucci family and in the remarkable U-Haul saga, where the father flipped between authoritarian, neglectful and indulgent styles across a wide age divide between older and younger children. (Both are featured in Chapter 9.) The final category is probably the ideal in many cultures, the authoritative parents, who are high on both support and authority.

In a family business this may guide the children in a planned way to becoming part of the business, or equally discourage them from doing so. Either way, this fourth style is reckoned by family therapists to be the most effective style in balancing the needs of the child and keeping the family together.[59] But we should be careful not to advance a one-size-fits-all model. Love and support can be oppressive if linked too closely with control, and some families become 'enmeshed' when their frames of reference are all internal, where everyone obsesses about everyone else in the family and the light of the outside world rarely seems to penetrate the tangle of their relationships.[60] At the opposite extreme are families where a climate of freedom has been cultivated to the extent that everyone goes their own way without regard for each other. The family is fragmented and centrifugal, with everyone flying off into their own individual worlds.

PARENTS AT WAR

There are other variations. Some are around the relationship between the parents. Where there is warfare, or perhaps an armed truce between parents, there can be a battle for allies among the children – producing a schism, a split down the middle of the family as the children are enlisted by either side. War is often waged through children in such families, with severe and damaging consequences for the development of the next generation cohesion in the family.[61] The Pritzker family (Chapter 7) suffered a split of this type.

It has been said that one of the biggest sources of influence on children is the unlived lives of the parents.[62] Mum and dad can offload the frustrations of their lives on to the lives of their children. Many highly ambitious individuals had their striving fuelled by the unfulfilled desires of parents whose lives were limited by lack of opportunity, resources, or their own parents' behaviour as blocking agents. These patterns can be thought of as 'scripts' for living that individuals pick up from various sources in childhood: parents, teachers and role models.[63] Adults often rebel against the scripts they have been handed – though this may happen as late as midlife – and break away from the life and career they have been living. Otis Chandler, the last family publisher of the *LA Times*, illustrates this starkly (see Chapter 7). In family businesses a growing child's script may be written around the future role intended for them in the firm. Clearly this has dangers if the next generation have adopted the narrative without owning it psychologically:[64] that is, if the kids know how to recite their parts but their real secret life is elsewhere. The very palpable danger is that they take on the business and then run it half-heartedly.

SCAPEGOATING

One common pathology in families is 'triangulation' – where two parties in conflict deflect their negative energy on to a third party – typically parents at war taking it out on one of the kids.[65] More general scapegoating also happens, where all family members identify one individual as 'the problem'. This ganging up makes the scapegoat the canvas on which are painted all the other members' frustrated desires. The individual so identified is often the weakest, slowest, most aggressive and so on: the one who deviates most beyond the range of what is considered normal or acceptable by the remainder of the family. This may be a child, but it can also be one of the parents, especially when the parents are in conflict.

The opposite side of the coin is favouritism, individuals who are singled out for special attention and support because they are perceived as gifted, special or most lovable. To return to the language of gene politics, all the parental investment becomes focused on the most likely source of payoff – the child who will be the most reliable bearer of the family genes. This does not always work out as parents intend. Edgar Bronfman Sr's choice of successor among his children illustrates this point (the Seagram case in Chapter 6). Even the most obedient child may rebel against the pressure of expectation, cast off the shackles, and disappoint the parents by taking flight in a new direction.

FAMILIES AS CULTURES

The idea of **family climate** captures these variations.[66] The concept of climate is an aspect of culture. It denotes the specific sets of beliefs and practices that are expressed and practised by a group; many of these consist of what is expected. Within a family, culture resides in the behaviours and attitudes that are taken for granted. So far we have concentrated on aspects to do with feeling – especially around love, control and identification. Family climate also has a thinking and an acting dimension.

The thinking dimension is the degree to which family members share the same world view and values. Clearly this has a bearing on their solidarity or their ability to achieve cohesion. Excessive cohesiveness leads families to retreat into their own exclusive world and culture – 'enmeshed' and impervious to the outside world. In family businesses a deadly consequence is failure to take external reality checks, which, as we shall see, leads to some business-destroying conflicts as demonstrated in the cases in Chapter 6, and perhaps most spectacularly in the Sakowitz case, where it dissolved a once-thriving Texan department store chain. In the opposite case, too little cohesiveness and the family members scatter to different areas of life and involvement, coming together in twos and threes occasionally but otherwise maintaining a norm of separation.

The acting dimension of family climate is the way family members conduct themselves and solve problems. This can be rigid or flexible. Rigidity comes from family members being locked into their scripts and roles – such as, tough dad, indulgent mum, achieving son, rebellious daughter. Rigidity may look like comfortable stability until the family comes under pressure. Then it becomes less adaptive.

The family has become sclerotic – incapable of altering its pattern to accommodate change. The Guinness family (Chapter 6) arguably fell into this trap by not adapting their skills to be effective stewards of their firm.

The novel and movie *Ordinary People* depicts such a crisis, where the accidental drowning of the eldest favourite son causes a family breakdown. Most affected is the mother (memorably acted in the movie by Mary Tyler Moore), who is unable to unfreeze her orientation from mourning the loss of her favourite child to the remaking of her relationship with her husband and surviving son. The key to flexibility is open communication and a willingness to adopt new behaviours to meet the requirements of the moment. In some families there are 'no go' areas of non-communication. Often for a good reason, but the more taboos you have the more difficult it becomes to deal with exceptional situations and circumstances. Can one be too flexible? The answer is yes – growing children need anchors and parents adopting stable roles.

The more general principle is actually that families need to adapt to life's changes. Any family will be dysfunctional if it retains a rigid format.[67] As children grow their needs alter. The relationship between parents also matures in different ways. The economic life and resources of the family do not remain constant. External events intrude on families continually, with a shifting range of demands, opportunities and threats.

THE FAMILY VESSEL CONCEPT

Let us now simplify all this into a single image. Imagine an earthenware vessel designed to carry liquids. It has a form, an identity and a purpose. This is the family. Most of the time it fulfils its purpose; occasionally it is dry, sometimes full to overflowing. It is robust, but not infinitely so. It can be wilfully smashed. It may also disintegrate under pressure. Imagine if such a vessel is subject to the violent ingress of liquid, for example from a high-pressure hose. Minor cracks and fissures that in normal use cause no problems now become liabilities. They are lines of fragility which become fissures that ultimately destroy the vessel. So it is with families. We like to think that adversity brings us together. So it may do, in the short term, but often families find themselves split asunder by the strain of coping with desperate times and events.[68]

We shall return to this image of the family vessel. For many families, owning a business brings more pressure than they can bear. A family needs to be resilient and adaptive if it is to bear the weight of owning and running a firm. Adaptation may start easy and become difficult. As long as the business is doing well it is easy for people to be happy, but as it becomes more complex and more people become involved, the room for conflict increases. The robustness of the family climate is tested.

It might seem as if we are just viewing families as nothing but bundles of liabilities. The theme running through this book is a family can grow in strength through successfully overcoming problems. This means that the most vulnerable family can be the one that has no stress at all – it will lack the adaptive strategies to cope when stress comes unexpectedly.

This book aims to help families find paths to adaptive success by facing problems and dealing with them. The cases we look at here come from those whose success came at a big price in terms of family harmony, or who comprehensively failed as businesses because of their conflicts. By looking at the paths they followed, we hope to bring insight and hope to all those who would avoid such fates. But first, let us look at two themes – two sets of inputs to family dynamics – that will recur as we tell our stories. They are culture and personality.

CULTURE AND PERSONALITY

THE RINGS OF INFLUENCE ON FAMILIES

Families do not just spring into existence – they are part of a chain of influence, or rather they are at the centre of surrounding rings of influence. Picture a series of nested rings, with arrows of influence between them. Each outer ring influences the rings within.

The first ring around the parents is their own parents, enshrined in their memories and instincts. We imitate as 'normal' many of the habitual practices of our parents, without too much thought. Sometimes the influence is negative – we react in an equal and opposite direction, especially where memories of childhood are painful. There may be a seesaw of parenting styles between successive generations: permissive parents' children grow up to be disciplinarians, and vice versa. Of course there are two parents, so the model adopted is often a negotiated agreement – a compromise. Sometimes the model of one parent is imposed on the other. Since we seek as marriage partners people with whom our values are aligned this is usually not a problem.[69] But as we have seen, where parents bring contrasting models and allow these to become points of conflict between them, the result may be unclear, unpleasant and unsettling for the children.

The next concentric ring is schooling. By schooling we mean teachers of all kinds and from all sources. Our parents control these inputs initially – the bedtime stories we are told are a kind of schooling, for they help to form our first ideas about family life, morality and much more. Television and the chatter of our friends likewise school us in what is 'normal' or to be taken for granted.[70] Formal education embeds this. In all cultures the classroom is where we learn in detail the rules of our society.

So the next concentric ring is our native culture – or subculture, more correctly, since we are subject to the strictures of our local clan before the wider rules of the tribe are imposed upon us.[71] The concentric rings widen to embrace broad ideologies and systems of thought that distinguish the worlds of different economic and political systems, faiths and ideologies.

Family businesses in their conflicts and adaptiveness draw upon the language and energies of these forces, even when they appear to be lost in the past or invisible to the actors.

THE UNIQUE FAMILY

So it is that the one finds differences between family firms emanating from diverse sources. Some are unique and local to the family, while other patterns have cascaded down from wider unseen cultural forces. Thus there is a world of difference between the sprawling diversified conglomerate of the extended Indian family, such as the Tata Group, to the long thin chain of father to son succession that can be found in the nearly 500-year-old Italian specialist gun maker, Beretta. Finally, there is another dimension to consider – time. Families aren't what they used to be, and all over the world they are changing. Economic prosperity generally triggers a fall in the birth rate, while social and health benefits bring increased longevity. The result around the world is the spread of the 'beanpole' family structure – all length and no breadth – with multiple generations alive at the same time but few siblings and cousins.[72] This profoundly affects the future form of family firms, restricting choices and changing the nature of intergenerational dynamics.

Family businesses are also springing up in areas where formerly they were prohibited, as in the former communist states, and in regions where globalization is radically restructuring social and economic life, such as parts of Africa and the Middle East.

It is a mark of the most successful family businesses that they have been able to ride the waves of culture change, each generation adopting the new ideas of their times. Of course this is also a point of failure and conflict, where the older generation gives way too late and places little trust in the 'new wisdom' of the up and coming generation. We shall see this unhappy saga and trail of consequences in several of our tales, notably in the Ford family, where it was not until the third generation that founding father Henry was ousted (Chapter 4).

HOW FAMILY MEMBERS DIFFER

All of these patterns are etched by culture on the identity of the family – some consciously, some subliminally. We often underestimate the degree to which our thinking is conditioned by others and by the circumstances that surround us. But there is still a source of uniqueness that above all others works its way into the fabric of the family and its firm – **personality**.

Personality is a mysterious and somewhat intangible concept, yet it is invoked in everyday speech to cover every foible and quirk a person may exhibit. Lately, however, psychology has taken great strides in unravelling and measuring its meaning and structure.[73]

It would be a tedious task to try to list all the ways one family member may differ from another, but such a list would resolve to a few themes. What is the person's outward style or character – in their display of energies? What is their emotional tone – positive, negative, variable, or stable? What are their key drivers, needs and obsessions, and with what strength are they held? Do they have inner conflicts? What is their 'thinking style'? What is their preferred pattern of relationships, in terms of closeness, variety and power?

Personality, as measured by psychologists, is considered to be a person's 'enduring dispositions': qualities of thought, feeling and action, that remain with us for most of our adult lives. It is a collection of filters, biases and instincts that lead us to prefer one situation over another or one person over another. But personality is only part of the story of how individuals in a family differ from one another. There are three other areas.

One is **ability and aptitude**. We differ in a range of what psychologists call cognitive factors, such as intelligence, logical reasoning and memory, which are a function of how our brains are wired. These matter in business, but how much depends greatly on the situation. In many areas of business you don't need to be super-smart to be an effective business person. Increasingly it is easy to get technology to help you out with tasks that were formerly the exclusive province of 'experts'. The best leaders know this, and try to surround themselves with others who have even greater skills than themselves.

The second area is **values and beliefs**. These come from various sources – personality for sure plays a big part. People's attitudes to authority, charity or community, for example, are closely connected with their needs for power, love and sociability. But a lot of our personal ideology comes to us from culture and the people who are significant to us. Consistent alignment to company-related values is vitally important in the family firm, but this rarely springs from personal values so much as it does from personality. That is, a family member's individual beliefs about what the family business should stand for matter less than do the style and manner with which they express those beliefs.

The third area is what we can call **self-concept**. This is how each one of us views ourselves – it is the judgement we make when we look in the mirror, or the idea about ourselves that we wish others to have of us. In some respects it is a story we tell about ourselves – a 'script' that we carry with us through life, which we try to act out. From time to time we rewrite the script. This happens when we decide that the script we have been following is not the real 'me'; usually because we come to realize someone else has written the script for us and we have believed and accepted what they handed down to us. Parents and teachers are the main culprits. Parents' intense attachment to their children can lead them to project on to them some heroic wish fulfilment. Remember what we said earlier about children living the unfulfilled dreams of their parents. Sometimes this is a bad script. We shall see several cases where parents have judged and misjudged their children and their capabilities. The overlooking of female children is one of the most common restrictive themes of parental scriptwriting.

THE BUILDING BLOCKS OF PERSONALITY

These factors are important, but personality – the way we think and feel – colours all aspects of experience. What is it and where does it come from? Psychologists are mostly agreed that personality has a five-dimensional structure, often called the Big Five model of personality.[74] It is combinations of highs and lows on these dimensions that defines much of our individuality:

- Emotions – how sensitive, anxious, pessimistic or liable we are to mood swings, versus unchanging, untroubled and thick-skinned.
- Extraversion – how sociable, dominant and in need of external stimulation we are, versus solitary, quiet-seeking and self-sufficient.
- Openness – how radical, change-seeking, creative and adaptive we are, versus conservative, traditional and structured.
- Agreeableness – how nurturing, forgiving and tender-minded we are, versus tough, justice-oriented and self-seeking.
- Conscientiousness – how dedicated, controlled and obsessive we are, versus easy-going, disorganized and laid back.

These five produce an almost infinite variety of personality patterns. None of these patterns is intrinsically 'better' or worse than any other, although we might strongly wish other people, or ourselves, to be of one type or another. The question we should really pay attention to is how well our personalities match the situations we are in: the challenges we face in our jobs, and the relationships and groups that we are attached to, including our families.

A family is a bubbling cauldron of human ingredients; each member has their own flavour. Sometimes the blend of personalities makes fine soup, but at other times it just doesn't mix right – unpleasant stuff floats to the surface. The recipe for a happy family comes partly from the ingredients and partly from the cooking. Strong personalities in a family can dominate the flavour – the family climate. Opinionated and outspoken members can monopolize attention, while more impressionable members merge into the background. Sometimes flavours clash, such as when headstrong individuals may struggle for control of the family.

THE PARADOX OF INHERITED PERSONALITY

Now here's a curious, paradoxical but vitally important fact about the genetics of personality that has a powerful bearing on family firms – it is that although a lot of our personality comes from our genes it does not run in families.[75] Personality is substantially heritable: more than 50 per cent of our character comes from our genes, while the rest comes from the unique path of our life experience, much of it from impressionable childhood. But because the inherited matrix of personality comes from unique combinations of genes, our children inherit quite different patterns of the same genes, and as a consequence they differ in personality.

Think of it in this way. The genes that make up your personality are like a hand of cards that you are born with and play during your lifetime – winning and losing tricks according to the strengths and weaknesses of the cards you hold and how you play them.[76] It is the same for your partner. Now when you and your partner reproduce, each of you is in effect passing copies of half the cards in your hand on to your child. They now are born with a fresh hand, made up of half your cards and half your partner's – picked at random. So it is that configuration of the new hand – the child's genetic profile – is unique. Thus can two peace-loving parents give birth to a fiery daughter; and two highly strung parents raise a calm and easy-going son. It happens.

The implications for family businesses are obvious. Don't depend upon your kids inheriting the traits that enabled you to build the business. Entrepreneurs do not breed entrepreneurs, except by the luck of the genetic draw – what we may call 'the gene lottery'.[77] Time and again we see family firms where it is strongly but falsely assumed that the combination of inheritance and schooling will make succession smooth between generations. Time and again the gene lottery overturns the applecart, or takes the family in a completely new direction. Among our cases, several illustrate this truth, such as Césare Mondavi's sons Robert and Peter's divergent styles and their inability to fulfil their father's desire for them to work in close harmony within the family firm (see Chapter 3).

INSIGHT AND CONTROL

But personality alone does not shape the family or the family firm. The mere coexistence of two strong personalities in a family does not condemn them to a life of ceaseless conflict. Personality, like any psychological force, can be controlled and disciplined. The control can come from within. If we are wise, we learn what our danger traits are and try to master them, to take control of the triggers that we know set us off down some unproductive pathway. Therapeutic counselling with troubled individuals tends to focus on these habits.

In family business some of the most powerful and helpful interventions come from advisers with a background in family therapy who are able to help families develop healthy communications and emotional self-discipline. External control can also be effected by rules and conventions. Family firms draw up codes of practice and family constitutions that will keep them on the straight and narrow paths of good decision making and best practice. Advisers can be useful catalysts to developing such documents and protocols. Many of the family wars we shall review could have been prevented by a little self-control, a little external discipline and some counsel from outsiders.

In the most complex cases the problems are multi-layered, and to solve them requires attention to a number of levels. Governance systems can help a great deal, performing many different functions. In the family firm they provide the means for reconciling diverse perspectives and building consensus among owners. It is a matter of harnessing the unique power of the family to best effect. In almost every one of the cases we shall review, a better approach to governance could have helped to keep the family and its business on track.

THE STORIES OF FAMILY WARFARE

This ends our review of themes and issues. Many of them will crop up in our journey across the battlefields of family wars. We shall be pausing, repeatedly, on the way to analyse how they came about and how they could have been prevented.

Here is the path we shall be following. It proceeds from the most primal forms of conflict to the most complex. At the primitive end we start in the next chapter with 'Brothers at arms', focusing on the sibling relationship that is often the most difficult and dangerous – brotherhood. Sisters are occasionally involved, but it is between the boys that many of the most commonly destructive flashpoints in family firms arise. We move on to consider the other primal point of conflict: the parent–child bridge and how it crumbles under the weight of mismanaged succession. This too is predominantly male – fathers and sons 'Fighting for the crown'. Our next stop takes us into 'The house that hubris built' – where we find leaders, not always founders, whose personalities burn brightly and dangerously for all around them. In the chapter entitled 'Heads in the sand – the insularity trap' we look at families who have become insular to the point where they lose their capacity to make good business decisions and forgo control. From here we move to the wider arena of family splits when we look at 'Schism – the house divided'. We conclude with 'Un-civil war', where tribes with diverse and divergent interests clash in multiple areas on the field of battle.

If this sounds daunting, fear not. Every case also contains lessons for the wise, and hope for other family firms. Our book will end as we started – in praise of the family firm and the unique benefits in wealth, performance, culture and commitment that it can achieve.

That comes later. First we must take a deep breath take our first plunge into the mêlée that is Family Wars.

3

Brothers at arms

The most dangerous word in any human tongue is the word for brother. It's inflammatory.

(Tennessee Williams, playwright)

Am I my brother's keeper?

(The Bible)

INTRODUCTION

Once upon a time there was a very charismatic and creative man who founded a corporation which grew to global proportions. His son, Adam, grew to be a fine young man, but his wilfulness and independence of mind led him to resist his father's authority. There was a major falling-out between them, and he set off with his wife to make a new life for himself in agriculture. He worked hard and forged a living for himself and his family, and was blessed with several children including two sons, Ken and Abe.

The firstborn, Ken, was dark, serious and very determined. His younger sibling, Abe, was by contrast a bright and sunny individual, much more naturally likeable and gifted, with an easy and generous nature. Ken was always jealous of the favour that seemed effortlessly to fall on his younger sibling. Meanwhile, granddad continued to exert a strong influence on the family, and it was to him that the boy Ken chiefly looked for most regard. His chance came when one day grandfather asked for the two boys to come and do some work for him in his business. For Ken it was a chance to outshine his brother, and he set to work with great energy. Alas for Ken, his sweaty toil was not enough. Yet again Abe proved that the expenditure of sheer effort is not enough. Through sheer skill Abe had shown he really knew how to add value to grandpa's project. Worse than that, granddad called the boys before him and told them both his verdict on their efforts. Ken was mortified to be told how disappointed in him his grandfather was, and that he should strive to be more like his brother.

Ken sat seething through the interview, and as soon as he was alone with Abe, he flew into a furious rage, turning on his brother with the words, 'There is no justice in this world,' to which Abe smartly replied: 'You are completely wrong. You should focus more on the lasting values that drive this business instead of always thinking of yourself.' This drove Ken to breaking point. 'To hell with you', he yelled and struck his brother full in the face. It was a mortal blow. Abe swooned and fell back, never to recover. Ken had killed his brother. The verdict at the inquest was manslaughter. Ken escaped a custodial sentence, but was forced to leave the country. He ended his days scratching a living in a remote and barren land.

So ends the story of the first recorded sibling rivalry in Western writing – for this is the saga of Cain and Abel, and their conflict before the Almighty. The story has been rewritten many times – in Steinbeck's novel *East of Eden*, in the soap opera *Dallas*, and in the movie *The Lion King*. In history and legend brothers kill or try to eliminate each other with alarming frequency: think of Michael Corleone gunning down brother Fredo in *The Godfather*, Romulus killing Remus, Shakespeare's King Claudius disposing of Hamlet senior, and from history, Césare Borgia removing his sibling rival.

This paints a gloomy picture of sibling relationships, especially between brothers, where the competition for resources and attention is magnified by the overdrive of male machismo. Yet we know this is only half the story. Brothers can work together wonderfully well. As we saw in the introduction, there are good genetic reasons for siblings to stick together. They have more interests in common than either of them has with outsiders. But the dynamic of siblings is that they come into conflict when they are locked into a single space, sharing resources to get to the same goal – there can only be one top dog. If they are able to differentiate themselves and find their own space it is easier. Hence siblings of opposite sexes find peaceful coexistence easier than same-sex siblings. It is also easier when there is a big age gap. And it helps if siblings have very different characters, styles and needs, which thankfully the gene lottery of family character often brings about.

But what happens when the sex is the same, the age gap is modest, and both have a desire to succeed in the same territory? The territory for many growing siblings is identity. It is as if the identity of one has to be subordinated to the identity of the other in order for them to get along. Of course the solution to this is the right degree of separation – then each can afford to build for themselves, and maintain good regard for their sibling. As we noted early, boys who are warring throughout childhood and teenage years often astonish their parents by becoming the best of friends as adults.

So what does a family business do to such brothers? It poses a special risk. Brothers can manage a firm successfully and happily if they are able to reach an accommodation that doesn't violate the interests of either. Often this will be acceptance by one of the other as the acknowledged leader – as was the case with the Watsons of IBM (Chapter 4), where Dick, as head of international operations, never stood in the way of his elder brother Thomas Jr. In many family firms brothers operate highly successfully in harness together, with divided labour and responsibility, but often with one person ascendant. The Hindujas, leading one of India's major conglomerates, come to mind; there are other notable examples in just about every economy.

Thus the recipe for family war or peace around brothers is a cocktail of character, age spacing, and circumstances that allow them to be aligned in some formation other than conflict. Parents play a big part – often unwittingly fuelling the potential for conflict by how they reward, punish and label their children. In the cases that follow, we shall see potent examples of this toxicity.

KOCH INDUSTRIES – DESTRUCTIVE REDRESS[1]

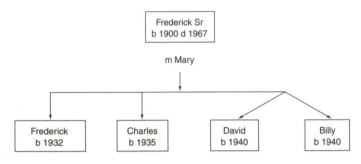

Figure 3.1[2] The Koch family

ORIGINS

The largest and most successful business families are not immune to feuding, as the history of the Koch family demonstrates. Founded in 1940 by Frederick C Koch, the company Koch Industries has grown to become one of the biggest privately owned family businesses in the world. Still in the hands today of second-generation siblings Charles and David Koch, who have built a business that has revenues of over $80 billion, the corporation spans a diversified range of industries including pipelines, fibres and polymers, and forest and consumer products. The company philosophy is based on 'a value system and framework for action that encourages employees to think and act like principled entrepreneurs'. The founder, Frederick, was a typical driven self-made entrepreneur, who, in the years leading up to the Second World War, with the aid of pioneering new refining technology pitched himself into a David and Goliath fight with the oil majors. It was not long before he saw the impossibility of this fight, so he retreated from his home market and decided to go to a more virgin territory – setting off to build refineries in Russia. His Russian experience helped shape his political views: to be strongly opposed to communist ideology, values that are perpetuated to this day by his sons who support libertarian political causes.

So far, so good. This is a conspicuous success story of business building, but behind the scenes there is a lot of heartache. Fred Koch, before he died, begged his children to 'be kind and generous to one another', to which, as if fearing the worse, he added that their wealth could be 'a blessing or a curse'. If he had misgivings, they were surely realized, for it presaged a family split, where two sides went off to pursue their respective interests, after a succession of major tremors. In the Koch case, this is not a saga of winners and losers. Along the road some members made more than others, but family harmony paid a big price. Faced with differing visions among the family owners, a division of the assets or sell out by one party is often preferable to trying to seal over the cracks, which can be both time and wealth consuming. The Koch's break-up arguably allowed the brothers to pursue their entrepreneurial instincts with even greater drive and to achieve outstanding results.

THE BOYS' WORLD

This was a family where the parenting regime was harsh – authoritarian rather than authoritative in the jargon of family theory. Fred Sr had the frontier spirit, and had become an entrepreneurial dragon, forging his way forward through calculated risk taking and a succession of legal and business battles with Big Oil. His four sons were brought up under a strict disciplinarian regime, and were expected to work for the firm through their holidays and at all times to live up to very highest standards of behaviour. The eldest son, Frederick, like Cain, earned his father's extreme disfavour over an alleged act that the father strongly disapproved of. Despite Frederick's strenuous protestations of innocence, Fred Sr, like a vengeful deity, concluded that he wished to sever all connections with his son, transferring his bequest on to his other offspring. The second son, Charles was the most ambitious; driven and hard working, like his father. As a youngster he pushed his brothers around when they played a game they knew as 'King of the Hill'. The youngest two brothers, David and William (Billy), were twins. Of the two, Billy was the forceful character, and bridled at the tough treatment he received from his dad, as well as the bullying he received from his older brother Charles.

As often happens when a strong man and emperor dies, he leaves a power vacuum. Hoping for peace on your deathbed is rather too late to build a climate of cooperation, and once authoritarians lose their power, as history has shown repeatedly – look at Iraq – the legacy is warring factions.

In the Koch case, the first move to conflict was when Billy secretly made moves to oust his older brother Charles from the board in 1980. His tactic was to gain control of the business through a proxy fight. It was not long before Charles got wind of what was happening, and with the support of David entered the fray, persuading some share-holders to switch sides at the 11th hour. Once victory was assured Charles summarily fired Billy and proceeded to buy out the two siblings who were no longer involved. This he was able to do, so that Billy and Freddie Jr could exit the business as rich men. The sale in 1983 provided the sellers with $1.1 billion and their lives before them. Charles and David were left to run the business as they wished. Charles and David now controlled 80 per cent of the shares in alliance with a long-time associate, James Howard Marshall II, who held a 16 per cent stake, with the rest owned by employees.

During Billy's unsuccessful proxy fight, Marshall's eldest son J Howard Marshall III had taken sides against Charles and David. Illustrating the capacity of poison to spread in family wars, the feud had been replicated among the Marshalls. Marshall Sr, disapprov-ing of his son's support for Billy, stripped J Howard of his inherit-ance, making his younger brother E Pierce Marshall his primary heir instead. The Marshall family hit the headlines again in 1995 when the patriarch J Howard died and his new wife Anna Nicole Smith, over 50 years his junior, sued his estate when she discovered he had left her nothing in his will.[3] The case, which was discussed regularly in Anna Nicole's reality TV show, went all the way to the US Supreme Court. The protagonist, who had been the 1993 Playboy Playmate of the Year, met an early death in 2007.

BILLY'S FIGHT

Following the 1983 buyout one might think everything was set fair for the future. Alas, it was not. Just as the dust appeared to be settling after the split, Billy raised his head again. He felt that the bank loans that the company had taken on for the buyout were paid down a lot faster than he had predicted. Billy believed that there might be grounds for suing his brothers on the grounds that he had been entitled to a larger share of the company's assets during the sale process. With this in mind, he commenced legal proceedings that turned into a huge protracted saga – dragging on for over a decade, involving teams of lawyers and costing millions of dollars.

For all these efforts, Billy failed to get the redress he claimed he was due. He still had the bit between his teeth and he wasn't going to let go. Just as everyone thought it was all over, he refocused his attack on another target – the company. At the time an investigation was being held by a Senate Committee that many argued was flawed. Koch Industries was accused of stealing natural resources from Native American Indians by using unreliable methods to measure oil pumped into their pipelines.[4] The company strongly denied any such impropriety. Billy, still in combative mood, joined in this action against the family firm. Finally in 2001, a line was drawn under the lawsuits. Billy Koch and Koch Industries settled their outstanding legal battles, and thus drew to a close a family war that had lasted over 20 years.

COMMENT

When the previous generation leaves the question of succession in the hands of descendants, it has to be expected that from time to time one group will not get along with the chosen new leader. In this case, Billy spent almost half his career fighting his siblings. In the drama of sibling rivalry, the story is of the younger sibling's revenge – seeking to overthrow the established order of the supremacy by portraying an older brother as dishonest and lacking in values and principles. With the benefit of hindsight, Billy's battle was doomed from the start, so why did he go to such lengths to get the world to share his deeply negative feelings about his older brother Charles?

It is curious how the residues of childhood are either washed clean by fresh growth of adult development, or they percolate up through the years to form more potent passions. It seems that the latter occurred here, with resentments from childhood – reconstructed memories of suffering at his brother's hands – providing a continuing source of motivation, beyond the money, to emerge victorious.

There was a consolation prize for Billy at the end of this saga, when in 1992 his boat *America* captured yachting's most prestigious trophy

– the Americas Cup. But history will record this alongside a lifetime of grievance and conflict. This is a family whose members could have quietly gone their separate ways accepting their differences.

THE RELIANCE STORY – THE MYTH OF UNITY[5]

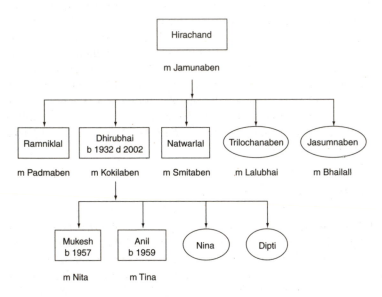

Figure 3.2   The Ambani family

ORIGINS

The Reliance story is probably one of the world's biggest business disputes conducted in the full glare of publicity. It concerns two immensely wealthy brothers contesting control of a vast business empire in India. It is the story of a bitter power struggle that had a surprisingly happy ending, which with a little wisdom could have been foreseen.

The Reliance Empire was founded by Dhirajlal Hirachand Ambani, also known as Dhirubhai, who was born as a second son to a poor schoolteacher, in a small village in the Indian state of Gujarat on 28

December 1932. Soon after he finished schooling, Dhirubhai decided to join his elder brother in Aden, Yemen, working first as an attendant in a Shell petrol station and later as a clerk in the oil company. Dhirubhai had an entrepreneurial cast of mind – meaning he had the wit to spot opportunities and the energy to pursue them. While he was adjusting to life in Aden, one day it struck him, with the fresh eyes of the newcomer to a culture, that the value of silver in Aden coins exceeded the price of the coin itself. Immediately he started to trade, quickly generating profits which he used in 1958 to set up a trading agency called the Reliance Commercial Corporation, importing polyester yarn and exporting spices.

Dhirubhai often incurred losses exporting spices while he tried to procure replenishment licences to import nylon. However, the imported products commanded a premium price, for Indians with their increasing disposable income at this time were developing a growing appetite for expensive clothes. After 10 years in Aden, Dhirubhai moved back to his native India. Seeing a growing opportunity in the textiles business he opened his first textile mill in Ahmadabad in 1966. In time Reliance textile products became the biggest-selling and most trusted fabric brand for Indian households – known as Vimal.

In the 1970s, Dhirubhai launched the company's first public offering of shares. Its success was to change the image of corporate financing in the country, and helped to develop an equity culture among the general public. The investors who were lucky enough to buy Reliance Industries Ltd (RIL) shares in 1977 would have seen each Rs 1,000 ($29) invested grow to Rs 165,000 ($3,419) by 2002. During this period of massive growth the number of shareholders increased, reaching 3.3 million by 2005.

In the 1980s Dhirubhai's two brothers, Ramniklal and Natvarlal, assumed the roles of joint managing director and executive director, while the founder presided as overall leader and chairman. His two other siblings were women, and since it was a conservative Gujarati family, they played little role in the business. When the brothers raised the idea of dividing Reliance among the three of them, Dhirubhai reacted with vehement disagreement. For him, it was an article of faith that the strength of the business came from its unity and indivisibility under his leadership. It would remain as one unit. To avoid further disputes and to underline his vision, Dhirubhai set about removing his brothers from the business, offering them large sums in compensation. This would not be the last time in the group's history that unity of leadership would be an issue.

ENTER THE BOYS

Shortly after, in 1981, Dhirubhai diversified into the plastics and polyester sectors and brought in his eldest son, Mukesh, a fresh MBA graduate from Stanford University, to run the project. Mukesh soon proved his skills and came to be regarded as the implementer of his father's vision. Mukesh was in many ways following the familiar first-born pattern described in the last chapter – following his father's footsteps quite closely as a serious, driven and business-oriented man. In 1983 his younger brother Anil also joined the business after graduating from Wharton Business School. Anil formed a sharp contrast with his brother – creative, highly sociable, with a taste for the high life. Of the two, Anil was the more media savvy and would become the public face of the Ambanis.

Dhirubhai was popular, having built good political and bureaucratic connections to underpin the success of the business empire. An important factor in the success of the business was that its globally competitive production facilities were built on a larger scale than those of its competitors. The company was managed professionally, although it was family controlled, and Dhirubhai gave his loyal managers a free hand and encouraged them to take initiatives and risks while insisting on excellence.

After suffering a stroke in 1986, Dhirubhai left the day-to-day operations to his sons, although he remained as the chairman of the Group. Being seen as a strategist and technocrat, Mukesh managed company projects and established new ventures, while younger brother Anil handled investments, financial markets and corporate communications. Anil's entrepreneurial business acumen marked him out to be a dealmaker. In the 1990s, Reliance diversified into financial services markets through Reliance Capital Ltd under Anil's leadership. At this time, the brothers were answerable directly to Dhirubhai, being the chief promoter and largest stakeholder, and chairman of Reliance Industries Ltd, the parent company.

Meanwhile Dhirubhai's health condition worsened, and following a fatal stroke he passed away in July 2002. In common with many ageing leaders, it seems he found it hard to believe in his own mortality, or at least its imminence, even when faced with the warning signs, for clearly he was not ready at the time of his leaving. He died intestate, without leaving a will. The management of the Rs 750 billion ($15.5 billion) empire thus fell automatically to his sons. All the family had for guidance were the stated wishes of the patriarch, which were his consistent commitment to the view that he did not want his legacy to be divided up.

THE SUCCESSION

In less than three decades, under the leadership of Dhirubhai, the Reliance Group had grown into a world-class company and accounted for 3 per cent of India's GDP. Following the death of the founder, according to the Hindu Succession Act of India, Dhirubhai's wife Kokilaben and her two sons and two daughters, Mukesh, Anil, Nina and Dipti, inherited the assets of the group. The children signed a deed of release to their mother, Kokilaben, and gave her the rights over the entire estate. The empire continued to expand under the leadership of Mukesh, who had taken over as the chairman and managing director of the group, while Anil was appointed as the vice-chairman and managing director. However, now the scenario had become two in a box – brothers whose sibling rivalry was going to be dangerously played out in the business arena. Anil – extravert, dominant and a successful entrepreneur in his own right – had no intention of being subordinate to his brother. Relations between the two were steadily worsening.

To create visible equality between them, Anil proposed that their mother become non-executive chairman, while he and Mukesh led the business as joint executive chairmen. Mukesh flatly rejected the proposition, and in 2002 took over as spokesperson for Reliance. This had always been Anil's responsibility, and he took Mukesh's action as an affront. He saw this as his elder brother trying to sideline him and override his authority. Meanwhile Mukesh continued to manage two of the group's companies, Reliance Infocomm (RIC), his brainchild, and Indian Petrochemicals (IPCL), while Anil ran two other companies,

Reliance Energy (REL) and Reliance Capital (RCL). The brothers continued to share leadership, somewhat uneasily, of the parent company.
This was the unstable configuration that sourced the power play and
deep rift that opened up between the brothers.

POWER STRUGGLE

In 2002, RIC, Mukesh's big baby, was expected to sell Reliance
Communications services to 5 million subscribers who would opt for
an upfront payment option. But he had misread the market. Instead,
only 1 million subscribers opted for this package, with most new
subscribers preferring to pay in instalments, creating a shortfall in
liquidity. Mukesh turned to the board of the parent company, RIL, to
fund the business, but faced the opposition of his brother Anil. The
board favoured Mukesh. Anil fumed, and made public his displeasure
by failing to appear at an important project launch in December 2002.
By now it was rumoured that Anil and Mukesh had started to avoid
each other on private occasions. They had moved into the familiar
spiral of escalating feud.

Much to the displeasure of Mukesh, in June 2004 Anil became a
member of Rajya Sabha (the Council of States and Upper House of
the Indian Parliament) by joining the Samajwadi (Socialist) party.
Mukesh was against the idea of any association of the Reliance Group
with politics. In his view the company's growth would be hindered by
any political alliances – it was against the ethos he believed should
drive a business. Mukesh's single-minded business focus contrasted
with Anil's instincts towards building a high public profile and visible
community involvement.

Immediately after, another event sharpened the rift between the
brothers. Anil announced that his division REL would start a gas-
based power project in the Indian state of Uttar Pradesh, a project that
would require investment from the parent company RIL. Mukesh, still
smarting from Anil's previous displays of autonomy, responded with a
resounding negative, saying that Anil should have sought the consent
of the Group board before making this announcement. Moreover,
Mukesh let it be known that he was not keen on RIL taking up the
modernization projects of Delhi and Mumbai airports, which he knew
that Anil intended the company to bid for. These investment-related

points of contention were, of course, the outward manifestation of the real battle between Mukesh and Anil, which was about who was to be the real boss of RIL and which one of them should determine issues of ownership and managerial control.

The dispute peaked in July 2004 when the RIL board passed a resolution in the absence of Anil, redefining the powers and authority of the leading roles in the business, conferring on Mukesh the role of executive chairman and with Anil as vice chairman and managing director. This gave clear leadership of the Reliance group to Mukesh, with all employees, including Anil, reporting to him. Anil exploded, protesting formally to the board that the decision had been taken without his knowledge and consent. It was a plan that had left him completely in the dark and playing second fiddle to his older brother.

Anil's personal life style also became the subject of wide criticism among the Mukesh camp, who maintained that Anil's liberalism was out of line with the conservative Gujarati traditions of the family. His friendship with film stars and politicians clearly made Mukesh and other family members uncomfortable. Dhirubhai had recognized the character differences between his sons, and deliberately given them divided roles to avoid this kind of collision. Now they were caught in this drama together, as the unwitting and unwise consequence of the family honouring the founder's legacy.

REPERCUSSIONS

Thus far, much of this had been going on behind closed doors, but rumours were circulating. Suddenly the fight burst into very public view when Mukesh, in answer to an Indian television channel reporter's question in November 2004 about the likelihood of a split between the brothers, admitted there were ownership issues. This triggered speculation about the future of the company, and the share price of RIL plummeted by over 12.6 per cent, the largest fall in the company's history. Speculation grew about a formal split, and the implications for the entire group of any change in ownership structure.

Anil shifted the focus of his attack to corporate governance. He alleged that the board had not adhered to accepted principles of practice and had failed to acknowledge his concerns. He hunkered down and produced a 500-page memorandum listing the alleged governance lapses at RIL, which he delivered to its directors.[6] A specific point of argument was around ownership issues and the granting of options in group affiliates. Anil questioned the value at which stock options in Infocomm had been issued in favour of Mukesh, and alleged that regulatory procedures with the stock exchange had not been followed. Later that year, Anil abstained in a vote for a proposal that the group buy back RIL shares from ordinary shareholders.

As the pressure mounted, the debate turned to which brother was the more able leader to protect the founder's vision and legacy. Mukesh's supporters argued that he was the architect behind major projects and that Anil's contribution was modest by comparison. Anil's supporters' riposte was that Mukesh's projects were supported by subsidies from RIL, the flagship company, whose success owed much to Anil as the financial brain behind RIC. Anil also continued to maintain that since his father's demise Mukesh had altered the ownership structures to his advantage.

The rift between the brothers became a matter of public concern, especially to the company's 3 million non-family shareholders, as the share price suffered. The image of the company and its reputation for governance and transparency were being damaged in the eyes of investors. Many felt that these disputes should not have been made public but rather settled internally. There was also a widespread belief that more professional management was necessary to improve shareholder value.

The first move to settle the rift came from Mukesh, offering to split Reliance Group with Anil. The deal he offered was for Anil to take REL and RCL as well as receive a cash payment. As a part of the deal Mukesh wanted Anil to withdraw from the RIL board, a proposal that Anil rejected outright. The proposed arrangement fuelled Anil's sense of inequity. But it was apparent that the dissolution of the Reliance Group was becoming inevitable. In early 2005, with a mounting sense of frustration Anil resigned as the vice-chairman and director of IPCL.

THE SETTLEMENT

Finally in March 2005, after numerous exhortations from various quarters, including the press, the mother, Kokilaben, stirred herself out of her shell of privacy and intervened, requesting two prestig-ious outsiders – the chairman of India's leading financial services group ICICI Bank, K V Kamath, and a family friend and chairman of the Indian branch of a US investment bank, Nimesh Kampani – to mediate between her sons. Kampani proceeded to conduct valua-tions and provided suggestions for a family settlement. In June 2005, Kokilaben announced that Ambani family's 34 per cent ownership of the Reliance group of companies would be split using a 30:30:40 formula, giving Mukesh and Anil a 30 per cent share each, while she would retain another 30 per cent, dividing the remaining 10 per cent between her two daughters, Nina and Dipti.

The mother's reluctance to make this move was clear. The last thing she wanted was to be instrumental in the carving up and possible devaluation of her legendary husband's empire so soon after his death. The solution did not leave the brothers entirely happy either, as they looked across the family and saw that the women in the family were now as a group the largest shareholders in the business.

In the settlement, Mukesh retained control over the original busi-nesses incorporating oil and gas, chemicals and textiles, while Anil took under his wing the telecommunications, energy distribution and financial service businesses. The existing shareholdings Mukesh and Anil held in each other's company would be swapped, along with $1 billion in cash to Anil. Kokilaben also insisted that both her sons sign a 10-year 'non-compete' agreement. With this settlement in the news, the group's share prices began to improve.

COMMENT

While the Reliance story has clearly not ended, the settlement unblocked the stalemate opening the door to achieving a successful outcome. The unbundling of the businesses and the possibility for the brothers to act as leaders in their own right, in their own style and with their own businesses, proved to be a formula that unleashed dramatic innovation and growth. Exploiting buoyant market condi-tions in India and with their new-found focus on their respective groups, the Ambani brothers' businesses are both powering ahead. A glance at the websites of the two groups shows both siblings staking a strong claim to being the bearer of Dhirubhai's legacy.

No family likes its dirty linen to be aired in public. But in this case it was inevitable that the media would take a keen interest in the story as it directly affected millions of investors. Yet the case illustrates how arguments carried out through public media get seriously amplified, not least because the media spin on comments and postures is something the parties have no control over, yet they will be inclined to take seriously as the authentic voice of their adversary.

The deeper story here is about individuality, and the folly of creating a zero-sum game by setting young men with different casts of mind but equal ambition in a shared competitive space. Sometimes it seems the wishes of parents are best ignored.

THE DASSLER FAMILY – RACING FOR SUPREMACY[7]

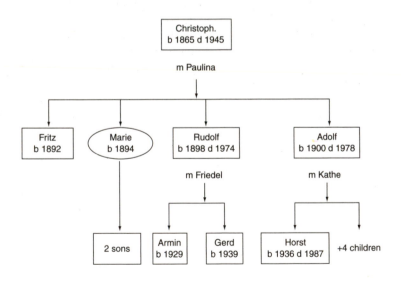

Figure 3.3   The Dassler family

ORIGINS

The Dassler family lived in the northern Bavarian town of Herzogenaurach, which had for centuries been a centre for the production of shoes. Adolf Dassler was born in 1900, and as a young lad was an active sportsman, setting up impromptu running races and competitions with his friends. The family were not well off, but hard-working. His father was a shoemaker, and to help make ends meet his mother ran a small commercial laundry from the back of their house. In the First World War Adolph, along with his two older brothers, joined the fight on the front. The Dasslers were fortunate to see all three sons return home after active duty. Adi, as he was known, returned with an ambition, and immediately set up a small shoe workshop in a space in his mother's washroom premises that had fallen out of use after the war. Adi devoted a portion of his time to experimental work in his beloved sport of running, dabbling in the manufacture of running shoes with spikes.

At first he and his friends were, in fact, the only customers for the product. By 1920 the venture was showing promise and the Adolf Dassler shoe company was set up. Of all the potential outlets for their products they spotted an opportunity in football, which was emerging as the most popular sport. The company started to sell its shoes and boots directly to sports and football clubs. But the big breakthrough happened when Adi managed to catch the attention of the German Olympic coach in the run-up to the 1928 Amsterdam Olympics. This budding relationship was the springboard to the company becoming the leading supplier of athletic running shoes.

ADI AND RUDI

By 1923 Adi was feeling the strain of success, and turned to his brother Rudolf to join the firm to focus on developing new business. Rudolf, two years Adi's senior, was a man cut from a different cloth. His expansive manners had proved unsuited to his first career choice, in the local police. He came to the realization that his skills would be better employed in sales. The brothers then officially became partners in July 1924, incorporating Gebruder Dassler, Sportschufabrik, Herzogenaurach.

Soon romance beckoned for Rudi, and in 1928, buoyed by the finances of the growing business, he married Friedl, a pretty brunette and with an easy-going personality. The couple moved into the large villa that the family shared in Herzogenaurach, where the new bride established a good relationship with her in-laws. A few years went by before Adi in turn decided to marry, in 1934. His choice was Kathe, a more assertive hard-headed character who found it a struggle to integrate into the family ménage of the communal villa.

The climate in the family started to become an emotional cauldron, through the chemistry of the contrasting personalities and the heat of their close proximity. On top of the contrasting characters of the wives, an ideological divide started to emerge between the brothers around their political beliefs and loyalties. This was the 1930s, and the region was not far from epicentre of the rise of National Socialism in Germany and the emergence of the Nazi regime. Both brothers became party members, but in differing ways. Whereas Adi was not committed, Rudi openly supported the ruling party's philosophy. There was an atmosphere of rising tension at the family villa, fuelled by the bickering couples. In the business too Rudi was becoming steadily more assertive, while Adi remained the linchpin of the company, the man with the knowledge that gave Gebruder Dassler its edge. Tension between the siblings was on the rise as the contrasting personalities of the brothers collided with ever-greater intensity. Rudi felt mounting impatience with his brother's detail-conscious tinkering, whereas Adi felt increasingly ill at ease with his brother's brashness and dominance.

THE SPLIT

With the advent of the Second World War the German state still needed industry to produce vital goods. Adi thus earned early release from the army so that sports shoes could be kept in supply. Meanwhile, Rudi was still away, posted to an administrative job at the customs service in occupied Poland. This disparity in fortunes left Rudi bitter and jealous. There he was, far from Herzogenaurach, while his brother was running the business. Rudi wanted to regain control, and bent his mind to a strategy for doing so.

The end of the war was not a good time for Rudi. He was arrested by the Americans and briefly imprisoned as a suspected Nazi sympathizer. But Adi also had a fight on his hands to clear his name so he could carry on with the business of making shoes. It was during this period – both of them, like many of their fellow countrymen, tender with the scars of the war – that they reached the tipping point at which they split. Adi's wife Kathe heard the rumour that Rudi had given the De-Nazification Committee false information, attempting to incriminate Adi. This infuriated her.

At this point Rudi and his family made the first move, quitting the family villa together with his mother Paulina, who by now was a widow, to move across the River Aurach to the other side of town. Marie, the Dassler sister, remained with Adi. She was also daggers drawn with Rudi, unable to forgive him for refusing to employ her two sons in the shoe factory, which would have kept them away from the war. Both had been killed in action, and she blamed Rudi.

With the split widening between them, the brothers decided to divide the firm's assets, with Rudi taking over the smaller factory on his side of town. The employees were left to decide which brother they would like to work with. Most of the sales team joined Rudi while the production staff largely stayed with Adi. In 1948 the brothers registered their respective companies. Each of them chose names that were to become leading brands, Adidas and Puma. The break was not only a major event in the family; it was a cause célèbre in the town, which was also divided in its support for these two local firms. The dispute heralded decades of rivalry in the fast-growing sports-wear market. Herzogenaurach became known as the town where people always looked down at your feet when greeting you, so they could see whose shoes you were wearing and therefore what camp you belonged to, before starting a conversation.

ESCALATION

The fight that set Adi and Rudi Dassler at each other's throats was to reach even greater heights as the second generation started to join the business. At first Adidas was spurred on by Adi and Kathe's son Horst Dassler, who displayed much of his uncle's commercial flair, successfully promoting the Adidas brand. Yet Horst in turn was to create a split in his family. The stimulus was his parents dispatching him to France to establish a new division based in the Alsace region. So successful was Horst that Adidas France grew in size to rival the mother company in Germany. Horst, a workaholic entrepreneur, had the bit between his teeth and set himself on a path to outdo his parent's business.

Horst's rise ruffled feathers, not least of his mother. Kathe, ever the tough one in the family, was determined to retain full control of the family empire. Horst then alienated his father, defying company policy by entering the market for sports clothing. As this internal wrangling went on unabated, the fight in the marketplace was also intensifying. During the 1958 World Cup in Sweden Puma filed a complaint against Adidas's advertising slogan. The brothers, who drove their respective companies hard, never relented.

The next generation was standing in the wings to continue to fight when the first generation protagonists had left the stage. Rudi, always the more difficult of the two brothers, also had a poor relationship with his eldest son Armin, whom he constantly berated. As the brothers aged, their relationships with their successors did not mellow. Indeed, as Rudi fell into terminal ill-health in the 1970s, he impulsively amended his will, excluding Armin from his estate, in favour of Gerd, the younger of his sons. Rudi died in 1974 and when the will was read, Armin was devastated at this final and unexpected blow from his late father. His brother refused to listen to Armin's entreaties and so Armin sought legal counsel. He eventually found redress, and was installed as the general partner of Puma, with Gerd holding a minority stake.

Another four years went by before Adi also passed away in 1978, to be buried in the same cemetery as Rudi, though conspicuously laid to rest in a different part of the burial ground. Although the brothers had met face to face a few times towards the end of their lives for private discussions, to the very end the families remained bitterly divided.

COMMENT

What are the lessons from this case? One of the most obvious is to consider character before you get in the box and start working with someone, especially if that person is your close relative. People who might have coexisted happily in separate spaces were not only forced into harness together, but in the same villa, along with a volatile concoction of spouse differences. The rivalry between mother and son that subsequently emerged is highly unusual, and yet springs from the same root as most parent–offspring conflict – the desire for control pitched against the desire for autonomy. Strong personalities make this a major liability.

In contrast to Reliance, here was a tale where making a clean break between business interests of warring brothers did not yield a solution. The reason was that they continued to be in the same competitive space. This suggests some more creative division of responsibilities across the empire might have worked, though by the time the split came there was probably too much bad blood. The ideological differences between Adi and Rudi Dassler were always going to make any kind of joint decision making tough. All of this leads to the conclusion that complete separation including non-competition agreements is probably the only way in a low-trust context, such as Reliance and the Dasslers experienced.

THE MONDAVI FAMILY – A BITTER CUP [8]

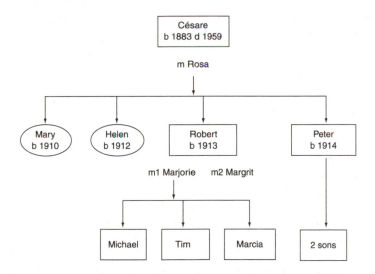

Figure 3.4   The Mondavi family

ORIGINS

The central character in this story is Robert Mondavi, an inspirational entrepreneur who pioneered a revolution in the Californian wine business that saw it emerge in the latter part of the 20th century as a region that is now recognized as one of the world's great sources of fine wines. Leading by example, he was able to demonstrate that the business acumen of his native US citizens could be combined with the best skills from the Old World to produce wines that could be widely marketed to people who could appreciate good quality in their glass.

It is testimony to the drive and determination of the man that Robert was able to implement his vision when he was well into his 50s. It was the 1960s, and he was armed with a vision of how he could go about merging the art of Europe with the savvy of North America. Robert was spurred into action by a desire to prove himself, and his rivalry with his younger brother Peter.

Robert and Peter were born in Minnesota just before the beginning of the First World War, the youngest of four children to parents Césare and Rosa Mondavi who had recently emigrated from Italy to the United States. Father was the provider and believed strongly in self-reliance, while their mother worked hard, helping the family make a living by lodging other immigrants as boarders in their house. Césare, wishing to make a better living for his family, saw the opportunity to go into wholesale supply of grapes to the wine-producing Italian community of America.

RIVALS

In their youth the siblings were already rivals, competing in the summer along with groups of workers in the family winery business to see who would nail together the most wooden boxes. With his strong fighting spirit and desire to win, Robert usually came out top, happily crowing over his brother that he was 'world champion'. During the 1930s the Mondavi boys were growing into young adults. Robert was the first to join the wine business in 1936, and immediately it ignited his passion. The family business took an important strategic turn in 1943, during the Second World War, when Robert persuaded his parents to acquire the Charles

Krug winery and move out of the wholesale business into higher-margin bottled wines. Césare made only one stipulation for his son Robert on buying the winery: that he should work together harmoniously with his brother Peter. So it was at the end of the Second World War that when Peter was discharged from the army he joined Robert at Krug.

The brothers were very different in terms of motivation, interests and values. Robert focused on the business, where he held the reins in terms of sales and marketing, with few outside interests, apart from getting married to Marge in 1937. His subsequent lack of attention to his growing children and to his marriage was to haunt Robert later on in life. His younger brother Peter followed a more balanced approach to life, leaving time outside his work, where he was responsible for all the production aspects of the company, to devote to his hobby – fishing – and his family. Robert, wanting to develop the business, constantly pressured Peter to produce better wines to improve the family firm's reputation for quality. When Peter did not deliver Robert was angered. Increasingly the two grew apart.

THE BROKEN CUP

With the death of the patriarch Césare in 1959 the family no longer had a peacekeeper and the divisions between the siblings widened. The family firm was no longer unified by a shared vision. Robert's ambition to be the best was not matched by Peter's honest but more modest aims. In November 1965 the Mondavis assembled for a family gathering, which turned out to be the stage for a fundamental point of fracture. Robert and Peter got into a fist fight over an argument about Marge's new mink coat, and whether it had been bought with company money (which it transpired it had not). Robert, now in his 50s, seemed to gather the negative energy of their decades of rivalry and let his emotions rip, landing several blows on Peter. The fight ended with neither apology nor handshake, even though it transpired that the original cause was a misunderstanding.

Indeed it divided the family and left Rosa the matriarch heartbroken. As a result of the bust-up Robert was forced by the board to take six months' paid leave from the company, leaving behind his brother Peter to manage the business. The fallout was a cloud of acrimony,

with Robert accusing the firm of wrongful dismissal and demanding he should be free to cash in his 20 per cent share in the business.
Robert fought his case in the courts to secure this claim, which he
eventually won after a decade-long battle.

The biggest change that followed from the family split in 1965 was
Robert's liberation to pursue his vision of founding a new and bold
high-quality wine venture in the Napa Valley. He set out to create the
best winery, producing fine wines that would sell by reputation and
not by price, emulating the finest European producers. At the outset,
because his financial resources were limited, he brought in a partner.
Some years later when he had achieved the settlement with his family
and the new business was beginning to flourish, he was able to buy
out his partner and become fully independent. The Robert Mondavi
Winery earned its spurs in spades, producing what the founder had
set out to do, and becoming an exemplar for other Californian wine
pioneers to follow. Mondavi's reputation grew to the point at which
Baron Philippe de Rothschild, seeing the potential in New World
wines, knocked on the door of Robert Mondavi when he decided he
wanted to develop a winery in California. In 1978 their partnership
winery Opus One was established; another venture that was to earn
high accolades among wine connoisseurs.

RIVALS, MARK II

With his freedom from the rest of his family Robert had been able
to push forward to ever greater heights. Now in his role as founding father of his own company Robert wanted to develop his sons to
become the future leaders of the firm. But the skills of business visionary and family steward do not necessarily go hand in hand. Part of
the issue was that Robert, like his father, wanted to see both his sons
Michael and Tim take a leading involvement in the family business.
By placing the two sons in open competition with each other he was
unwittingly reproducing his own past and driving a wedge between
them. Often, when they made a mistake, he would dress them down
publicly, humiliating them in front of employees.

Robert's apparent lack of any 'soft' side was a liability. He seemed
oblivious and unconcerned about the problems that his harsh behaviour caused. Michael, the elder and more extrovert of the siblings, was

perceived to be the natural leader. Tim, the younger and more reflective brother, had been reluctant to join the family business, remembering the family fights between his father and uncle. Robert played around with different leadership models and eventually installed his sons as co-CEOs in 1993, following the public flotation of the business. He had been afraid that in choosing one of his sons for the role that the other would leave the company. But this decision muddied the waters. During these years the business was growing fast and was beginning to over-extend itself. The co-CEOs were lacking in the required discipline and clarity of decision making. Co-leadership in this case was struggling to provide either of these important management attributes.

Robert's strong suit clearly lay elsewhere than in developing a family business continuity plan. The Mondavis' approach to succession planning was to try every solution in the book. Part of the reason behind the failure to get to a lasting solution was the senior generation hanging on to power. But equally the next generation, particularly Michael, never fully rose to the challenge. Perhaps their father had too zealously tried to mould his sons to reflect his view of the world, rather than just instilling in them good ownership skills and bringing them on as stewards. Maybe their sister Marcia was the leader that they should have had. She served on the board of the company and had strong views; for example it was she who challenged the proposal to float the business.

In fact the initial public offering (IPO), which was designed to help the business finance growth, marked the opening of the final chapter for the family business. This period culminated with the loss of independence of the firm a decade later when the business was taken over. By the time the company was put up for sale in 2004 both of the brothers had left the company. Michael's reign of leadership was unsuccessful and in 2001 after a relatively short period at the helm he stepped down as CEO. Although he remained as chairman of the board he had become a lame duck leader and the board ousted him in early 2004, with no evident opposition from his father. With the board firmly in non-family hands the decision to sell the business in the face of an offer from a larger competitor went through unopposed, bringing to an end the family business. If there was to be a consolation prize for the sale of the business, it was the public reconciliation of Robert with his brother Peter, by then both in their

90s, announcing that they would co-produce a barrel of wine for a charity auction.

COMMENT

Again we see the ill wisdom of parents forcing siblings into the same space when the children's modus operandi is more competitive rivalry than cooperative behaviour. In this case the error was compounded, for Robert recreated an even more difficult conjunction for his own children by forcing them into co-leadership. Clear and distinctive separation of roles between the family members working in the business would have helped.

For people with visionary gifts and temperament, like Robert, the answer is to bring in professional leadership and create a real partnership for business success. Not least among Robert's deficiencies seems to have been emotional intelligence – the ability to manage his own emotions and to read the emotions of others. His decisions about his children arguably reflect this.[9]

Let us finish this saga of fraternal rivalry with the story of a rival North American wine producer, and one of the world's biggest, the Gallo family.

THE GALLO FAMILY – VINTAGE CONFLICTS[10]

ORIGINS

The family name Gallo has become synonymous with the wine industry in California, and its history in viniculture goes back to the early part of the 20th century. Today, Gallo is the world's second largest wine producer, closely following the new owners of Mondavi's Constellation brands. The Gallo family were one of the first movers in the industry, and their name is indelibly associated with the development of the California wine business.

Before the advent of Prohibition in the United States in 1920, Joe Gallo was the owner of small businesses in the hospitality sector, including the Gallo Wine Company (founded 1907 with his brother), which earned him and his family a comfortable living.

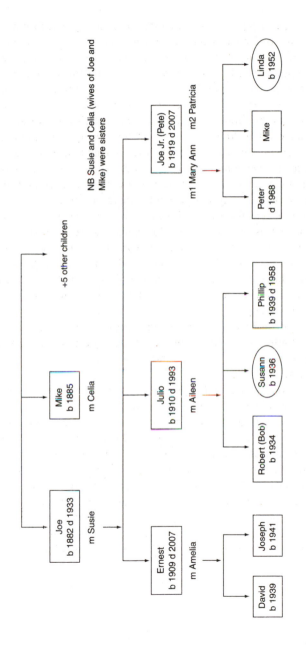

Figure 3.5 The Gallo family

In 1908 Joe married Susie, the daughter of an early California winery owner Battista Bianco, while his brother Mike was in love with her sister Celia, whom he eventually married. Joe's marriage proved to be a tempestuous affair, with Susie twice filing for divorce but each time retracting her threat. With more luck than foresight, Joe closed his liquor business and the hotel and saloon they owned in 1918, and reinvested in the production of wine grapes. This turned out to be a smart move when Prohibition was ushered in, for wine grapes were in high demand among both home winemakers and bootleggers. Joe Gallo was a smart entrepreneur who built a good business and who was able to keep any brushes with the law to a minimum, for his was an industry very closely scrutinized by the authorities.

Susie produced three boys; Ernest, Julio and Joe Jr, also know as Pete. Joe Jr was born in 1919 a full decade after his oldest brother Ernest, who was just one year older than Julio. As a father Joe was frequently absent, and difficulties emerged in his relationship with the two eldest boys, Ernest and Julio. Much of their childhood was spent in the care of the Biancos, their maternal grandparents. It was a tough life for the oldest boys, without much freedom or material wealth, though it gave Ernest his first insight into winemaking, witnessing his grandfather filling the earthenware jugs of the Basque shepherds who came down from the surrounding hills to buy his grandfather's home brew.

Things were different for Joe Jr. He arrived in times of greater plenty, and to a looser regime – being allowed to do things in his youth that his brothers had been denied. As the Prohibition years passed, the young Gallos grew up being expected to spend a lot of time when out of school toiling in the vineyards. The arrest of their father in 1923 on charges of violating the Prohibition laws was an embarrassment to Ernest and Joe, so there was relief all round when the charges were dropped later in the year. These events during their formative years had a strong influence on the two older siblings – it seemed to urge them towards creating their own distinctive identities and distancing themselves from their parents' generation.

FATHER AND SON

The elder son Ernest was inclined to stand up to his father Joe, and the gap between them grew ever wider. Joe could be rough and uncouth, and would often shout his son down if they disagreed. Ernest's resentment of his father was growing steadily all the while. Yet Ernest, ever observant, learnt the tools of the trade from his father, which also fed his ambitions to succeed. Eager for a stake in the fruits of his work he started to push his father towards giving him a stake in the family business, but was rebuffed repeatedly. Eventually in 1930 Ernest decided to have it out with his father, and confronted him with an ultimatum: give me a partnership with equity or I quit. He didn't get the answer he wanted. Joe exploded with rage and pulled out his shotgun, threatening the boys. At this point the brothers fled the home, leaving their mother to bear the brunt of their father's anger.

The breach was not permanent, and they came back a few months later at their parents' begging. Meanwhile, the older brothers observed that Joe Jr was being treated much more softly by their father. Although Joe Jr still looked up to his older brothers as heroes, they were jealous of him. Also, Ernest had found a new departure in his life by marrying Amelia Franzia in 1931, daughter of another prominent Californian winemaking family.

Then came a bombshell that was to change the family forever. In June 1933 Joe and Susie were found murdered at their homestead. It was and still remains a mystery how they had died. The coroner recorded a verdict of murder–suicide. This threw a pall of gloom over the family. Of the brothers Julio was the most upset. Ernest's way of coping was to immerse himself ever deeper in his plans for the business, in readiness for the repeal of the Prohibition Act that was due later that year. Grape growers were all readying themselves for the new era that would emerge when they could start to trade as wineries. Meanwhile the parents' probate had to be settled and Ernest was the appointed administrator.

Their mother's will stipulated that her estate was to be divided in equal amounts between the three brothers when they reached 21, whereas their father Joe died intestate. One of the main assets of the estate was the vineyards, a key element in the plan for the two older brothers to establish their new winery. To get the requisite licences they needed to be active in the grape-producing business. At this stage the older siblings were their brother's legal guardians, with full powers to manage Joe Jr's affairs. His elder brothers treated him much as their father had treated them, working him relentlessly out of school hours and keeping him in the dark about the state of the business or its history. Joe Jr innocently signed all documents put in front of him, including a consent form granting full powers of attorney to Ernest and Julio.

At this time, the assets from their parents' estates were put into a partnership, Gallos Bros Ranches. Half a century later the issue of the division of the estate would be disputed in court by Joe Jr.

ERNEST'S ERA

The years that followed saw Ernest gradually putting a firmer stamp on the business as its leader. At the start he and Julio strove together as partners, taking it in turns to work their one tractor for 12-hour stints, but their relationship was becoming increasingly uneasy. Julio was still suffering in the aftermath of his parents' death. He had experienced several mental breakdowns during the period, to the point of being hospitalized on several occasions during the years of the Second World War.

When he eventually returned to the business the brothers had a potentially fruitful division of labour, with Ernest, the indefatigable salesman, brilliantly promoting the product and acting as business leader, while his brother Julio in the engine room managed the vineyards and oversaw the winemaking. But Ernest lived by the 'Three Rs' motto he drilled into his sales force – rigorousness, relentlessness and ruthlessness – which meant unceasing pressure on Julio to deliver the production that was needed to support the growing success of the company in the marketplace. With the siblings' relationship failing to improve, Julio started making threats to resign and seek dissolution of the partnership, but without ever making that move.

Meantime, as soon as the war ended, Joe Jr left the army and came back to work in the family business. Although Ernest offered to hire Joe to head up winemaking, dangling a carrot of potential partnership, he chose to work under Julio in the vineyard operation. Joe settled into his new role as employee and staff member. A few years later in 1950 any financial links he still had with the family were ended when the Gallo Bros Ranches partnership was dissolved.

Meanwhile, the 1950s and 1960s saw the company transformed. They moved from the chief supplier at the bottom end of the market to something closer to respectability, through the cushion created by a new best-selling product. This was Thunderbird, named after the Ford sports car, a cheap lemon-flavoured fortified wine. It was through its outstanding success that E&J Gallo were ahead of the pack by the end of the 1950s.

At the same time as the wealth of the Gallos was growing, the next generation were emerging as adults. The door was open to the family members joining, without much reflection as to where their talents and abilities actually lay. This was problematic. Ernest's two sons, David and Joey, struggled to make a mark in the shadow of their father. He gave his sons a rough ride, including confidence-draining public dressings down. Although Ernest wanted his sons to succeed him, at the same time his desire to be the dominant top dog was unquenchable.

The perception within the firm that nepotism was ruling key appointments was sapping morale in the company. Staff turnover was high and rising. Hiring young family members extended to Julio's branch, where both his son Bob and son-in-law Jim Coleman came to work for the firm. Then another tragedy struck: Julio's youngest son Phillip committed suicide. He was said to have been experiencing psychological problems. With this further blow to his fragile state of mind, Julio started again to entertain the idea of breaking away from the family firm, but with the encouragement and support of his younger brother Joe Jr he was persuaded once again to hang in with the family business.

DISPUTED TERRITORY

An incident in the mid-1960s ignited further tension in the family when the brothers decided to consolidate their glass bottle unit, through which Joe Jr held a minority interest in the wine group. Ernesto and Julio would not allow their brother to exchange his shares in the subsidiary for a small stake in E&J Gallo, but insisted on buying him out. This led to a dispute over the size of the payout, and only after threatening legal action was Joe's family able to get a price for their shares that they considered to be satisfactory. However, this incident was only a skirmish ahead of the conflict to come over bigger issues.

More tragedy was to visit the family in 1968, when Joe's eldest son Peter, fighting in the Vietnam War, was killed in combat. Spurred on by the sudden void in the family and free from any close ties to the activities of his older brothers, Joe and his surviving son Mike redoubled their efforts to build their own business activities. One of their activities was to supply grapes from their own vineyards to the Gallo winery. In the early 1980s they decided to branch out into the food business, and launched a new cheesemaking operation, the Joseph Gallo Cheese Company, which took hold in the market. Ernest was present at the launch to congratulate his youngest brother, but a year later the situation had soured. Ernest now accused his brother of violating their trademark rights by marketing the cheese under the name of Gallo.

In 1979 Gallo had acquired the trademark rights to Gallo Salame, a cold meat brand that had been on the market for many years, apparently wanting to protect the usage of the Gallo trademark in fresh foods. Ernest called Joe to a face-to-face meeting which Julio also attended, to discuss the trademark issue. The outcome of the meeting was the beginning of negotiations to establish a licence agreement from the winery for Joe's cheese company. But a compromise was never found. Ernest took an increasingly hard line and the dispute escalated in 1986, with Gallo wines taking the battle to court, accusing Joe's company of violating their trademark rights. During the process of discovery for the trial, a document came to light that Joe believed indicated that he was entitled to a third share in his mother's estate. On learning this, Joe was incensed and immediately filed a counter-suit claiming damages for his exclusion from the assets of his parents' estate.[11]

But Joe was out of luck. His arguments made no headway in the courts. In the final outcome, Joe's legal battles were both unsuccessful. He lost the right to use the Gallo name for his cheeses, and failed to prove any wrongdoing by his brothers in relation to their late mother's estate. To add injury to the situation, two years after the court battles finished Joe Gallo's grape supply contracts to E&J Gallo were terminated. Over half a century after the death of their parents the brothers' interests were finally completely separated.

ENDGAME

Today, Gallo still rides high in the marketplace and the company thrives in private ownership, controlled by the descendants of the founding family. Having been predeceased by their brother Julio who was killed in a car accident in 1993, Ernest and Joe Jr died in 2007 within a month of each other. With their passing, the strains and ructions of earlier generations were finally laid to rest, while the family and the business moved on. The Gallos play an active role both in the governance and management of the business. In contrast to the Mondavis, they have consistently placed considerable importance on attracting, retaining and motivating high-quality non-family talent, which has stood them in good stead. By being adaptive and through adjusting their corporate strategy in line with the changing trends in the marketplace, Gallo remains the largest family-owned wine company in the world.

COMMENT

This is a story of family enterprise where at first a sibling partnership works well, because one brother recognizes that his sibling has the drive and the vision to lead the business. The difficulties arose through neglect of the interests of a younger sibling, culminating in the damage that inevitably comes from a legal showdown.

The source of the difficulties can in part be laid at Joe Sr's door: a role model for persistence and resistance, he forced his high-achieving son, Ernest, to break free and forge ahead. It taught the boy virtues and vices in equal measure – the latter being poor judgment of character in the treatment of his children and failure to comprehend their needs and difficulties.

Indeed that has been a theme in all the cases in this chapter – poor male parental role modelling, deficiencies in emotional intelligence, bad decisions about children's roles in the business, and unchecked (sometimes even encouraged) rivalry between male siblings. We shall see elements of this pattern reproduced as we proceed, for this study suggests it may be one of the most common and fundamental hazards to family business.

4

Fighting for the crown

Parents are the bones upon which children sharpen their teeth.

(Peter Ustinov)

INTRODUCTION

There is a dream that many family firms successfully live out. In it, loving well-balanced parents build a business and a home side by side, giving their children the blend of guidance and choice that enables them to find themselves before they find their careers. This means some trial and error – especially error, for there is no discovery without risk. They acquire life and professional skills which they are then welcomed to use in the business at whatever level they can aspire to.

Whether family leadership succession will be an unbroken sequence depends on the gene lottery and the ability of the business to offer the right opportunities. But even in the absence of family executives, responsible ownership can be a viable aspiration for every family in business.

To avoid being at the mercy of the gene lottery – that is, not having to count on dad, mum and kids all having congruent temperaments and casts of mind – families needs sound parenting. Then they can withstand a modicum of ill-fortune. Many of the protagonists in our cases lack essential elements of effective parenting or control, and find themselves at the mercy of internal divisions, hostilities, temptations and all the travails that can divide a family.

We are entering Shakespearean territory where foolish old kings make a hash of the handover of power, and warring princes are willing to go to any lengths in order to gain absolute power. Between the dream handover and the bloodbath there are many varieties of mixed quality, such as the dynasty who continually strive to put on a brave face to the outside world, papering over the fissures that run through the family, and doing their best to conceal the eccentricities and manifest deficiencies in character of the protagonists.

The chief difference between a monarchy and a family firm is that the latter generally has more choices and fewer resources. Royal families are fenced in by laws, traditions and the weight of public scrutiny. Family firms – astonishingly to some observers, ourselves included – can start acting like royalty, taking on unnecessary rules and strictures and getting in a mess because of the way they've tied their own hands.

But even in family firms where there is nothing manifestly wrong in the family, ownership and leadership transitions turn out to be testing. Succession is generally acknowledged to be the Achilles' heel of family firms, especially at certain phases of their development.[1] We have observed that transitions between generations can be played out over a time frame that is very long, stretching sometimes for decades. Take the case of the Carlson family.[2] Owners of one of the world's largest travel and hospitality groups with properties such as Radisson Hotels, they endured one of the longest transition periods ever seen in moving from founder Curtis L Carlson first to his son-in-law, then back into his hands and finally on to his daughter Marilyn, who leads the company at the time of writing. The process of passing the baton to a member of the second generation lasted over two decades in this case.

In Chapter 2 we outlined the deep causes of conflict, especially the evolutionary roots of sibling and parent–child conflict. In Chapter 3 we showed how the sibling bond can strangle a business, and the theme recurs in several places in this chapter, so universal is the duality of brotherhood and sisterhood. But here our attention is mainly on the less recognized conflict between parents and offspring. This is often the stuff of tragedy. It seems unnatural for parents and children to be at war, but however much they love each other, the fact remains that the interests of parents and children are often divided, and sometimes fatally for a family business.[3] Fighting for the crown is the summary label, but underlying it are battles for control and autonomy, for freedom and power, and for often competing destinies.

The presence of substantial wealth in many family firms does not help the situation. Rather than being a support and a buffer enabling parents and children to make optimal choices, which it would in an ideal world, in the real world it seems often just to raise the stakes.[4] We find in many cases the senior generation who were chiefly responsible for growing the family wealth clinging onto the reins of power for too long, even if it is legally their right. The question is, are they still adding value? Sadly, often they are not.

Typically, the senior generation assume they are adding value, by virtue of their accumulated experience and wisdom. But the often unspoken issue on their minds is their own quality of life. Power is addictive; people find it hard to abandon one lifestyle for another. Older people also know, just by looking around them, how fast their contemporaries' energies seem to dissipate when they retire.[5] The pleasures of endless golf rounds are illusory, especially after one has been involved in weighty decisions and carried successfully the burden of a business and all the lives that depend upon it. Besides, often such 'emperors' of the senior generation have been so immersed in the business that they haven't even had time to learn how to play golf, or develop any other consuming interest. Unable to separate themselves from the company, they become immovable objects.[6]

Owning and running a substantial business is a little like being a demigod, no matter how you dress it up in the language of stewardship and care. And when did the gods ever want to resign their heavenly thrones? The fear of death lurks in the recesses of their consciousness. The mind can readily dream up lots of really good reasons for hanging on under such a disincentive to letting go, without realizing what you are running away from. There is also the very practical barrier in small, young firms, that they may have not had enough time to build a sufficient nest-egg of personal savings for retirement.

Mostly, though everyone knows what is going on, all too often no one is willing to talk about it. In family firms there is often a complete lack of succession planning, even when the seniors are quite advanced in years.[7] Either way the next generation can see the writing on the wall and drift away from the business, leaving it without a family future. In the cases we look at here they are more tenacious and frustrated – banging on the parents' door to let them in. Nor do they always have right on their side. The next generation can over-egg their case – imagining their parents to be more senile and incompetent than they really are, and believing themselves to be more capable of taking over than they really are. In short, it is not just the seniors who are prey to self-serving delusions. These psychological games are complicated by ownership arrangements. Usually, the deck is well and truly stacked in favour of the senior generation, either directly or indirectly, where family members' hands are tied by shares being held in trusts.

The process of handing over is thus a complicated matter. There are three interweaving strands to be untangled:

■ the transfer of ownership;
■ alteration to the balance of power, accountability and responsibility;
■ most important, the psychological transition from one role to another.

It is no wonder when all this is going on that the eye can be taken off the ball that is the business. Successions in all firms are a distraction, but in family firms, although they are typically more infrequent than in widely held non-family firms, they are more momentous and all too often beyond a point of fatal fracture.

Another barrier to succession is the gene lottery. In many cases seniors, by luck or judgment, have built a successful enterprise, but what are the qualities of the next generation to be effective leaders or responsible owners? Imagine being proud and loving parents who know in their heart of hearts that the children are just not cut out for it. Their love and fear of damaging the parental bond can lead to dissembling, delay and any number of other minor dishonesties. Sadly, research bears out the very real risks. Although studies have demonstrated that family ownership brings a performance premium[8] – what we can call the added value of 'family capital' – there is powerful recent evidence of the performance risks of family succession, especially when male primogeniture operates: that is, the eldest son is required to succeed.[9]

Governance systems that have to bear the weight of these challenges are often not up to it. They can lay down rules and procedures that force succession in its timing and aspects of process, but how they are operated matters a great deal, especially around the handling of emotions and resolution of conflicts. Many families lay down policies that govern the conditions for entry into the family business. A typical policy will cover such issues as educational standards for family members aspiring to work in the business, minimum age and work experience criteria for applying to join the firm, and hiring procedures. Some families want clear demarcation lines set between management and the board, implementing policies that debar family members from taking up management roles in the business, and restricting their involvement in governance.

The Henkels of Germany are one example of a highly successful business family who maintain a policy where family do not normally have access to working in management positions in their publicly listed company.[10] In a more extreme example William Randolph Hearst, the first great newspaper magnate of the United States, who died in 1951, set out in his will that he did not believe that any of his heirs was competent to run the business.[11] He established a trust, where the family maintained a minority of the votes, with day-to-day control of the company put in the hands of non-family management. Any of his heirs challenging his wishes, as set out in his will, would be disinherited. On paper Hearst's plan appeared very simple, but 40 years after his death the family was in court fighting over the direction of the family trust. His plan – to keep the family out of the management of the business, providing clear guidelines as to how the company should be run – backfired years down the line. Subordinating the views of the family as owners to the non-family trustees was arguably a step too far. Not even as mighty a man as Randolph Hearst could rule from the grave, but amazingly and foolishly many senior family business owners try to do just that. It is a poor substitute for planning succession with a realistic appraisal of the options and human resources.

Now let us tell some stories that illustrate these themes, and consider how might things have turned out better.

THE McCAINS – WHEN THE CHIPS ARE DOWN[12]

THE McCAIN DYNASTY

The McCain family were part of the wave of emigrants from the British Isles who began farming in the fertile lands of Eastern Canada in the 1860s. H H (Henry) McCain was an innovator and a genuine entrepreneur – a man who looked opportunity in the eye and then grabbed it by the tail. His first venture concentrated on apple growing on his farm in Florenceville, New Brunswick. He also set up a general store, and was one of the first merchants in the area to pay farmers for their produce in cash rather than goods. He had three daughters and one son, Andrew Davies (A D). The gene lottery fell favourably. A D from an early age proved to be hard-working and intelligent, earning him responsibilities beyond his years. In 1910, Henry and A D started potato farming, and called their enterprise the McCain Produce Company. Potatoes became the most important cash crop in the area, and the McCains grabbed the opportunity to export their produce to the United States and beyond. A D worked tirelessly, and by the time Henry passed away in 1920 the business was flourishing. Along with the growth in their business the McCains had developed a reputation as benevolent capitalists, generously supporting local community activities and projects. Mrs A D ran a social service agency supporting the Florenceville community.

A D and his wife Laura had six children: Marie, Andrew, Robert, Eleanor, Harrison and Wallace. The gene lottery this time dealt a matrix of personality types that was to be an important leitmotiv for the family saga. The eldest, Marie was quiet and timid by nature; Andrew and Robert were solid, somewhat staid types, while younger sister Eleanor was quick-witted, funny and talkative. The two youngest siblings, Harrison and Wallace, were like twins, growing up very close to each other – they even shared the same bed, as did their elder brothers, until they went to university. A strict work ethic was instilled in all the children by their parents and mediocrity was not tolerated. The McCains never lavished money on the children. If they wanted something, they had to earn it. Mrs A D, as she was always known, was a strong and dynamic woman who ruled the McCain family with the same authority she exerted as a natural

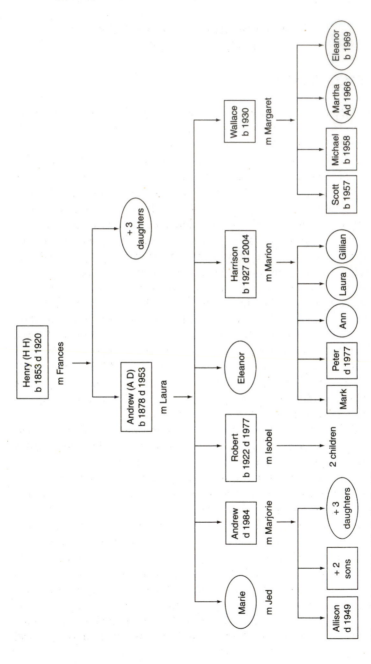

Figure 4.1 The McCain family

leader of the Florenceville community. A D, for his part, although a quieter and more subdued character than his wife, was no pushover, but a strong-willed man who commanded his children's and his employees' respect.

HARRISON AND WALLACE

Throughout their school years and into adulthood, it was the two youngest McCain brothers, Harrison and Wallace, who stood out. Harrison was a quiet and studious child, who not only flourished academically but was also an energetic athlete. He showed leadership qualities even in school, and in adolescence developed an uncommonly strong interest in politics. Wallace, his 'twin', was the family jokester and somewhat of a rebel, who needed constant prodding to get him through his schooling. Yet in time he too flourished, largely by virtue of his enormous capacity for attention to detail. Both boys met their marriage partners at college: Harrison married Marion 'Billie' McNair, the sophisticated and well-connected daughter of the New Brunswick premier, and Wallace married Margaret Norrie, a strong and independent woman. At university the brothers were also building their social networks, which included an important relationship with the successor of a major industrialist, K C Irving, in whose firm they both obtained their first jobs on leaving college.

A D McCain died in February 1953, aged 74, with the business on his mind right to the end. But Harrison and Wallace decided not to join the family business after their father's death, and chose to continue working for K C Irving. A D died intestate, which required his estate to be divided as specified by law. His widow Laura received a third of the assets, and the remainder was divided equally among the six children, giving them each a one-ninth share in the family business. Laura would not tolerate family dissension, and filling the void left by her husband, she took on the mantle of unifying force in the family. The running of the family company fell largely to older brothers Andrew and Robert, with active support from Laura, in the role of company president. Laura had known that her husband kept a mistress, but when A D passed away, typical of her determinedly rational outlook, she showed sangfroid in defending his memory so as to retain family unity. In short, as a steward through this transition period she was exemplary.

McCAIN FOODS LTD

Meanwhile, the two youngest siblings were itching to start their own enterprise, and it was the high-achieving Harrison who took the lead by quitting his job to start looking for opportunities. With the financial cushion of his inheritance he could afford to take a little time to survey the scene. However, it made Laura nervous to see her son unemployed, and she implored eldest son Robert to help come up with some ideas. Robert noticed that the General Foods Birds Eye label had started packaging frozen foods at a plant in Maine just over the border, including the manufacture of frozen French fries. He put to Harrison and Wallace the proposition that there was a business opportunity in processing fresh potatoes in New Brunswick and going into the frozen food business.

The younger brothers jumped at the idea of setting up such a venture, both investing C$30,000 for a one-third stake, with Andrew and Robert both contributing C$20,000 for a sixth share each. Additional finance to their C$100,000 start-up capital was raised via a bank loan, supplemented by a federal grant towards the cost of a new cold-storage plant that was needed to warehouse the company's products. Harrison was already available to start work preparing the ground for the new business, and Wallace soon joined forces with his brother to oversee the building, construction and installation of the plant and equipment. The brothers formed Opco ('Operating Company'), an umbrella group under which McCain Foods, Carleton Cold Storage and future McCain subsidiaries would operate.

The board was filled with family members, including the four brothers plus sister Marie's husband Jed Sutherland, a practising dentist. In the early stages of the McCains' frozen-food venture it grew rapidly under the shared leadership of Harrison as president and Wallace as vice president, selling most of the produce to the catering trade. Harrison from the start was highly confident and led from the front. He was the McCain seen in the public eye, whereas Wallace was more of a details man focused on the business operations. Year by year the business became more profitable and the company grew steadily. Meanwhile, the cattle and farming company founded by their grandfather, McCain Produce Co, which grew crops for the new processing plant and continued to ship seed potatoes worldwide, was still being run by Andrew and Robert. They remained more provincial in their outlook, sticking close to the land that they had lived on and to the farming community they had grown up in.

One of the McCains' best strategic moves during the 1960s was to focus their international development efforts on the British market, rather than attempting to go next door, to the United States. This turned out to be an inspired choice, for they entered the United Kingdom at a time when fast food restaurants were springing up all over the country. By the 1970s, McCain Foods had grown into a sizeable vertically integrated operation. In 1971 the brothers changed their titles to better reflect the jobs they were actually doing in the business: Harrison became chairman and Wallace president.

Later, in a move that possibly foreshadowed the growing inability of the brothers to work together, they started to compartmentalize the business, splitting their responsibilities along geographic lines: Harrison took charge of the United Kingdom, Europe and their transport business in Canada, while Wallace directed operations in Canada, Australia and the United States, all markets in which the company was now working. McCain sales grew strongly during this period.

UNEASY PARTNERSHIP

Harrison and Wallace worked hand in hand as a sibling partnership team. Harrison liked to play the role of the patriarch, though he had a temperamental streak. He focused on business development and finding talented people to staff the growing business. Wallace, with his meticulous attention to detail, kept the factory running, ensured costs were under control, and continually searched for ways to improve productivity. In all his dealings, with employees and suppliers alike, Wallace was tough but scrupulously honest. In those early days governance was relatively unstructured and the brothers rarely had board meetings. They sought informal consensus to make the most of their decisions.

It is curious but true that people often find it easier to stick together when striving to improve their condition than when swathed in the cushions of wealth and luxury. As the personal fortunes of the McCains grew, so did the cracks in their once-solid relationship. The first fracture point between Harrison and Wallace, the formerly inseparable 'twins', started to become visible. Of course they were not

twins, and just like any siblings their interests could be divided as
easily as they could be united.

While their wealth might have been comparable, their status was
not. Harrison's social standing had been given a major boost when
he was appointed to the board of the Bank of Nova Scotia in 1971.
Wallace disapproved of his brother taking time out of the family
business to pursue other professional activities. A second more seriously divisive issue around ownership planning arose at the same
time. Three of the brothers agreed to a plan for transferring their
shares into trusts. The fourth, Harrison, increasingly a man of distinction, stood out against this move. His view was that you shouldn't
automatically trust your family.[13] Wallace was shocked. What could it
signify that his once so close brother could be so low in trust? Might
this not mean that Harrison was untrustworthy himself?

Let us take note – trust is the most important five-letter word in
business, and it is the cornerstone of the family firm. Trust is like
an oak tree. It takes years to grow but can be cut down in an hour.
You sow the seeds of mistrust and in the future you will reap a bitter
harvest. For the McCains the process of losing trust in the family had
started to set in.

ENTER THE NEXT GENERATION

Harrison and Marion had five children; two sons and three daughters: Mark, Peter, Ann, Laura and Gillian. None of their five offspring
would establish a successful long-term career path in the family firm.
To a large extent the reason lies at the door of their dominant father.
There was not much light for growth under the shade of Harrison's
increasingly looming presence, and all found it better to develop their
lives away from the family company. Also, while the hiring policy
for male family members was very loose, with easy access to jobs in
the firm, the McCain daughters were not welcomed. Laura seemed to
have the skills and to be the most motivated to work in the family
company, but she only stayed in the firm for a very short period
before leaving to set up her own seafood business.

Wallace and Margaret had four children: Scott, Michael, Martha
(who was adopted) and Eleanor, and their success rate in career terms
was destined to exceed Harrison's children. The first-born son Scott,

a regular guy who loved hockey and socializing, was to become the vice president of production in McCain Foods, but Wallace's other son Michael proved to be the most ambitious. Academically bright and brimming with self-confidence, it was Michael of all the McCain children who demonstrated most interest in joining the business.

Michael openly expressed his ambition to one day succeed his Uncle Harrison. He did not do so in any kind of weak-minded way, but with a belief that family should prove themselves, and that the current hiring policy was too lax, protecting the weaker family members by placing too little emphasis on performance. Michael also knew that it would be very difficult to rise to the top because of the tension that existed in his relationship with his uncle. He sensed early on that they would be engaged in a fight. It was a case of the young stag versus the old bull. His mother, Margaret, seeing this cloud of conflict on the horizon, wanted her youngest son to get out of the family business before a clash occurred. Meanwhile, other family members were eying the same prize. Michael's cousin, Allison, from the Andrew McCain branch, an engineer by training, applied to his Uncle Harrison to join the business. Harrison's agreement to hire his nephew was taken without his brother Wallace's knowledge.

In many families such a move would be welcomed without a stir, but in the low-trust atmosphere that was emerging between the brothers, Wallace perceived this as an attempt by Harrison to line up a potential successor and rival to Michael. He thought that in Allison his brother had possibly found a surrogate for his own children who had ducked out of the race. Poison was beginning to seep in and to fill the atmosphere in the family firm.

THE TENSION RISES

Thus began a period of rising tension among the siblings. Then suddenly an illness struck the second of the brothers, Robert, who died in 1977 at the age of 55. His loss was a blow not only because the family had lost the person who had given the idea of the business to his younger brothers, but also because Robert was a unifying force in the family. On top of this, the situation revealed deficiencies in the firm's governance procedures. There was no guidance on how to resolve the question of who should succeed Robert on the board, for he had died suddenly and unexpectedly leaving no succession plans in place. The family at this point invited their family lawyer Roger Wilson to join the board. Their desire to have closer support from their attorney at such a time was understandable, but Harrison and Wallace knew that appointing close advisers to the board was not sound practice in governance terms. A slate of independent directors would have been more valuable at this stage. The brothers did however make a gesture to the minority family shareholders and started small dividend payments, the first in over two decades. Soon however Harrison and Wallace slipped back into their normal mode of running their fast-growing business, without attending to questions around governance and succession planning.

It is in the nature of conflict that it often churns like an underground river, while the protagonists busy themselves working the land above it, maintaining an aura of not being distracted by its gurgling – that is, until it erupts through some exposed fissure. So it was with Harrison and Wallace, steadfastly ignoring the issues between them while they continued to drift apart. But cracks started to emerge through which the tension burst.

One visible incident occurred when Harrison was inaugurating a new plant in France in October 1981. Harrison held a press conference during the launch party, failing to invite or even inform Wallace, who had been intimately involved in the groundwork to get the factory up and running. This piece of neglect was compounded some years later in 1988 at an awards ceremony in Toronto, honouring Canadian business leaders, which Harrison had won but again didn't invite his brother to attend. Wallace found out independently and was determined to be there, so he pointedly booked a table, to which he invited his own list of company executives. But Harrison trumped him at the last. When Harrison went to receive his award and make his acceptance speech, he introduced all the people at his table but made no mention of his brother. For Wallace this was a very public humiliation.

Meanwhile, McCain Foods had grown to become the market's largest French-fry maker, employing more than 18,000 people, with 55 plants around the world. Harrison and Wallace worked in adjoining offices connected by an unlocked door, and they often talked on an intercom or shouted through the open door. Decisions in the business were taken by consensus, and the brothers continued to work together as a team, despite the antipathy bubbling away beneath. The one issue that openly divided them, however, was the subject of succession. Over the years, Harrison felt his brother Wallace was becoming blinded by his regard for his son Michael.[14]

THE CRUNCH

Wallace for his part thought Harrison was becoming corrupted by power, and that he would hang on as long as humanly possible, effectively stifling the ambitions of the next generation. By now the standoff between the two brothers was beginning to negatively impact the corporation. In 1988 their largest competitor in the United States was put up for sale and McCain didn't even enter a bid, thereby surrendering an unrepeatable chance to try and acquire a bigger slice of the US market.

With the relationship between the siblings heading towards breakdown Wallace decided to try to find a solution with the help of external intervention, hiring Professor John Ward, the eminent family business scholar and consultant. This was not the first attempt. Two years earlier, another family business consultant had proved unable to broker a lasting peace between the brothers. Ward saw the primary need to be greater objectivity and detachment, by establishing a board with a majority of independent directors, requiring the brothers to both back off from their respective positions. The directors' task would be to decide on a plan for leadership succession. Predictably perhaps, trust between the brothers was at such a low ebb that they were unable to agree on the board structure, let alone on candidates for the non-executive director positions. Ward's intervention was doomed. Although his remedy was correct in theory, it failed because it did not pass the first hurdle of assent by the warring brothers. When the patient is in no mood to take the medicine, the physician's wisdom is for naught.

Wallace had expressed his wish to appoint his son Michael as the CEO of McCain's US operations, a new post the organization was due to fill. In fact Michael had been running for some time the largest of the three US divisions, McCain Citrus, the fruit juice business, significantly growing its revenues and returning it to profitability. But Harrison dismissed Michael as unfit to run the division, strongly expressing his preference for a non-family appointee.[15] Wallace was adamant, and using his powers as head of the US Division went ahead in October 1990 appointing Michael. This evoked in turn a strong reaction from Harrison, who immediately called a board meeting to discuss the appointment.

Come the meeting, Harrison appeared to have dropped his objections, but when the agenda reached any other business Wallace spoke up. He read out a prepared statement defending his actions in promoting his son Michael. But going one step further, he declared that his relationship with Harrison was on the rails and that trust between him and his brother had evaporated. Harrison responded that if he could not get his brother to back down over the appointment, he would seek wider changes in the organization.

By now battle lines were hardening, and it was becoming apparent to Wallace and his wife Margaret that they no longer commanded family support. Harrison and Wallace each held a 33.5 per cent share in the company, with the remainder divided among a couple of dozen other McCain relatives. Harrison's restructuring proposal included setting up a two-tier board that would shift power away from him and his brother to the rest of the McCain family shareholders. His proposed board consisted of one non-family member alongside two representatives from Wallace's family, two from Harrison's and one each from Andrew's and Robert's families. Andrew's and Robert's families backed this scheme. As for succession, Harrison proposed that he and Wallace would each draw up a list of three contenders for the CEO position that they would refresh periodically, and upon retirement of either of the brothers, the family-run board of directors would select from the list of contenders. Thus Harrison's solution would give the leading role to the family to resolve differences, in contrast to the Ward proposal for neutral external non-family directors. Who was right? Which could be most easily swayed by the politics of coalition building?

The brothers argued over the issue for almost a year, until the board ruled that if the brothers' differences were not resolved by October 1992 the board would meet again to decide to fire either Harrison or Wallace, or indeed both of them.

THE OUSTING OF WALLACE

The succession battle by now had become openly vitriolic and extremely messy. Wallace proposed three options to break the logjam:

- split the operations of the company geographically into two separate units;
- implement what is known as a buy-sell type agreement, under which ownership control can change through the highest bidder being able either to sell or buy shares;
- sell the company outright.

Wallace let it be known that he had no desire to be thrown out of the business or demoted to play second fiddle to Harrison. Harrison unsurprisingly rejected Wallace's proposals, sending a letter to board chairman Andrew McCain describing Wallace's proposals and asking the directors to decide on a course of action. Matters had now reached boiling point. Following a quick-fire series of board meetings it was decided Wallace must step down from his CEO position.

The board was determined to go ahead with its decision to sack Wallace. The decision was backed by all board members except Wallace's sons. He had only one last card to play. He offered to buy 17.5 per cent of McCain shares from his relatives to try to gain a majority shareholding in the group. With the share offer for the first time a value had been put on the company, but Wallace's bid to buy the shares expired without any takers. The outcome left Wallace and his family sidelined. At this point Wallace and his family decided to sell their shares to the company and make a full exit from the business. Thus ended the long struggle of the McCain siblings. The split ended the brothers' relationship, and while Harrison continued to lead the original business well into his twilight years, Wallace and his family, staying true to their entrepreneurial values, acquired a large stake in Canada's largest producer of breads and processed meats, Maple Leaf Foods, starting a parallel dynasty that thrives to this day.

COMMENT

This looks like another case of sibling rivalry, which of course it is at one level, but this is more than a case of brotherly rivalry. It really revolves around a changing adult relationship, a fascinating case of dual leadership gone wrong. Dual leadership models are much more common in the family business arena than elsewhere, and often they work well, with brothers, cousins, uncles, parents, as well as family and non-family, sharing leadership.[16] Sometimes joint titles are held, such as co-CEO. In other cases one is designated chairman and the other CEO. It really doesn't matter. What counts is how good the match between personality and roles is. How does the relationship evolve? How conscious and in agreement are the partners over their respective roles? How sensitive are they to each other's needs and rights? What kind of process regulates their interaction?

This alliance seems to have been entered into with nothing more than force of will and convenience, and the devil take the hindmost. Here two close siblings entered a space that was too crowded for them and too psychologically unregulated – by either of them. Harrison could have shown more restraint in his thrusting ambition, Wallace more openness in his attitude to family rights and obligations. Here the fighting for the crown was a surrogate battle fought out by the seniors on behalf of the next generation. In the absence of any effective governance to regulate the relationship and the process for decision making, it should have been up to the brothers to enter a constructive problem-solving mode. Not easy when your daggers are drawn.

Another lesson here is that advisers are only as good as the way in which they are used. What is especially pertinent here is that the family sought advice, got it, but were unwilling or unable to adopt it. This seems extraordinary and irrational – but think about it. Perhaps this behaviour is more common than we like to admit. Do people not go to their doctor and then ignore the advice? Why? Because they went for some reassurance that they did not get, or they were prescribed medicine that would be too painful to take. The sacrifices to their current life style were too great. We cannot read the minds of the McCains from this distance, but the good advice they received would have created a complete reversal of their accustomed and preferred pattern of action, which was to keep outsiders at arm's length and to trust in the good fortune that hard work and force of will had brought their family in the past.

The lesson for advisors is, don't take it for granted that people are open to your reason. It is not at the level of rationality that the battle has to be fought and won. Hearts before minds!

IBM – THE WATSONS – A STRUGGLE FOR IDENTITY[17]

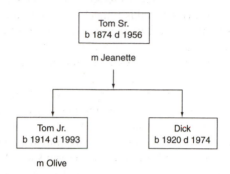

Figure 4.2   The Watson family

ORIGINS

IBM is today perhaps the epitome of the modern public corporation, where rationality rather than sentiment calls the shots strategically and culturally. It seems hard to countenance, much more even than in the Ford story, that IBM was a family-run business for the first half-century of its existence. This does not make it a fully-fledged family firm, since the Watsons, whose dynasty we are concerned with here and which spanned two generations, only held a small percentage of stock in the company. However, so widespread was the equity that the holding of the CEO, Tom Watson Sr, was sufficient to give him the clout of absolute ruler of the business. Tom Watson was another powerful and strong-willed entrepreneur. But so too was his successor and son, and it was on the narrow plank of their modest shareholding, stretching over this enterprise, that the two Watsons fought out their father–son battle.

The story begins in 1874, when Thomas Watson was born into an American family of Scottish descent. He could have chosen to follow in his father's shoes and work in the family's lumber business but instead, with his father's encouragement, he ventured out into the world from their village home in the north-eastern United States. Settling in the city of Buffalo and desperate for a job to repay his debts, he managed to persuade the manager of the local branch of the National Cash Register

Company (NCR) to give him a job as a salesman. Here he learnt some key lessons. Perhaps the most important were personal qualities of resilience and persistence in the face of tough and unyielding markets. Like many leaders he benefited at this critical time from having a mentor, his boss John Range. He learnt the art of salesmanship, acquiring a good deal of commercial acumen, plus how to take abuse from a tough and demanding boss. He quickly earned promotion in 1899, moving to manage the NCR office in Rochester, NY.

NCR was enjoying phenomenal success, largely due to its founder John H Patterson, a flamboyant entrepreneur who earned a place in the hall of fame of American business heroes with his mission to supply the nation with cash registers. Patterson was a man of strong principles. These he relentlessly drilled into the staff at NCR, including the young Watson. As a training ground for an ambitious young businessman on the rise, there was no equal. It was tough, but Watson thrived and rose rapidly to become the national sales manager. But his boss, for all his virtues, was a man who would brook no rivals, and high achievers had a low survival rate in the organization. So it was with Watson. In 1913 Patterson, irrationally fearing any powerful employee that he thought might take the company away from him, fired Watson. He left the organization heavily bruised but with an orientation to business in values and methods of working that bore a close resemblance to his former employer – total dedication to the business, unrelenting demand for allegiance from staff, a penchant for paternalism and a brittle style that was never easily humoured.

Out of work, Thomas Watson was a man with a good deal of valuable tacit knowledge, and it was not long before he was approached to run Computing-Tabulating-Recording (CTR). At the time CTR, which had been built through the amalgamation of some loosely related businesses, was heavily indebted and in bad shape. Watson swiftly set about reshaping the CTR assets, renaming the company IBM and creating a sense of common purpose in the business. It was at this time that Watson and his young wife Jeanette Kittredge started their family. Thomas J Watson Jr (Tom Jr) was born in 1914.

TOM JR'S TRIALS

Tom Jr did not enjoy an easy childhood under the domineering influence of his high-achieving father. His self-esteem wilted under the pressure of his father's high expectations, continually being told he would not make the grade. Tom Jr's sense of powerlessness was heightened by his impotence to protect his mother from his father's attacks on her during his fits of ill temper.

Indeed the parents' relationship was struggling, and only when his mother threatened Tom Sr with a divorce did he sit up and take notice. It is a mark of the man's character that he really did shape up and start to treat his wife and family with respect. For Tom Jr this meant his father's interest in his development, which manifested itself in helping him secure a place at college.

Alas, Tom Jr did not excel as a student. He scraped through Brown University, and at the age of 23 he was again assisted by his father, who found him a position in the sales school of IBM. Here he led a protected life. When he was sent out into the field he was shielded from the harsher reality of the business by being put to work on soft target accounts. Meanwhile, Tom Sr had reverted to type. Disappointed by his son's lack of achievement, he wasted few opportunities to demean or criticize him. It was always unambiguous who the boss was. That was how Tom Sr wanted it to be.

But the bond between these two emotional men was complex. When Tom Jr married Olive in 1941 he asked his father to be best man at the wedding. This was the time of Pearl Harbor, and for Tom Jr the US entry to the Second World War triggered a welcome release from his family and his job at IBM. It turned out to be life-transforming. Tom Jr had learnt to fly as a student at Brown, discovering a passion for which he had a natural talent. In the forces the young man's latent intelligence and acumen were spotted by Major General Follett Bradley, Inspector General of the US Army Air Corps. Bradley took Watson on as his aide, and the working relationship turned out to be a kind of psychotherapy for Tom Jr, whose confidence started to grow by leaps and bounds. Free from the oppression of family life, he had started to become his own man.

FIGHTING FATHER

The end of the war saw Tom Jr lined up with a job as a pilot with United Airlines, but his mentor General Bradley encouraged him to think that he would be capable of stepping into his father's shoes to run IBM. At first the idea was shocking to him, but by the time of discharge in 1946, he was ready to re-enter the firm with renewed confidence. This episode demonstrates the huge value that successors can derive from external experiences before starting their careers. It also shows the benefit of having the encouragement and guidance of a mentor and honest councillor. Tom Jr set to his work with gusto, but very soon felt hampered by his immediate boss, a man little older than himself. The path to the top seemed blocked. Tom Jr tried to resign from the company but succumbed to entreaties from his father to stay. For Tom Sr the natural order of parental supremacy was intact. And then Tom Jr's boss died suddenly of a heart attack, at the age of 43.

Tom Sr was at this time aged 73, a CEO well past the normal retirement age, and in contravention of the organization's rule that mandated retirement at 65. Tom Sr's aura was powerful and fearsome. The ferocity of his angry outbursts was legendary, and increasingly they were directed at his son, for Tom Jr now reported directly to his father, frequently summoned from the floor below by the imperious ring of the buzzer Tom Sr had installed in his office. Tom Jr's role often consisted of supplying public justifications for the decisions his father had taken. On occasions when he disagreed, a blazing row would ensue. But ever more confident, Tom Jr was no longer a pushover, and the fights between them became ever more savage with the passage of time.

Relations took a turn for the worse when Tom Sr brought his younger son Dick into the company and gave him wide responsibilities. In fact Dick became responsible for running the entire non-US business, a decision that Tom Jr fiercely opposed. The leadership of IBM was becoming a cocktail of rivalry in which the Watsons were constantly at strife. These fights were often public. At one meeting Tom Jr voiced some opinions regarding his brother's side of the business and his father told him to mind his own business. Tom Jr responded in anger, shouting that the company should only have one boss. Following that incident he thought that he was going to be fired by his father, but neither was prepared to jump over the edge.

Apologizing to his father by letter defused this situation, but every month some new issue would set off another violent argument between father and son. Letters made public after Tom Sr's death show he was deeply fearful that his sons were chasing him out of the business, something he was determined to resist. By the 1950s Tom Sr, now in his late 70s, was starting to mellow and the atmosphere was becoming a little calmer in the office. But the father was still testing his son, making him fight every step of the way to the top of the ladder. Tom Jr had learnt too that the best way to diffuse his father's anger was simply to accept his repeated criticism.

Eventually Tom Sr succumbed to his son's pressure and appointed him president in 1951. But Tom Sr regretted the move no sooner than he had agreed it, and left the office the same day without speaking to his son, not even to utter one word of congratulations. Until his death in 1956 Tom Sr kept his hand in the business, making life difficult for his son to the last. It was only shortly before his death that Tom Jr was appointed CEO.

COMMENT

The Watson story is unusual for the intensity and complexity of one family relationship that eclipsed all others. It was a love-hate bond from which neither father nor son could detach themselves. Tom Jr was clearly a man of high intelligence and resourcefulness – a fitting successor to his father, were it not for the insecurities that clearly plagued both of them. Is there a lesson for family business? There is, especially if one reflects that IBM was a corporation that was acting like a family firm when in truth it wasn't one. Had the Watsons owned IBM outright, then the insecurities might have eased some-what, though Tom Sr was always going to be a man who would not know how to let go. But real ownership can help, insofar as it enables leaders to cultivate the art of stewardship; maintaining the business for future generations. The Watsons – especially the father – fell into the trap of dynastic narcissism, caring about personal fate more than the business.

BATA SHOE – A STRUGGLE FOR STRATEGY[18]

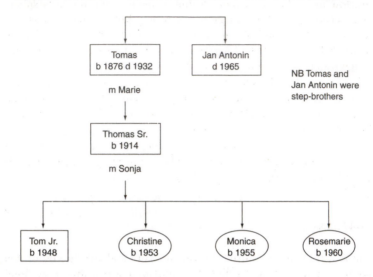

Figure 4.3   The Bata family

The Bata story illustrates that patterns of letting go can be repeated in succeeding generations, and the importance of timing the enforcement of succession.

The Bata Shoe Company is still going strong after more than 100 years, with over 40,000 employees in 69 countries selling over 200 million pairs of shoes each year, but the path has had its rocky patches, not least around highly problematic succession issues. The business was founded by Tomas Bata in Zlin, a town in Moravia in the modern Czech Republic. Tomas held a passionate faith that the business he had created was not solely an instrument of wealth creation but also a vehicle for supporting the development of society through the architectural and social reform movement of 'constructivism', popular in the 1920s. Zlin had become the focus for the company's commitment to creating a modern urban society through investment in contemporary architecture and amenities. Tomas's vision for the company saw it offering customers value for money and the communities where it operated improved living standards. These goals are still frequently referred to in family meetings. During its history the company faced serious obstacles, including surviving under the communist regime that followed the Second World War. At the end of the Second World War the company's operations in Czechoslovakia were nationalized.

THOMAS BATA SR

Thomas Bata Sr's life changed profoundly with the loss of his father Tomas, founder of the firm, who died intestate in a plane crash in 1932. Thomas Bata Sr, then only 17, was not ready to take over responsibility for the company, so instead the leadership fell to his uncle, Jan Bata. However, young Thomas had grown up working in the business and he was determined eventually to succeed his father. He was a popular and energetic person with a down-to-earth attitude that he was essentially a shoemaker despite his enormous wealth. But when Thomas came of age his uncle clung to his position and refused to accede to an orderly handover. This turned into a war of attrition, fought through the courts, for the ownership rights of the Bata Shoe assets. Eventually, in 1966 at the age of 47 Thomas Sr succeeded in winning title to the company's shares, but only by virtue of his tenacity and persistence.

Thomas Sr married Sonja Wettstein in 1946, a Swiss woman 13 years his junior who had trained as an architect. Sonja became his energetic business partner, and together they began to build the new Bata Shoe Organization from a fresh base in Canada. Sonja was a powerful influence, serving on the Bata board and in every way a key person in decision making. Together they built a highly decentralized organization, with a conservative culture in which people addressed senior executives by their last names. However, under Thomas Sr's leadership they were missing opportunities to fully exploit Bata's potential, and insufficient muscle was put behind its brand during times of aggressive competition from emerging global modern footwear labels like Nike and Adidas (see Chapter 3).

TOM BATA JR

While the company moved forward, the Batas were also growing their family, with new additions including a son, Thomas George

Bata (known as Tom Jr), and three daughters, Christine, Monica and Rosemarie. The conservative culture of the business and its Central European origins decreed that there was no place for women in management, and it was Tom Jr who was groomed to run the company. The three daughters did, however, serve on various boards of Bata regional companies but without playing active roles in day-to-day business.

Tom Jr was given the best training money could buy: an English boarding school education followed by a degree from the University of Toronto. At his parents' encouragement, he worked for several years in a rival shoe company to learn the business, which he followed with an MBA from Harvard Business School. Thus, before he joined Bata he was as fully trained as a modern manager could be. Tom Jr moved swiftly up the ranks and in 1984 at the age of 70 Thomas Bata Sr decided it was time to step aside so that Tom Jr, then 36, could take over as president and CEO of Bata Ltd. But the Bata parents were not about to relinquish their dominant roles in the company. Bata Shoe now contained not just one or two but three outsized personalities: Thomas Sr, Sonja, and now the thrusting presence of bright and determined Tom Jr.

Although Tom Jr possessed managerial drive, he was introverted in style and had yet to demonstrate his abilities as a leader. To get on with the job he needed separation from his gregarious father. But as Thomas Sr grew older, Sonja emerged as a stronger force in her own right, at first informally and then as a member of the parent company's board. When Tom Jr wanted to float part of the company's operations onto the stock market, Sonja objected. She was proud of Bata being the world's largest privately owned shoe maker and didn't like the idea of going public. Other differences in views surfaced with his parents and the board, and eventually Tom Jr decided he'd had enough and quit, even though many believed he had the right approach. Working in the shadow of his parents was not tenable, and he had no appetite for fighting a losing battle with his elders who, he felt, were just not ready for change. Tom Jr recognized that it was best to take a step backwards and distance himself from the company and its day-to-day operations, at least for a period of time.

THE OUTSIDERS

If Bata was a tough place for a son to work, it was even harder for outsiders. The company hired a new non-family president, Stan Heath. No sooner had Tom Jr left in 1993 than Heath's management team crafted a different direction for the company. But they found it challenging to implement a new strategy with so much resistance from local managers. Thomas Sr fell into the habit of checking up on people, enquiring about lower ranking managers' opinions of Heath. For Thomas Sr it was always a struggle to retreat from day-to-day operations. Heath believed that the company must concentrate more on marketing and outsource a large part of its manufacturing, but he found it difficult to convince Thomas Sr to surrender the operational side of the business when his lifelong mission had been for Bata to be 'shoemaker to the world'. The external management hired to drive the company's strategy forward was severely out of synch with its owners. The company was at an impasse.

Heath could see no way forward. Feeling both undermined and resisted, he took the only constructive course of action he could envisage – he quit. After Heath's resignation, Tom Jr and a newly appointed non-family chairman, Jack Butler, set up a committee to study the problems in Bata's operations and recommend corrective action. They ran into the formidable barrier that was Sonja. After a series of strong disagreements with her, Butler also resigned within just six months of joining the firm.

The company continued without a CEO in post for three years. Then in 1999 there emerged a new non-family candidate to take over the leadership of Bata, Jim Pantelidis, a respected retail executive. However, he lacked the support of the third-generation siblings and in particular Tom Jr, who was still a board member but had been excluded from the recruitment process. They questioned his ability to tackle Bata's deep-seated strategic problems given his background as a 30-year oil veteran.[19] Yet his biggest challenge was the same as had dogged his predecessors: how to perform the balancing act of mediating between Thomas Sr, Sonja and their son Tom Jr – all people with powerful convictions.

CHANGES IN OWNERSHIP

In November 2001, Tom Jr and his three sisters fired the new CEO and decided to bring about a change in ownership structure of Bata. Although Tom Jr was willing to step in and manage the company operations, he was hampered by a trust structure that excluded Bata family members from exercising direct control over the organization. The siblings believed the company had dropped in value as a result of poor leadership over a decade, and were convinced that a new owner-ship structure would help them get onto the path to recovery. Their goal was to preserve the best of the company's historic values and to create a new beginning for the business through a new strategy.

This time the parents and the non-family trustees were willing to listen, and accepted the argument that a new structure was needed to survive the changes in the shoe industry. Now Tom Jr was able to assume the role of CEO in a reconstructed seven-member board, which included three Bata family members and four outsiders, with Sonja Bata holding the Bata charitable foundation board seat. With this new structure, the company's destiny was once again in the hands of the Bata family. The family were able to set aside the problems that had arisen during the long years of transition from second to third generation, and for the business to go forward with greater confidence as a family company and with a common sense of purpose.

COMMENT

The Bata case is living proof that even serious succession conflicts don't have to destroy a business. Bata Shoe was undoubtedly helped by the fundamental strength of the business. Without that the business and family harmony might have collapsed together. It was Tom Jr's insight that a time would come when he would have to win the argument, seize the leadership and transform the ownership and governance structure in order to protect the company.

The most serious lessons of the Bata case, however, are to do with family unity and the role of non-family executives. Where family members have a combination of divergent voices, forceful characters and a very hands-on approach to operations, it is about as difficult as it can get for an incoming non-family executive. It seems as if the Batas weren't ready for outsiders, and the outsiders weren't ready for them. This was compounded by the incomplete succession process that took place – with the senior generation second-guessing and obstructing leadership. The owners were hampered in taking decisions by means of a governance architecture that was not fit for purpose. Tom Bata Jr spotted the issue and set about simplifying the structure, to establish more direct input to decision making at family owner level, balanced by greater external scrutiny by bringing a majority of independent directors onto the board.

5

The house that hubris built

As for the men in power, they are so anxious to establish the myth of infallibility that they do their utmost to ignore the truth.

(Boris Pasternak)

INTRODUCTION

Hubris is a Greek word meaning overweening confidence and pride. In the Greek tragedies it denoted the character flaws that bring about the eventual destruction of a hero and those entangled with him. Many of the problems in this volume have their roots in the identity of the leader. Some are founders – towering figures who arrived somewhere or other with empty pockets and big dreams. From the sweat of their brows they made money and then made more. They tirelessly, single-mindedly and doggedly built their empires, brooking no obstacle and clinging to visions of possibilities. What they assumed on the way was that the power of will is an invincible force that can carry all before it. They learnt that if you want it you can have it.

It was into a world gasping for more inventions, better products, new services that these creative entrepreneurs strode. We do not need to get bogged down in academic arguments about whether entrepreneurs are born or made – these were men of their times.[1] Whatever instincts and gifts they were born with were applied and then honed at the wheel of experience. Not all our cases are founders; some are the children and grandchildren of founders. It makes no difference. The gene lottery can throw up such individuals at any point in a family business's history.

But there is a price to pay. Hubris is a property of people with extreme personality profiles, notably individuals who exhibit high levels of self-regard, achievement striving, ambition, appetite for power, dominance and analogous traits.[2] These are often people who are admirable for their achievements. They build empires, but they are not the people you would most want to have as a long-term house guest. Although it would be a stretch to say these qualities are personality disorders, in certain respects they can resemble some of the profiles that turn up in psychologists' consulting rooms. Indeed it has been argued that many executives exhibit mild forms of the personality disorders psychologists see in their clinics. One team of researchers looked at the following six types, comparing practising managers and convicted criminals in their propensity towards them:[3]

- Histrionic. These are individuals with superficial charm. They are insincere, egocentric and manipulative.
- Narcissistic. This is the grandiose person; focused exclusively on themself; lacking in empathy for others; highly independent and exploitative in relationships.
- Perfectionist. These people display an excessive devotion to work. They are often rigid, stubborn and dictatorial.
- Anti-social. The behaviours of this type border on the patho-logical – they can be prone to physical aggression, irresponsible behaviours with a casual attitude to laws and rules.
- Borderline. The borderline type is impulsive and theatrical. They are emotionally unstable, and liable to suicidal gestures and attempts to use others through their emotions.
- Passive-aggressive. Members of this last type are seething with unresolved resentments and hostility. This is often concealed, and they are expert at putting others in the wrong and inducing guilt in them. The often do this by making exaggerated displays of contrition for their sins.

The researchers found the first three disorders to be more common among managers![4]

Some victims of hubris seem to have been infected since childhood with the drives that bring about their downfall: so it is a combination of the gene lottery plus upbringing. Others seem initially less extreme but become unbalanced through their adult experience. Repeated good fortune fuels their self-belief, so that, as in the Greek legend of Icarus, they fly ever higher and closer to the sun that will melt their wings and bring them down to earth. One of the penalties of success is the amplifying effect it has on the wilful personality.[5] Thus leaders come to believe they are immortal – failing to write their wills, even at advanced ages, and taking huge business risks. They believe that their judgment is infallible and that whatever goes wrong they can make right. They think they can shape relationships at will and get people to do whatever they want them to do. Most fatally, they believe that their choice of successor or partner will work exactly as they wish.

The gifts of the powerhouse founder and visionary often have a huge vacancy where you would want to find the ability to reflect, the empathy to read character, the impartiality to make reasoned judgments, the humility to bind people together, and the stewardship to preserve and respect the differences of others.[6]

What can be done for such people? The answer is not a personality transplant or some coaxing into the unfamiliar territory of the mind. You cannot change personality, but you can change behaviour. These people, more than any others, need counterbalances. These can come in the shape of another person in the family hierarchy, such as a parent or sibling that they respect and may defer to. Alternatively the balancing influence can be from a non-family confidante such as a business partner, board member or adviser. But here's the problem – listening to and trusting someone whose view on the world is quite different to one's own is a challenge, as we shall see.

THE FORD FAMILY – PARENTAL OPPRESSION[7]

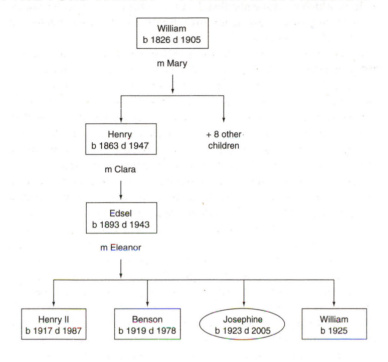

Figure 5.1   The Ford family

YOUNG HENRY

So much is the Ford car business a part of industrial history, still standing as an icon of the modern age, that one tends to forget its family
origins, and indeed the continuing relevance of its heritage. As a family
story it rates high in passion – a saga of a powerful entrepreneur who
lost his only son and heir prematurely, was forced by his daughter-in-
law to abdicate power, and left a trail of psychological debris.

   The Ford story is also a testament to business success via the classic
values of hard work, ingenuity, ruthless persistence in the face of
obstacles, and a blindingly intense single-mindedness. These were
the qualities that built America, and Henry Ford was their epitome.

But there is a dark side to these qualities of entrepreneurial determination, which he also embodied. Not least was his spectacular failure to have any awareness of his own limits and his total neglect of succession management.

Henry Ford was born in Dearborn, Michigan in 1863, eldest son of Mary and William Ford. He was educated locally and at an early age developed an interest in engineering. His mother encouraged Henry's passion, for example letting him use her darning needles to make screwdrivers for fixing timepieces. When Mary died while giving birth to the Ford's ninth child, the family was devastated. Young Henry had lost his chief supporter. Driven by his passion, the young man worked days and nights on his inventions and studied in his spare time to acquire the business skills that he thought he would need to succeed. He fought hard, often against the odds, becoming one of the greatest entrepreneurs of his era. Through his focused determination he established the automobile industry in North America, arguably initiating a new era in the industrialized world.

But he was an obsessive personality, a sort of 'mad genius'. It was his practice to take all the credit for the company's successes, giving no recognition to the contributions of others, even decreeing that press releases from the organization would only mention his name. After the Great Depression, when Ford's high-wage policy was no longer tenable and labour negotiations got tough, Henry Ford became a *bête noire* of the unions. Later in life his obstinacy never subsided; to the last he was rejecting change in the business long after it had become a necessity.

His life embodied these contrasts. He pioneered the introduction of mass-produced automobiles, transforming society, and even earning within industrial sociology, an 'ism' – 'Fordism' – for the mass-production factory system that was imitated throughout the industrialized world. Yet he was a stubborn man who wouldn't take no for an answer. During the Second World War he was tarred with the brush of being a Nazi sympathizer, partly because he vetoed his son's decision to support the war effort by producing Rolls-Royce aero engines for the British. Later in life, his persistence became his Achilles' heel – following his gut instincts to stick to outdated policies. The best-known example, perhaps, was his stubborn insistence that the company produce only one model of car. Ford, a victim of his own iconography, was blinded to how fast the market for automobiles and public preferences were changing. He left the door wide open for General Motors to steal market leadership from under the company's nose.

EDSEL

Born as the son of this legendary father, Edsel Ford's challenge to achieve distinction was enormous from the outset. For sons of towering figures the best advice is, get out from under the shadow: which means, take an independent path and find your own way to make a mark. But Henry's looming presence was more than a shadow. It could grip, and so it did. Edsel's father anointed him very early on as his successor to lead the Ford Motor company. Henry forbad his son from enlisting to fight in the First World War on the grounds that he was needed for the business. From a very early stage it became a certainty that Edsel would join the family firm, which he did on leaving high school. Henry didn't want his son to go to college. He claimed that his own success proved that work experience was more important than education. Yet the most important experience Edsel needed for success in business was denied to him by his father, and that was experience of real power. Throughout his career Edsel was the executive who was the boss's son.

Henry's refusal to countenance strategy change, and his deafness to the advice of people around him, was the backdrop to the family tragedy that was to unfold. In the early 1920s, under pressure from the rapid growth of GM's Chevrolet brand, spearheaded by Bill Knudsen, a former Ford executive whom Henry had let go because he thought he was 'too good' for Ford, Edsel commissioned a redesign of the Model T car. His father reacted strongly against his son's plan and ordered him to 'rub it out'. In awe of Henry's fearsome wrath, Edsel backed off, putting on hold any more initiatives to modernize. Henry undoubtedly loved his son, but could never let go any opportunity to put Edsel down, in private or in public. Try as he might to act out the role of president, Edsel was faced with the choice of either fighting his father openly or pursuing peace by disengaging. A more sensitive soul than his father, he chose the latter path of least resistance.

Edsel adjusted his priorities, backed off from the company and focused on his private life. He had decided that he couldn't shake off the malign influence of his father, and as long as he was at work he continued to be a victim of his father's erratic behaviour. Colleagues came to appreciate Edsel's qualities. Despite being the perpetual crown prince, they admired his integrity in seeking to champion better labour relations. But Edsel's escape routes from his father included a taste for alcohol, and his fondness for drink started to take a toll on his health. In 1943, just before he turned 50, Edsel passed away from cancer. Henry had lost his only son, leaving a bitter void in his heart and his life.

HENRY HUNKERS DOWN

The Ford dynasty however was not yet finished, and Henry acted to reassert his power, by firing many of Edsel's supporters and associates. Perhaps he needed to shake off the sense of loss, following his son's death. Meanwhile, his inflexibility and outdated business ideas were more than ever hampering the business. There was a crying need for fresh leadership but Henry's response was a step backwards, elevating one of his old cronies, Harry Bennett, to be his right-hand man. Perhaps what attracted the ageing patriarch to Bennett was the image of strength that he felt had drained from himself. Bennett had a ruthless gangster-like image. He would be the company's tough guy; Rasputin to the ageing Tsar.

Meanwhile the Ford dynasty was continuing, with the third generation now joining the company. First, Edsel's eldest son Benson joined the firm, followed in 1941 by his younger brother, Henry II. Henry was much more talented than his elder brother. Henry senior recognized this capability in his grandson and reacted to it negatively, again as a neurotic fear of threat to his familial supremacy. First, the old man tried to freeze his grandson's progress, ignoring him when he showed up for work; and even preventing him from moving into his late father's office.

Henry II for his part was driven by a need to make amends for his father's crushed career at Ford, which he suspected might have led to Edsel's premature death. Henry II and his mother blamed grandfather Henry for this tragedy. But Pearl Harbor and America's declaration of war intervened to put this emerging drama on hold, as both brothers were drawn into service. Meanwhile the war at Ford had barely started.

YEAR OF THE LONG KNIVES

The battle for succession sprang to life in 1945 in the form of an outright confrontation between Henry's protégé Bennett and Henry II. During the previous year a codicil to the founder's will had come to light that established a trust to control Henry's shares after his death for a full decade. The secretary to the trust was none other than Bennett. Henry II, seeing his career at Ford soon coming to an end, confronted Bennett. The battle lines were clearly drawn. On the one side was Bennett, the non-family leader and company heavy, backed by the immovable presence of patriarch Henry. In the other camp was the young scion Henry II with the support of much of the family. At a meeting the following day Bennett stunned everyone by publicly putting a match to the trust document. The odds were no longer stacked against the next generation.

Thus far the younger generations had avoided confrontation with the founder, but now they sensed that the moment for change had arrived. It was Edsel's widow Eleanor, controlling over 40 per cent of the shares inherited after her husband's death, who delivered the ultimatum to Henry. Abandoning her deference to her father-in-law she gave him an ultimatum – either hand over power or she would sell her shares. It also helped that the founder's wife Clara had lectured Henry that he was destroying any hope of family unity by opposing his grandson. Henry, effectively cornered, reluctantly conceded the appointment of his grandson to the presidency of the company. However Henry II would only accept on the condition that he could 'make any change I want to make'. His grandfather bristled but had no choice. At a board meeting the following day a letter of resignation that Henry II had ordered to be prepared for his grandfather was read out. Henry, a frail and crushed man, did not go quietly. He even shed tears in public. His business life had ended, and two years later, with nothing left to live for, his corporal life ended. He died at home on 7 April 1947 at the age of 84.

COMMENT

Henry was eulogized by the world's leaders for his historic achievements as an industrialist. Rightly so, for he had revolutionized manufacturing production and founded a mighty business. Today, Ford continues to be a powerful presence in the market, and still retains an element of 'familiness' in the form of residual minority family ownership. There is continuing board-level involvement by family members, with the chairmanship occupied by family member Bill Ford Jr at the time of writing. But how much mightier it could have been had Henry come to the simplest of recognitions as a leader – that the future cannot be like the past. Businesses must move on, and succession is part of progression. It is hard for a pioneer to see, perhaps, when a once great and unique vision needs to be revisited, or even more difficult, that oneself, as a powerful leader, needs to accept the challenge of new perspectives.

Leadership and personality are closely intertwined. They make greatness. They also embody flaws that need to be dealt with. It is interesting in this story that it was a woman and in-law, Edsel's widow, who broke the impasse over succession. Would that it had happened sooner – in Edsel's own troubled history – that his mother might have either moderated his father's behaviour or helped Edsel to escape. That the founder no longer held all the levers of control in his hands may have saved the Ford dynasty from being completely crushed by market forces, for it was only the succeeding generations' awareness as owners of the need for change that saved the company.

THE DART GROUP – AN EXCESS OF WILLPOWER[8]

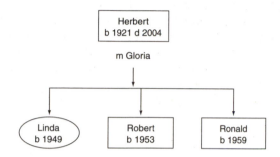

Figure 5.2 The Haft family

ORIGINS

The Dart Group case echoes the reluctance to let go that we have observed in other cases in this book, such as the McCains and Ford. In the Dart case we see the conflicts are multiple and fought out in a public arena. The dominant father eventually finds himself isolated from his family, having fired one son, fallen out with the other and divorced his wife. The *New York Times* justly likened the battle in this family to a real life version of the fictitious Dallas soap opera.

Herbert Haft was a visionary businessman who trained as a pharmacist and opened his first discount drug store in 1955 in Washington DC. From this he grew the Dart Drug chain to 75 outlets before selling out in 1984 to reinvest in other entrepreneurial ambitions. These were wide-ranging. He established discount retail formats in other areas, including alcoholic drinks, auto parts and perhaps most significantly in books, using the fruits of his success of Dart as a springboard to launch these other operations. Herbert was also shrewd in finance, and via his investments and dealing making he was able to spot the opportunity for 'greenmail' attacks on two large retailers, Safeway and Stop & Shop. In these manoeuvres he succeeded in earning a reputation as a corporate raider, and managed to earn $250 million for the Dart Group. His eldest son Robert played a significant role alongside his father as his business partner, and was instrumental in many of these deals.

Unfortunately, this was yet another case of strong-willed fathers and sons finding a shared harness impossible to bear. Robert's credentials for business were strong. Early in his career, while studying for his degree at Harvard Business School, Robert had written the business plan for the discount chain Crown Books that he and his father had founded. As a team they had managed to chalk up some notable business successes before family tensions started to split them asunder. But Herbert was beginning to feel threatened by his son's leadership capability and independence.

HERBERT'S IRE

The flashpoint came in April 1993 when Robert, committing the sin of publicly revealing his thoughts, made statements in an article in the *Wall Street Journal* that a change of guard in the company was imminent and that going forward, business would be conducted in a different way. To Herbert, this was like reading his own obituary. One can understand his anger. The move by Robert was provocative and challenging. It also exposed the deficiency in planning around ownership and succession in the business.

Herbert was in no mood for reconciliation. The following day Robert received a fax from his father's lawyer firing him on the grounds that 'he was trying to take the business over'. Matters were about to become uglier when Herbert also removed his wife of 45 years, Gloria, from the board. She promptly turned the tables on her husband by filing for divorce on the grounds of infidelity and physical abuse, and suing the company for wrongful discharge.

Herbert's response to these calamities was to turn to his second son, Ronald, enrolling him as an ally in his fight against Gloria and Robert. Ronald, who was very different from his father and had been estranged from him for some while, had little business leadership experience. This made him a bizarre choice to replace Robert as president and CEO. Herbert also proceeded to alter the ownership structure by issuing Ronald with share options that substantially increased his stake in the company. This diluted the stakes owned by the other family members, including Gloria, who saw the potential value of her divorce settlement plunge.

Unsurprisingly, this sparked a succession of legal battles, drawing in the other family members. Linda, the eldest sister, who had no formal role in the company, entered the fray, taking sides in the first round of skirmishes with her father and brother Ronald. But within a year Herbert had fallen out with Ronald over a disagreement on a real estate deal. Perhaps this was predictable because in terms of character the two were 'as different as you can be' according to Ronald. By now the infighting among the Hafts was beginning to take its toll on the operating businesses. Crown Books, without strategic direction, went into decline and eventually was forced into bankruptcy protection. After Herbert had sold his interests there was a brief revival of the chain, before it was forced to file for bankruptcy again in 2001, when it finally went out of business.

DECLINE AND FALL

The swift decline of family unity and its business purpose led family members to see their interests best served by cashing in their chips and making an exit. For the Hafts, conflict prefigured business dissolution. Robert, Linda and Gloria sold out in 1997 for $41 million, and Herbert himself followed suit within 12 months, settling for $20 million. Ronald also left, with a smaller payout but retaining control of the family real estate interests. What might have been the outcome in this case if the Hafts had stuck together? A fighter to the very end, Herbert's last venture was in the dotcom boom, funding an online pharmacy where he ended up in competition with his son and nemesis Robert, who had already set up a similar business. These business ventures offered one last chance for the father and son to square off as rivals in the marketplace. As it turned out both ventures were dissolved in the rapid deflation of the internet bubble at the turn of the 20th century.[9] In the end Herbert, like an emperor who is unable to lay down his arms, died in 2004.

COMMENT

The Haft case illustrates again the folly of megalomania – the founder parent who is unable to countenance any vision other than his own.

We could moralize that only the most selfish father could so openly seek to destroy the career of his own son, but that would be a superficial condemnatory stance. For here we see a phenomenon that is especially a risk where the age gap between father and son is not great. The father, understandably, may not be ready to hand over power when the son feels ready. The problem does not lie in the feelings of the family members but in their response to them.

There is a deeper theme here that is peculiarly male. It is the fragility of many men's sense of identity, often beneath the most powerful exterior.[10] It is clearly irrational for men of power, wealth and success to doubt their own strength, and for most outsiders the idea would be incredible. Yet men often feel that their worth and value is always on the line. Their past successes count for nought – it is only the current challenge or the next one that matters. This kind of deep-seated insecurity is a monster that can never be fed enough – even one's own children can become threatening. What can be done? Little less than psychotherapeutic intervention – otherwise reality is the hard taskmaster, when it exposes the character flaw that brings the house down around the person's head.

The more practical lesson of this case is that power and assets need to be the subject of intelligent, sensitive and open conversation, in a structured framework that allows integrative decisions to be taken. The Haft case shows how failure to do this is ultimately contrary to self-interest. It is amazing how fast business success can evaporate once will, attention and focus are absented by the prior claims of primitive family emotions.

CHÂTEAU D'YQUEM – THE PERILS OF CONDESCENSION[11]

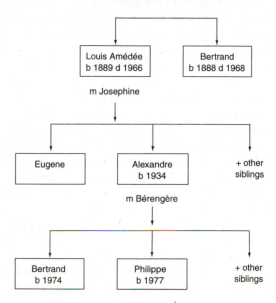

Figure 5.3   The Lur-Saluces family

THE BLOODLINE

Turning from the New World to the Old, we find many family businesses of venerable age. This story relates to a family that had been producing a sweet-tasting wine since 1593 that is known as Sauternes from Bordeaux, France. Their brand was sold under the world-famous name Chateau d'Yquem. The wine itself is drawn from the over-ripe late-harvested grapes that have reached the 'noble rot' stage.

Alas, the noble rot extended to the family, which after three centuries foundered – another victim of division brought about by the single-minded posture of the family leader. In this case the cause of the rift was the disaffection of family owners, a group who were largely taken for granted. It was felt that the leader of the family business had ignored his fellow shareholders, stretching their loyalty and family allegiance to the point where all they wanted to do was to sell out. You might think owning one of the world's most sought-after wines would be something that any family would be most proud of, and would wish to hold on to; even more so after centuries of family stewardship.

The entry of the de Lur-Saluces family into the business can be dated to 1785, when Louis Amedée de Lur-Saluces married Joséphine de Sauvage d'Yquem, a direct descendant of the original founders of the estate. It was the habit in such aristocratic families that in each generation one member of the family would be identified as custodian of the family legacy, bearing the responsibility of maintaining the age-old winemaking tradition, for which this region of France is world famous. In the Lur-Saluces family this was an exclusive arrangement. Other members of the family, even if they were part-owners of the business, regarded the family winery as something that did not really concern them, and had little to do with their lives.

By the latter part of the 20th century the clan that owned Chateau d'Yquem was divided into three groups. The largest group by number of family members, but with a minority of the shares, was the Hanguerlot branch, some of whom lived on very modest means. Meanwhile the controlling interest in the business was divided between two other branches of the Lur-Saluces family. The eldest son Eugene, who was childless, had inherited the biggest single stake in the company, with 47 per cent of the shares. His younger brother Alexandre was the chosen heir of his uncle Bertrand and became leader of the family firm, but with a smaller 9 per cent equity stake. Along with all the trappings that came from being head of one of the world's great Bordeaux chateaux, Alexandre also inherited the title of count. The imbalances between the three family groups meant the Lur-Saluces' centuries-long stewardship was at risk, if nothing was done to stop the rot.

NOBLE ROT

In this case the stimulus was supplied by the actions of the count. Almost from the outset, his stance from the lofty position of his title was imperial. His undoubted devotion to his mission left him little space to attend to his relationship with other family members, not even sending them the occasional bottle of the family's famous product. This was perceived as disdain by his relatives, who seethed with jealousy and resentment. As is often the case with soured relationships, small matters assume major proportions. Take for example the anger of the shareholders not working in the business – aggrieved at the peppercorn dividends they were receiving – when they heard that a large sum had been set aside to build new VIP bathrooms at the chateau.

Matters started to come to the boil when the count took steps in 1992 to strengthen his position so he could pass on the business to his eldest son Bertrand. This backfired badly. Other shareholders, including his daughter and other son, neither of whom was working in the business, decided they wanted out. Their shares were now up for grabs. The count, underestimating the strength of feelings within the overall family, had seriously miscalculated. It is hard to tell whether he chose not to consider the wishes of others in his family, including his own children, or whether he was just too distracted with other priorities, but the effect was the same. He also found himself facing his brother Eugene who was ready to sell part of his shareholding. So fundamental was this move to sell out that it spelled the beginning of the end of the stewardship by the Lur-Saluces family of their famous chateau. But the count continued to cling to power.

COUNT OUT

It was at this point that one of the world's richest businessmen, the successful family business entrepreneur Bernard Arnault, chairman of the LVMH luxury goods empire, stepped onto the stage. The chateau looked like a tasty acquisition, and a combination of charm and chequebook power were sufficient to persuade a large part of the neglected outsiders to sell up. This was an irresistible chance for a financial windfall on the shares they had inherited, but which had never given them a meaningful return. It was payback time. In November 1996 Arnault sealed a pact with enough of the shareholders of Chateau D'Yquem to acquire a 55 per cent stake. LVMH, with a majority, was now positioned to wrest management control from the count.

True to character, the count expressed aristocratic outrage. He claimed Arnault would ruin the reputation of the chateau, and launched a two-pronged defence. One was a fruitless 30-month-long legal action in the courts; the other was a public relations offensive. His attempt to portray himself as a David locked in a contest with a corporate Goliath won him some support from observers who liked to portray the leader of LVMH as a capitalist ogre. But instead of his slingshot felling the giant, it was the count who got seriously wounded and left isolated on the field of battle. The other Lur-Saluces family members had turned irrevocably against him. Some interpreted his warfare with Arnault as no more than a calculated ploy by a man who was trying to save face and make sure that when he exited that he would do so on the most favourable financial terms possible.

In 1999 the count finally conceded, when both he and his son Bertrand agreed to sell their 9 per cent stake, after reportedly extracting a higher price than the other family members. But Alexandre was not out of the game. He cut a deal that meant that even though his brother still owned a sizeable minority stake in the company, only he, the count, would retain a seat on the board as a director.

The peace deal that had been struck with his sworn enemy, LVMH, resulted in a settling of differences and rallying together that was necessary to take the business forward. In 2004, approaching his 70th birthday, the count finally retired from the company; gently forced out by the board which had reduced the mandatory retirement age from 75. Thus the last ties with the Lur-Saluces family were broken. A highly reputed non-family manager was appointed as his successor to take over the chateau. In parting, the count, in an expression laden with sour grapes, remarked that his family members harboured 'childless jealousy' – not the sweetest note on which to end over four centuries of proud tradition.

COMMENT

This is a more classical story of hubris than we saw in the first two cases. The leading figure placed himself, like Coriolanus in Shakespeare's play, in the position of one who did not need to give an account of himself. He was indeed a member of the nobility engaged in one of the most ancient and noble arts of business: viniculture. We might sympathize with someone who feels they hold an ancient trust, but the danger is that this stance can alienate people with more everyday concerns, such as family members looking for a return on their ownership. The rules, rights and obligations of office in any role should not occlude the human side of enterprise.

The perils of monarchy are in the way the monarch wears the crown. Nothing decrees that humility or awareness of one's family is impossible, but the institution is an invitation to patrician oversight, should the monarch be so inclined. The most effective family business owners are aware of how easy it would be to inspire fear and adoration from a position of lofty superiority. They know that this holds the danger of sycophants, toadies and yes-men acting as 'mind-guards'; keeping the truth from the sovereign leader.

In the Lur-Saluces case the stance of the count had an even more fatal flaw – it concealed from him the thoughts and feelings of people around him, including his own family. What could have happened differently? Well, maybe someone with courage to stand up to him could have warned him about the consequences of ignoring and overriding the wishes of others, but even this is doubtful. Some powerful leader personalities run on wish fulfilment and the right to make history as they want it to be, rather accepting it as it is. Perhaps the only answer is to have mechanisms that guard against letting leaders have unchecked power.

THE REDSTONE FAMILY – THE LEADER'S IRON GRIP[12]

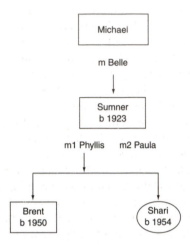

Figure 5.4   The Redstone family

SUMNER'S EMPIRE

This story is about one of the world's great media dynasties with all its pressures and expectations, as well as opportunities, potential rewards and big pitfalls, and at the top a towering hubristic leader. The saga also demonstrates how an heir's response to inheriting the mantle of leadership will vary according to their personal qualities. Some take it in their stride. Others struggle to find their own identity and autonomy. Put all that into the context of a family-controlled media conglomerate with an octogenarian leader and you have the stuff that Hollywood blockbusters are made of.

The Redstone family empire grew out of founder Michael Redstone's movie theatre business. The family holding company, National Amusements (NAI), owns a chain of 1,500 movie theatres worldwide that grew from the original business that Michael Redstone established. The business subsequently expanded massively in scope under the leadership of Sumner Redstone, its second-generation controlling owner.

Sumner, with the skills of a gifted entrepreneur, created his business empire through wise investments and some well-timed moves. In 1987 he stepped out onto the big stage, making a successful hostile bid to gain control of Viacom, a media company, and a prize that he had been eyeing for a long time. In 2000 he completed another mega deal to acquire CBS, the former parent of Viacom, for $39.8 billion. As a result of these deals the assets that were controlled by the family holding company NAI incorporated the CBS television and media networks, as well as Viacom, the media content business that includes such high-profile divisions as MTV, Paramount Pictures and the DreamWorks Film Studios.

FAMILY AND BREAK-UP

The control of NAI was concentrated in the hands of the Redstone family, Sumner and his two children Brent, 55 and Shari, 51, who each held a one-sixth share. Shari, who has similar drive to her father, has run the family holding company NAI, as well as sat alongside her father on the boards at CBS and Viacom as vice-chairman. Elder brother Brent on the other hand never found an equivalent niche. Not really adapted to the business life of the family firm, he drifted between executive roles in parts of the family empire without ever shining – a classic case of person–position misfit. It was no doubt hard for him to accept that he was not cut out for a career in the family firm, but Brent had to admit this was the case, swallow his pride, and get on with his life. But as we have seen in other cases, emotional baggage that has never been fully unloaded can come back to haunt you.

There is always a catalyst. In this case it was the parents' divorce. Brent's frustration with the family came to the boil when his father requested support from his children during legal divorce proceedings, asking Shari and Brent to relinquish their voting stakes during the divorce so that he could retain control of the company. Like the business battles that Sumner fought, this was an ugly and messy separation. The Redstone couple had been married for 52 years, and with the split came a deluge of emotion, a catalyst for Brent's alienation from his father. Instead of going along with Sumner, as the patriarch had all too confidently expected, Brent took his mother's side and refused to cooperate with the proposed scheme. Not so Shari, who lined up alongside her father.

She was subsequently appointed CEO of the family holding company, giving her supremacy in company terms over her older brother. Sumner's divorce not only led to the end of a marriage but created a rift in the family, dividing father against son as well as brother against sister.

LOCK IN

As a result of his decision to side against his father, Brent became a prisoner in his own family business, locked in by his minority one-sixth stake, without any means of realizing the wealth his portion represented. The shares were held through a trust and produced no income. While a sale could have been an option, the family shareholder agreement stipulated that shares change hands at book value, which would make selling out a bad deal. Brent would forgo a substantial part of his fortune.

Confronted with this dilemma, Brent took the time-honoured course of alienated family business members and went to the courts to fight for his rights. Perhaps he thought he could force a compromise on price to allow him to make a gracious exit.

This did not happen. Faced with his ever-powerful father he was not in a position to strike any bargains. Sumner still showed few signs of relinquishing power, presiding in 2007 at the age of 83 as chairman of each of the three main corporations, NAI, CBS and Viacom. His tenacious grip on the firm is captured by his claim 'Viacom is me ... that marriage is eternal, forever.' For Sumner, as for many other owner/leaders, the companies he controlled were deeply entwined with his personal identity. He was a master in the art of seeing off enemies and challengers in the business battlefield, all the way through retaining absolute power. But like many stories in this book, this is an unfinished saga.

COMMENT

Again we are in the domain where leaders act as if they are immortals, clinging to power beyond what many would consider a natural tenure. Here our leader straddles the business like an emperor from a bygone age, where challengers, whether bloodline or otherwise, were summarily removed from the stage never to return. Sumner has seen off some big fish in the battles he has fought, firing CEOs who got in his way and threatened his grip on his empire.

The trap that his son fell into was perhaps inevitable. There was little chance that Brent was going to be dealt any favours. Only filial loyalty, such as Shari was prepared to offer, was tolerated by dad, and not even family harmony would be allowed to stand in the way of Sumner retaining absolute power. The case illustrates the importance of a good fit between family members' orientations and their roles in a firm. Brent could have been supported earlier in developing a career of his choice. The patriarch's desire to have his children around his knees while he occupies the throne won't work for many families, and especially when the senior generation is unwilling to let go.

Here the family dynamic is triangular, which gives it special properties. In a three-party relationship there is always the possibility of a two-against-one alliance. In a family when a parent and child ally against the other child – especially when the excluded one is a first-born male and the alliance is between father and daughter – the scene is set for serious conflict. On the one side is the father, reinforced in his belief in his right and with the clear power of both parenthood and majority. On the other side is the dispossessed first-born, motivated by a powerful sense of his right. In this case the father held all the cards, and the outcome was the destruction of family relationships but not the business.

There are many simple ways this could have turned out differently. For sure, Sumner could have spent more time inquiring into the needs of his children and supporting them. And at a practical level it is of little use to have a shareholder agreement such as operated here that makes exit impossible.

SOLID WASTE AND THE WAXMAN FAMILY – GREED, DECEPTION AND DESTRUCTION[13]

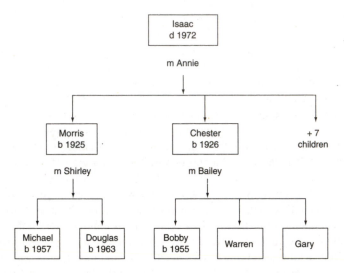

Figure 5.5 The Waxman family

ORIGINS

This is the story that pits two brothers and their families against each other in a war that culminates, like many others, in the courts. Underlying this conflict, however, there is more than money and personal enmity: there is a clash of values and philosophies.

The story begins in the early 20th century when Isaac Waxman arrived in Canada from his native Poland to start a new life, soon to be joined by his wife Annie. To earn a living he started at the bottom of the scrap heap of consumer society: trading in used rags, bottles and scrap metal. The business became more focused over time, and his sons Morris and Chester, born in the 1920s, joined their father in the family company, which had been incorporated and traded under the name of I Waxman and Sons.

The two second-generation brothers Morris and Chester worked side by side in the business but were contrasting characters. Morris, the older boy, a quiet and reserved young man, keenly interested in the technology of recycling and a constant tinkerer with inventions, ran the operations. His younger brother Chester was a much more dominant and expansive character, a garrulous salesman and trader, driven by big ambitions. He headed up business development. Between them, the brothers held a controlling interest in the company, with their father Isaac, as president, holding only a small portion of stock. Morris often struggled to express himself and deal with written communications, and in business dealings he was happy to completely trust his brother. This meant he often signed papers that Chester presented to him without detailed scrutiny.

FIRST DIVISION

The first indication that all was not well between the brothers was an incident over the division of their father's small shareholding in the company after his death in 1972. Morris had handed back to his father some of his shares a few years earlier in a special arrangement that allowed Isaac to continue to officially hold on to the position of president of the company. When Isaac died and his estate was divided in equal parts between his sons, the outcome was that Chester owned a larger portion than Morris, thus gaining control of the firm. Morris was not happy with this situation, and put pressure on his brother to amend the shareholding structure. Chester relented, and in 1979 they once again became equal owners of the business, as their father had intended.

During the same period the third generation were starting to join the business, but with the two branches applying quite different philosophies in terms of hiring policy. Chester's three sons, Bobby, Warren and Gary, followed their father, joining the firm at an early age after dropping out of college. On Morris's side, a greater value was placed on education and preparing the children for life through learning. His two boys, Michael and the younger Douglas, both went to university, with neither of them showing any interest in joining the firm on leaving college.

THE STRUGGLE FOR OWNERSHIP

The question of future ownership was an issue that increasingly preoccupied Chester. He realized that the present 50/50 ownership split with Morris meant that his three sons would eventually end up with smaller stakes in the business than their two cousins. So he put forward a plan to divide ownership of the firm into five parts, with each member of the third generation getting a 20 per cent stake. Not surprisingly, Morris rejected this proposal. Undaunted, Chester realized that his branch could just as easily extract value from the company though salaries and bonuses.

Although Morris was opposed to the bonus scheme that was proposed, Chester had him sign a board minute authorizing this new form of remuneration in the company.[14] The first bonus pool was C$250,000, with all the monies going to Chester's sons. Further chunky bonuses of over C$1 million were to flow in 1981 and 1982 to the three cousins, which Morris was later to claim happened without his knowledge. In 1982 Morris's son Michael became associated with the business, taking on the task of building up Solid Waste Reclamation Inc, a business he owned with his brother Douglas that had been spun off from Waxman and Sons.

Despite business success, Chester was still unsatisfied with the status quo, and he decided that he would make a new move to get control of the company by buying out his brother. He presented Morris with documents to sign, which as usual his brother autographed without close attention to their content. In one of them he sold his half stake in the business to the other side of the family. Morris's inattention to this business was partly a result of his ill health, for he had been diagnosed with heart problems and had undergone surgery. It was only during his recuperation in 1984 that he claimed he awoke to what had happened, believing his brother had betrayed him. Morris, convinced that he had been cheated by his brother, confronted Chester, but was brushed off. But Morris was not going to give up, and persisted in trying to persuade his brother to hear his complaint, with Chester continuing to stonewall him.

WAR IS DECLARED

Five years on, after persistent attempts to secure his claims for justice against his brother, Morris decided it was time to get matters of his chest and confide in his son. He called Michael into his office and told him his story. Michael's reaction was immediate and volcanic. He stormed into his uncle's office and threatened him and his family with violence if the situation was not resolved.[15] Michael's emotional reaction did not yield repentance in Chester; it merely stoked the fire of conflict.

During all Morris's ineffectual pleading to regain his ownership rights Chester assumed control of the company's finances, with his sons collectively receiving C$27 million in bonuses in the 10 years up to 1993. Company assets were sold, culminating in the disposal of the main business in 1993 for C$30 million. During this sale, Chester and his sons were able to secure their incomes by obtaining long-term employment contracts with the new owner. Morris and his family stood on the sidelines as helpless witnesses to this spectacle.

To the outside world Chester impressed people as a charming personality. He was a pillar of the local community, noted for his philanthropy. Morris on the other hand kept a low profile and stayed in quiet isolation. Now, with Michael by his side he launched out to defend their rights through the only means they could. For them it was a last resort, but they went to law in 1988. The reaction from Chester's branch was swift, firing Morris from the business, and to make it even harder, cutting off Morris's benefits including the health insurance that he relied on to pay for his medical bills.

The case itself took five years to wind its way through the courts, but in the end Morris and his sons got the justice they sought and their father was reinstated as 50 per cent owner of the company. The appeal court upheld the judgement that included an order for Chester to pay C$50 million in compensation to his brother Morris. Many of the explanations Chester had advanced during the months-long trial, which were summarized in a 439-page ruling, were judged to be fabrications. But the Waxman family and business had paid dearly for its family war. If today you visit Solid Waste's main office you will see a portrait of Isaac proudly standing with his two sons by the side of one of the Waxman company trucks. In Morris's version of the picture Chester, his nemesis, has been airbrushed out.

COMMENT

What is one to make of the Waxman siblings? The distinctive styles
and values of Chester and Morris could have made for a great sibling
partnership. Instead, they descended into a battle that was crude and
almost farcical, had it not been so tragic. Morris, the inattentive and
other-worldly brother, was vulnerable to the unchecked ambitions
of Chester. Nowhere between these poles did there seem to be an
ounce of vision and leadership beyond the material wealth at stake.
Where did Chester's at-all-costs ambition come from? It is difficult
to psychoanalyse from a distance, but Chester resembles elements of
the types we discussed at the start of the chapter – a product of both
ingrained personality dispositions and the pressure of circumstance.
For as we have see in so many other cases in this book, the presence
of wealth and opportunity seems to pump some characters up more
than others.

For at a simpler and more material level this case clearly fits the
Darwinian paradigm we introduced at the start of this book – where
genetic interests are absolutely divided between brothers, multiplied
by the fact that both of them had children. People's shared interests
in their own offspring are genetically twice the magnitude of their
interests in their nephews. Thus the forces pulling them apart were
stronger than those pulling them together. But it didn't have to be so.
There was enough wealth to go round had Chester taken a position of
stewardship rather than competitor.

Our faults lie not in our stars but in ourselves.

6

Heads in the sand – the insularity trap

Families have many ways of being dangerous.

(Ernest Hemingway)

INTRODUCTION

Not every family war dissolves in a pool of blood. Some just waste away. They start in rude good health; begin to practise small abuses of lifestyle that make them sluggish, myopic, and worse, complacent about the security of their existence. They become like sick people who never visit the doctor because in the bubble of their delusional world, there is nothing to worry about.

In the family firm, this is the other side to the coin that makes families strong, close and self-sufficient. The bonds of kinship, as we have observed, are the lattice upon which the magical powers of the strongest family business cultures are woven. But these are bonds than can squeeze the life out of a family by suffocation. In many of the cases we have seen, a by-product of internal conflicts can be a growing obliviousness to external reality. And once you start to slide, the descent can be precipitous and unstoppable.

As we noted in the Introduction, the desire to look after your own is in its place fine, laudable and a strength. Nepotism is ingrained in human nature. It's in our genes to look after our own.[1] It's as old as time. We are programmed to be wary of strangers and to put outsiders to a severe trust test before we let them in. In some cultures – notably in much of Asia and Latin America – families are large inclusive affairs. Under these circumstances people can be insular while still embracing a wide kinship network. It has risks, but it is a common pattern in the extended family.

In the West especially, as well as in many other parts of the world, family size is shrinking. This makes insularity a strategy of diminishing options. It becomes ever harder to justify the appointment of a favoured son or daughter against the external talent pool, and the negative connotations of 'nepotism' become stronger. For many people outside family firms, it is seen as a form of social cheating. But there is a case to be offered in favour of the practice. Having an unbroken line of kinship running through a business can be a vector along which knowledge and values are transmitted from one generation to another.[2] This is an enormous source of power to the family business.[3] There is also the idea that kin will identify more with their task, be more loyal, commit more of their heart and soul, and not entertain illusions that they are especially fitting to be favoured. The last point is important – family business leaders often combine unusual degree of both humility and pragmatism, especially when they know that they will have to call upon outsiders with qualities they lack to be able to serve the needs of the business.

In fact, this kind of realism and openness could be said to be the precondition for nepotism to succeed. And this is where many families fail through insularity. They either seek the input of outsiders too late, or they pick the wrong people to turn to, or both – as we shall see in the stories that follow.

In these case histories we shall see that their insularity was not a direct cause of business failure, but variously a cause of diminished options, biased perceptions, poor judgments, and vulnerability to the random threats of turbulent business environments. In all the cases that follow we can see firms that were riding the crest of a wave of success, oblivious to imminent risks and hazards. Thus Guinness at one stage was the world's leading brewer. Steinberg Inc was the largest food retailer in Quebec, Canada. Sakowitz was Houston's most prestigious department store chain. The *Louisville Times* was once one of the most respected regional newspapers in the United States. Seagram held the commanding heights of the distilled spirits market. From these positions of pre-eminence, all of these businesses eventually slipped out of the control of the owning family or lost their way. These families' efforts to retain family control over their strategy and investments without qualified outside assistance were never completely effective. Events drifted out of their grasp and their crises escalated. Their leadership model was heavily reliant on family members for inputs to most of the key decisions. This was sometimes a conscious and deliberate choice; in other cases isolation came about by default. Underlying this lack of foresight were deficiencies in planning, and the checks and balances that good governance and risk management bring.

THE GUINNESS STORY – SLIDING INTO SCANDAL[4]

ORIGINS

The Guinness family were one Europe's historic brewing dynasties, and emerged from Dublin in the late 18th century to become an industrial powerhouse in the 20th century. The company grew fast, feeding the thirst of the working-class masses in Ireland, and then smartly capitalizing on its home-market strength, expanding overseas to sell its rich and malty stout ale around the world, and build a brand that still is venerated today. Indeed, it almost invented modern brand building with its innovative and award-winning advertising campaigns from the late 1920s onwards.

EARLY SUCCESS

Family members active in the early days showed strong entrepreneurial drive, founding in addition to the brewery a finance house, Guinness Mahon, which grew to great prominence. The family became an engine of success. The bloodline was brimming with confidence and gifts that carried members to distinction in other walks of life beyond commerce and finance, including politics, sports and the armed forces. As the beer empire expanded, gradually and quite naturally the business came to play a smaller part in the life of a family whose wealth had grown considerably.

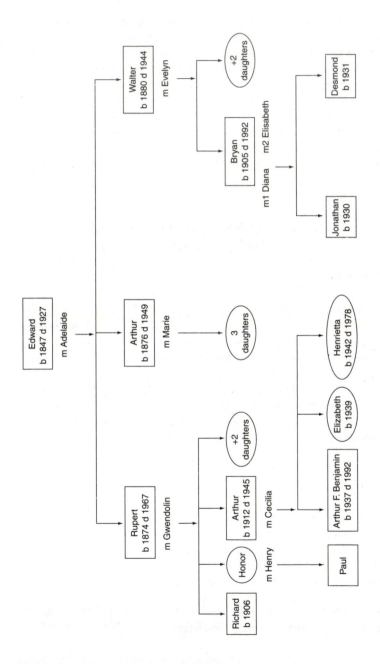

Figure 6.1 The Guinness family

Moreover, the Guinnesses had become members of the Irish and British aristocracy and were flamboyantly enjoying their elevated social status. Sir Edward Cecil, the first Lord Iveagh, was counselled by his friend the Prince of Wales and future Edward VII to 'buy some shooting in Norfolk'. He ended up acquiring, in 1894, Elveden Hall, a sumptuous 23,000 acre country estate that would welcome in the coming years most members of the Royal Family and dignitaries from England and elsewhere. Symbolically, owning the estate placed the Guinnesses alongside the Rothschilds and the Astors as one of the elite families of the day. The banking Guinnesses, while not in the same league in terms of wealth, also vigorously enjoyed the trappings of the English country social life.

Meanwhile the company still had to be directed and managed. Family continued to be involved, but with successive generations came a slackening of involvement, motivation and loyalty. The family did bring in non-family talent to help manage the growth of the company, but it wasn't until 1945 that they hired their first manager from a non-brewing background, in the person of Sir Hugh Beaver. Up to that time the only non-family senior staff were the highly qualified scientists working in the brewery. This helped to embed a corporate culture that was clearly product-led.

During the earlier stages of the company's growth the family maintained tight control over the ownership of the business, and it was not until the fifth generation that the shares started to become widely dispersed among family members. Although the company was originally floated in 1886 by Edward Cecil, the first Lord Iveagh, he still controlled over half the equity. When he passed on ownership he divided the shares equally between his sons. Even though ownership was becoming more dispersed, the family clung on to power and control. This was not because they were greedy for command, but more from a sense of patrician duty. From their perspective, the company had brought them great fortune and they felt a responsibility fell on them to continue as stewards.

THE PATRICIAN ERROR

The flaw in this reasoning was that it seemed to be a tenet that was held irrespective of whether family members had any formal education or training to enable them to carry such a responsibility. They were born Guinnesses, and that was a sufficient call to service in the eyes of the family. Moreover, this was bound by traditional norms. Even with the family tree growing wider and wider with each passing generation, male primogeniture (the succession of the first-born male) was still the norm when selecting their heirs. This was uncontroversial, since it was time-honoured and the family believed that it was probably the best way to stem possible dissension from relatives. The fact that it offered no guarantee that the best-qualified person got the job was a price worth paying.

This blend of insularity and complacency extended to board representation. Family members were not appointed to the board on the basis of their competence. For example, Bryan Guinness, later Lord Moyne, who joined the company's board in 1935, had been trained in the law but had given up practising at an early stage to become a farmer. Sadly, the boards of too many family firms today still reflect this kind of family placement without regard to competence. The cost of insularity is usually not borne immediately, but is a risk to future adaptability, as the Guinness case vividly illustrates.

The comfortable feeling of confidence and consistency that pervaded the Guinness leadership was also a disincentive to let go. The senior generation was getting into the habit of overstaying their welcome – in several cases clinging onto power well beyond their period of peak ability. Rupert Guinness did not hand over as chairman until 1962 when he was 88. The difficulty was compounded by the winnowing of family male ranks during the Second World War, when Rupert lost both his youngest brother and his son Arthur. However, convinced that the chairmanship was the prerogative of his descendants, he hung on until his grandson Benjamin, who was appointed to the board in 1958 at the tender age of 21, succeeded him as chairman a mere four years later at the age of 25. Benjamin Guinness had no formal training for the position, and besides, he was a shy person with few of the qualities one would associate with strong leadership.

His term as chairman turned out to be a period when the family, even though they were heavily represented on the board, began to lose their grip on the business as they became further and further removed from the activities of the group. This was directly caused by the combination of Benjamin's reserve and the remoteness of the other non-executive family directors from the business. This created a leadership vacuum, for in effect no one was setting out a vision and strategic direction for the business. The board remained family-dominated, while day-to-day decisions were being taken more and more by non-family managers without the benefit of any proper system of accountability and board control.

By the 1970s the need for stronger family input was recognized. The obvious candidate was Jonathan Guinness, the eldest son of Lord Moyne (Bryan Guinness). Jonathan was a man of outspoken right-wing political views, and the family baulked at the prospect of his leadership. He might have been able to offer strong leadership, but did he have the qualities to unite the family and the board? We shall never know. He did however publish a book, *Requiem for a Family Business*, that engrossingly recounts his family saga.[5]

LOSS OF LEADERSHIP

So now the family involvement in Guinness Brewing was reaching its final chapter. Non-family executive presence had been steadily increasing as the company grew. Much of this growth was through mergers and acquisitions, further swelling the non-family executive ranks. But without leadership the company was losing its focus, and all the while the distance between the family and its operations was widening. Rudderless, important decisions were often being taken ad hoc by people who lacked proper authority and more importantly, direct accountability. The company's financial fortunes started to suffer and, following a diversification spree in the 1970s, profits from the newly acquired businesses collapsed in 1980, causing a financial crisis at the firm. The family directors, who now only controlled about 20 per cent of the stock, seemed powerless to halt the slide.

Into this vacuum stepped the man who would bring to an inglorious end the Guinness family business empire and reputation. His name was Ernest Saunders. His reign started successfully with a turnaround of the company's performance by refocusing the business around its core brand, the famous stout beer. This cleaning of the stables set the firm back onto a growth trajectory, and the company began to contemplate strengthening itself through acquisitions. The first significant move was in 1985 with the purchase of Bells Whisky.

When Distillers Company, the long-established but vulnerable leader of the Scotch whisky industry, was put into play as a result of a hostile bid, Guinness emerged as a white knight, taking over its larger rival. But this turned out to be Guinness's darkest hour, for Saunders became implicated in a share price-rigging scandal. The takeover was a success in terms of developing the company and the brand, but culminated in the ignominious trial, conviction and jailing of its CEO, Ernest Saunders. The family, now relegated to minor shareholders in a much enlarged group, could only stand by and wring their hands in embarrassment – passive and inert bystanders to the scandalous irregularities perpetrated in the name of their family firm right under their noses.

Today, the name of Guinness survives as a brand owned by Diageo, the world's largest distilled spirits marketer.

COMMENT

This story illustrates a well-known phenomenon called 'the failure of success'.[6] This means that companies who ride the crest of the wave of market success are the ones that are most at risk to the unexpected. They are also the ones that are least inclined to reform and anticipate future changes and challenges. Understandably, people say, 'If it ain't broke don't fix it.' It is especially risky if success predominates the formative years of company growth. For Guinness, their outstanding early success was rather like a person who had been outrageously spoilt and pampered as a child. In due course the child grows into a lazy teenager, who continues to believe into maturity that they are special, invulnerable, and that the world will deliver to them the living it owes them.

For sure, with the world thirsting for their products, the Guinnesses were lulled into a belief that success would always come their way. Male primogeniture as a practice might have appeared like an easy way to settle the important matter of who was to lead in each succeeding generation, but it is notoriously risky. The Guinnesses seemed doubly oblivious of the fact that running a complex business is not a job for amateurs operating on intuition and goodwill, and second that the gene lottery offers no guarantee that the male primogeniture rule will deliver people with the requisite capabilities.

The Guinness case is a simple story of patrician detachment opening the doors to what economists call 'agency problems' – the separation of owners from managers, leaving the latter in a position where temptation, bad judgement, and even criminality can run unchecked.[7] The answers lie in three familiar domains: family self-appraisal, strong leadership and good governance. Each could have arrested the decline, raised awareness of the threats and taken timely action to avoid them.

THE SAKOWITZ STORY – THE UNCHECKED LEADER[8]

ORIGINS

The rise and fall of the Sakowitz department store family business in Texas offers a stark illustration of how the cycle of creation and destruction can evolve, mirroring an unfolding family dynamic. The company origins were modest, with the older of the two founding siblings, Tobias Sakowitz, opening the first store in Galveston, Texas in 1902. He immediately invited his youngest brother Simon to join him. The two brothers were the offspring of a Jewish émigré family that had come to America in the late 1800s to seek a better life. Tobias had been the last to arrive, waiting while he accumulated the cash to make the journey from Russia to join his family. On arrival he took his first job as a window cleaner, and subsequently acquired a position as clerk of a clothing store. Tobias paid his mother Leah for board and lodging, money that she managed to set aside over the years. It was from these savings that she was able to find $750 to bankroll Tobias's embarkation into business.

By 1909 the brothers had made good progress, and were able to expand by buying their second store in Houston, which they named Sakowitz Bros. As in many family companies, the biggest asset was the tireless energy and effort of its principals, as the brothers led by example to build success. By the time the second generation was ready to join the business the company had entered a new phase, relocating in 1929, just before the stock market crash, to occupy 70,000 square feet of new premises, 10 times larger than their previous space.

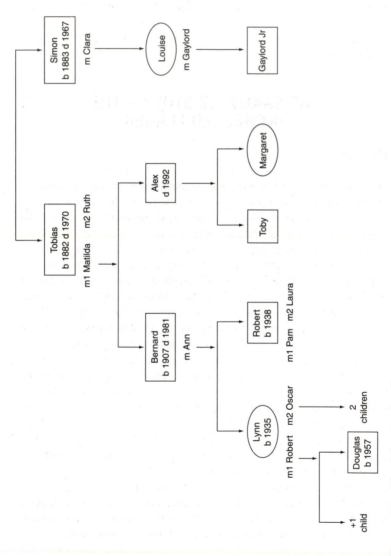

Figure 6.2 The Sakowitz family

Tobias's son Bernard viewed himself as the natural heir to the leadership of the company. His brother was pursuing a career outside the family business and his uncle's branch of the family had no male offspring. He looked the part, but found it hard to accept his father's stipulation that he would have to work from the bottom up. Bernard had joined the business with a good business degree and also completed an executive management training programme at Macy's, a premier retailer in New York. At university he had revealed his taste for leadership and power through his involvement in student politics, and managed to get elected to an executive position in the student body. He relished the status and personal attention that this brought. Thus he stood on the threshold, expecting the power of the family business to fall into his hands. He hadn't reckoned with the possibility that he might have to share the reins of management. His unwished for rival was Gaylord Johnson, husband of his cousin Louise, appointed to work in the firm alongside Bernard, also with the title of vice president.

TWO HEADS WORSE THAN ONE

This openly nepotistic hiring policy did not create a problem for employees, who recognized and accepted that this was the way that the firm operated. But they did see with disquiet that these two heads for sure were not better than one, for it was soon apparent to all that Bernard and his brother-in-law Gaylord were not a cohesive team and did not get on with each other. The friendly and unpretentious nature of Gaylord's character contrasted sharply with the arrogance that exuded from Bernard. This clash in personalities did not impair the company unduly during a time when the business and the economy more widely were both booming. The business was following the curve.

One decision that the father and son team of Tobias and Bernard could take credit for was expanding into the suburbs, opening the first large suburban department store in Houston in 1959. Meanwhile, a classic split was emerging between those working in the business and those who were not. The firm was continuing to operate a no-dividend policy because Bernard, who was now firmly in the driving seat along with his son Robert, favoured using spare company cash to reinvest in the business. On the other side, the family branch headed by Tobias's younger brother Simon started to question the liquidity policy, demanding a financial return on the shares. This is a common issue in family businesses, where the 'insiders' choose to run the company on cash with no debt. It often creates a major incentive problem for the 'outsider' family shareholders, as was apparent here.

To unblock the stalemate between the two family branches over this issue, Simon's branch agreed to a $4 million buyout, leaving ownership and control in the hands of Bernard's clan. The buyout was financed by a 20-year interest-bearing loan, with the final payment due in 1984. Straight after the deal Simon, who still came to work at the company, was stripped of his salary by his nephew. This was viewed in the family as a humiliating and ungrateful act by Bernard. It looked like pure vindictiveness, and created a sense of loss and bitterness that thereafter deepened the separation between the two founding branches.

ROBERT'S ERA

There was also a sense that where the first generation had always sacrificed for the good of the business, Bernard and his son Robert were acting more in line with their own personal visions and ambitions: pursuing a considerably more aggressive and high-risk strategy, and forcing a sea-change in the values driving the business. This meant, inevitably, a less than clear differentiation between their personal affairs and the company's.

Meanwhile Bernard's younger brother Alex, who had pursued his own successful career in academia, was concerned that his minority investment was never going to yield a return, since he had never been paid a dividend. He was also thinking of selling out. However, the company finances were now severely strained as a result of the buy-back of shares from Simon's branch. The financial squeeze was only resolved through the intervention of Bernard's wealthy son-in-law, Oscar Wyatt, who bankrolled the buyout of Alex by personally guaranteeing the stock purchase note.

Oscar, a very colourful character, had entered the family in 1963 by marrying Robert's sister Lynn, a woman two years older than him, with two sons from an earlier marriage. Oscar, a self-made multi-millionaire entrepreneur from founding a highly successful energy company called Coastal Gas, had himself married and divorced three times.

The beginning of the end of the Sakowitz business started in 1975 when Bernard, now in his late 60s, passed the baton of leadership over to his only son, 37-year-old Robert. The transition was at a time when the firm was under increasing pressure, compounded by the cashflow crunch brought about by the share buy-in. Competitors from outside Houston had woken up to the market potential of the booming city, with firms such as Saks Fifth Avenue and Neiman Marcus opening sharp-looking department stores on Sakowitz home territory. This segment of retail was beginning to consolidate, and increasingly around the country, independent department stores were selling out to larger chains. Sakowitz looked more and more out of step with the times. For Robert, taking over from his father as president was the achievement a life-long ambition. Little did he suspect how he was about to be tested.

INTO THE RED

As long as the business remained healthy any lack of family cohesion was no more than background noise. When these arguments found their way in the headlines of local papers it was more of irritant value than fundamentally damaging, and certainly nothing to blow the Sakowitz family business off course. But the vessel principle was taking effect – the idea we mentioned in Chapter 2, that pushing high-pressure fluid into an earthenware pot will test and find out its flaws and turn them into fatal fissures. This is what started to happen during the late 1970s and early 1980s. The risk of being a case of shirtsleeves to shirtsleeves in three generations was increasing fast.

Robert Sakowitz, in the euphoria of his ascendancy, was not the kind of person to act conservative and play it safe. He wanted to make his mark, and so boldly decided to set the company on a course of expansion. The risks were high, but Robert, with the confidence of the boy to whom wealth had always come easy, forged ahead regardless. The pressure rose as borrowings escalated, stretching the company debt burden to intolerable limits. The expansion took the form of an ambitious extension into the market of Texas's other boom town, Dallas. So the first Sakowitz store in Dallas opened to a fanfare in 1981, and initially trading was good. But the economy was moving into recession, and the move began to look a step too far.

This was not just a market failure. The crisis was also driven by Robert's desire to cash in on private real estate investments, which included a stake in the land where the new store was located. There is nothing intrinsically wrong with business plans that capitalize on investments, but there was significant disquiet in this instance over whether this plan was in the wider interests of the firm's shareholders. Robert was also incurring very heavy expenses. He jetted around the world on behalf of the business, occasionally on the supersonic Concorde transatlantic route.

But Robert's spending was reality resistant and didn't drop its tempo when the market began to move against him. The oil boom that had been powering the Texas economy through the 1970s hit the rails in the early 1980s, and by 1984 Sakowitz was slipping into deep red ink. A $3 million loss was reported that year on sales of $120 million. Alarm bells were already ringing with suppliers, who were starting to demand cash upfront before merchandise was delivered. Robert's strategic and financial hubris was being exposed.

AFTER BERNARD

Trouble was also brewing in the family, and started to come to the surface following the death of Bernard in 1981. As long as their father was alive Robert and his sister Lynn coexisted in relative harmony, apart from a little rivalry between them in ostentation, as competing doyens of Texan high society. Lynn was both glamorous and vivacious. With her glowing personality and great wealth – between them she and Oscar were seriously rich – she attracted much attention from the media and gossip columns.

At Bernard's death the family climate changed dramatically. The catalyst was the reading of the will, which revealed that he had left all his shares to Robert and his cash to Lynn. Lynn's husband, Oscar Wyatt, who had helped Bernard and Robert to purchase the shares from Alex's branch, was outraged. He believed that Bernard had been influenced to change his will, reneging on an alleged unwritten commitment to split his assets equally between his son and daughter. Bereft of the presiding patriarch, and his power to keep the peace, out came the knives. The epicentre of conflict was between the brothers-in-law, Oscar and Robert.

In her book about the family, Jane Wolf is uncompromising in characterizing Robert's leadership style within the business as 'weak and ineffectual'.[9] We cannot judge the justice of this claim, nor her reports of his constant meddling in the day-to-day decisions in the company and incapacity to delegate responsibility. He would not be the first leader to pay excessively close attention to the business, nor the first to do so at the neglect of relationships and people issues. But if, as was reported, you acquire a reputation for arbitrary and often demotivating treatment of staff through rewards and recognition, then team building becomes extremely difficult. Even as the business was teetering on the brink of collapse, Robert continued to invest large sums of money on a series of private investments unrelated to the main business. This included an oil deal in 1983 from which he benefited considerably,[10] enabling him to purchase a new mansion in 1984.

SHOWDOWN

In 1985 there came a showdown, when the company's main creditors, led by Chase Manhattan Bank, which was holding a $27 million note from Sakowitz, declared the company in default and demanded immediate payment. This action forced the firm to file for bankruptcy on 1 August, to protect it from its creditors. Robert was quick to claim others were responsible for this drastic turn of events, seemingly in denial about his part in the disaster.

But soon Robert would be fighting on two fronts; trying to steer the company out of its financial crisis and dealing with the ire of his brother-in-law Oscar Wyatt. Oscar was infuriated by Robert's stance, feeling doubly aggrieved. He felt his sister had been deprived of her rightful inheritance and it was now worthless. Oscar was also having to pay off the note he had guaranteed to enable Robert to buy out the Alex Sakowitz branch. For Oscar, this was the last straw. In December 1986 he decided to launch an attack on Robert through the courts, suing him for 'milking the assets [of the firm] for his personal advantage'. Robert vigorously disputed the basis of this legal challenge, but it came as a serious blow to him, now down on his knees – nursing a failing company and increasingly isolated from the rest of his family.

DEATH THROES

Under US bankruptcy law the business had a limited period of protection under the statute known as Chapter 11, a window of time for reorganization and rescue. Initially there were some glimmers of hope, but there were few signs that the firm was going to come through any reorganization successfully. To rescue a bad situation against a gloomy economic backdrop, Robert began negotiations to bring in a new investor, including provision for him to retain a share in the business to the exclusion of the other Sakowitz stockholders (that is, his relatives). The proposal stipulated that they would have their shareholdings eliminated in the proposed recapitalization, leaving Robert alone retaining a holding. This one-sided proposition naturally incensed his relatives.

Oscar and his faction wanted an equal and opposite outcome, with Robert playing no further part in leading the company as an executive or investor. To attempt to stop him they launched a further family lawsuit, this time initiated by Oscar's nephew Douglas Wyatt, one of the next-generation family members, who was trying to block a merger going ahead on the grounds that Robert was putting his personal interests ahead of other family shareholders. Douglas Wyatt was the second son of Lynn from her first marriage. He was a total contrast to Robert in terms of character – a sensitive and somewhat naïve individual.

Meanwhile Robert's strategy for saving the company from going under began to show signs of promise, as the new investor injected enough capital into Sakowitz for the business to continue pursuing its turnaround strategy. Alas for Robert, his choice of new investor was as ill-fated as his other decisions. The white knight, an Australian real estate group, suddenly declared itself bankrupt, a twist of fate that cut at a stroke the business's final life-line. By 1990, without this support the company faced an acute cash shortage. The unsecured creditors were unwilling to patiently hold back, and petitioned for the business to be auctioned. No buyers emerged, and so the company was liquidated and the doors finally closed on the Sakowitz department stores during August of that year, ending three generations of the family retail tradition in Texas.

As the curtain closed on the business, the family legal wrangles gathered pace. Robert raised the stakes yet again by counter-attacking his sister and her family through the courts. Not surprisingly, such a mighty feud attracted the attention of the local press. The *Houston Chronicle* reported the first day of the hearing under the banner headline: 'You scratch my face and I'll scratch yours.' During the hearings the two sides of the family did not speak to or even acknowledge each other. The case brought by Douglas Wyatt was unsuccessful, so he launched an appeal. At this point the lawyers did what the family had been unable to do: they got a dialogue going that eventually led to an out-of-court settlement. But the damage was done. A family and its business lay in tatters, with no winner, except perhaps the lawyers.

COMMENT

We have invoked the 'vessel principle' to explain how weakness can be destructively exploited by pressure. This again is a key theme here – in this case a cyclical pattern where leaders create the pressures that they then struggle to cope with. One lesson is that someone should look more closely at the vessel before the pressure gets applied too severely. Insularity means just this – a failure to look at the business realities and see how they are changing.

There are two key psychological elements in the Sakowitz case. One is that the leader gets cut adrift from other potential sources of advice and support that would complement and cushion his decisions. The other is that the leader's character and drives play badly with his leadership challenge and choices. It is the stuff of tragedy down the ages – where the king (Lear and Coriolanus in Shakespeare) are deaf to the advice that could help them, and cut themselves off from the people who would moderate their character flaws. The fall of the Sakowitz enterprise owes much to the insularity and isolation of its leaders. They exhibited an exaggerated self-belief. These is an attribute of many highly successful leaders, who are saved from disaster by countervailing elements that guard against these flaws proving fatal. In the Sakowitz case, character flaws became fatal liabilities because of the absence of any corrective mechanisms or influences. Without this, the strong and positive values of the first generation could not become ingrained to the point that they became a guiding beacon for the family's development – a key characteristic of successful family firms.

THE STEINBERG STORY – FALLING APART, TOGETHER[11]

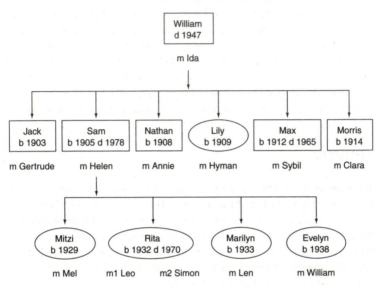

Figure 6.3 The Steinberg family

IDA'S BROOD

For our third story in the theme of insularity we remain in retail-land, a place where many great family businesses have originated and grown, some to world-beating success, such as the American grocery giant Wal-Mart, and Ikea, the Swedish furniture store. Now we turn to a firm that stood on the verge of great success but then comprehensively lost its way. The saga of the Steinbergs of Montreal offers a clear illustration of how the roller-coaster of fortune can be brutal when a family has no recourse to external agencies that could help it resolve internal dissent over strategy and identity. This family, like so many others, built their business on simple values of hard work, determination and sacrifice. From their very modest beginnings as an immigrant family arriving in Montreal from Russia before the First World War, the Steinberg family set themselves up as retailers in order to make a living.

In the early stages Ida, the matriarch, was the mainstay and driving force, laying the foundations for the future success of the family. As well as running the business, Ida raised her six children as a single mother, her husband Vilmos having left the family home when the children were infants. As a character, Ida was a force of nature, and she rose strongly to the challenge of raising the family single-handed. Her strong work ethic and her belief in sacrifice and mutual support were deeply ingrained principles, themes that would suffuse the family firm for many years to come.

Her second son Sam was in his mother's mould, sharing her passion, drive and commitment. Sam eclipsed all his other siblings in terms of competence and maturity, and they in turn readily placed their trust in him. Although he was second born, it was Sam who was effectively a surrogate father to his siblings. Throughout his life Sam enjoyed being in the limelight.

THE RISE OF SAM

Sam's career in the business started as a teenager helping out in the store. These were tough times, especially coinciding with the Great Depression, and work took precedence over education to make ends meet. At 14 Sam was a precocious child, and instrumental in acquiring the lease to the shop next door as the first step to expanding the business. He progressed rapidly, propelled by willpower and entrepreneurial talent. It is hardly surprising that he was able to take on the mantle of leader of the family organization without being challenged.

By the onset of the Second World War the company was controlled by Sam and his wife Helen. She was his first cousin on his mother's side of the family. The young couple were married in 1928. She was a great support for Sam but kept a low profile in relation to the business, focusing almost exclusively on raising their family. However Sam, characteristically, saw a business opportunity in his new extended family and formed a partnership with his father-in-law, who ran a local fruit shop. This consolidated his status as the undisputed family leader and entrepreneur. When his father-in-law died in 1930, majority ownership of the company moved into his hands, with the rest of the shares divided among his siblings.

The firm was thriving and had all the makings of an emerging successful supermarket chain. Although Ida passed away in 1942 during the wartime period, her life-time efforts created a platform of values on which Sam could continue to build the family retailing success story. Steinberg's was by its nature very much a family enterprise from the outset, with Sam in the lead, creating security and wealth for his family, his siblings and their offspring.

Sam led the firm with great gusto, with his only other interest in life being his family. Typical of many successful family businesses, the profits from the organization were reinvested to help the company expand rather than being spent supporting luxury lifestyles. As a leader Sam's style was freewheeling and informal. Decision making was spontaneous. Sam relied on his entrepreneurial instincts to dictate the direction the company would take. The family admired and trusted their charismatic leader, and put in his hands unlimited scope and power of decision to address issues of company policy, as well as their personal financial affairs. The family's voting shares were held in trusts, and only Sam voted the shares during his lifetime, maintaining an iron grasp over the company. His power was absolute and unchallenged. It was a tight ship with a sole captain, and as long as the passage ahead was smooth, things remained in good order.

GROWING PAINS

But ambitions for growth meant that this untrammelled autonomy could not continue. Expansion meant the firm required additional capital. Steinberg's first external share capital had been raised in 1955 by way of a preference share issue. This was followed in 1958 by a partial flotation of non-voting shares on the Montreal Stock Exchange. Access to outside liquidity would also make it possible for family members to sell their shares when they needed money, to buy new homes and fund increasingly expensive lifestyles.

Rapid expansion always tests the capabilities of a business, and the first sign of the vessel leaking was abnormally high staff turnover, especially alarming when it was from the ranks of management. Sam may have been a charismatic and flamboyant entrepreneur, but he was not the greatest motivator of people. His maverick leadership style tended to ride roughshod over people, demoralizing his employees and undermining the authority of his key managers. Thus where there should have been team work there was haemorrhaging of talent, an unaffordable risk in a growing firm that needs a strong and cohesive executive cohort.

The effects started to show up in business performance. There were also a number of strategic failures, such as the misjudged acquisition of Grand Union stores, designed to deliver geographical expansion into Ontario, and a new venture into a discount department store chain named Miracle Mart, which lost the group over C$100 million. Sam believed that these diversifications would provide protection for the family fortune, which had become heavily reliant on the core supermarket business. But each new venture away from the core business stretched the thinning resources of the business and increased the level of risk. None of this was helped by the fact that Sam's management skills were not a match for his entrepreneurial instincts. Blinded by the demands of the moment, he lacked the insight or humility to recruit and retain the outside talent that the company so badly needed.

A NEW GENERATION

Sometimes a strong personality like Sam can be the focus of sibling conflicts. The Steinbergs were lucky in this respect. Although pushed around by their brother, they accepted him as the dominant force of his generation and remained loyal and largely docile. His wife Helen was also accepting and supportive, but not so the next generation. Sam and Helen had known hard times from their childhood as barefoot immigrants, but that was not their children's experience. Their every desire was lavishly indulged, and when it came to their development their parenting was of the 'indulgent' or laissez-faire type.

Sam and Helen did not encourage their four daughters to get a good education, and even in the absence of a male heir Sam had no expectation that his daughters would work in the family company. Nonetheless the eldest, Mitzi, shared her father's drive and ambition, and once she had raised her family she decided to further her education. Persevering with her studies, she qualified as a lawyer. So it was that Sam turned to her for help in 1973. Needing to sort out one of his ailing businesses, Miracle Mart, rather than seek the assistance of skilled external professional managers, Sam preferred to keep it in the family, and he approached Mitzi, fully aware of the fact that she had no commercial experience. Mitzi agreed, although she had only recently been admitted to the bar.

The same insular instinct also led him to consider his sons-in-law as preferable to outsiders, and two of them joined the business: Mel Dobrin and Leo Goldfarb, husbands respectively of Mitzi and her younger sister Rita. These two men also happened to be best friends, and were happy to find their way into the executive ranks of Steinberg supermarkets. Sam favoured Leo to be his successor, a man of entrepreneurial personality whom he saw as in his own mould, but this plan was shelved when Leo and Rita's marriage started heading for the rocks. Leo resigned from the company. This cleared the way for Mel to be the prime candidate as successor CEO. This suited Mitzi, as strong a character as her father, who was promoting Mel's cause.

Mel Dobrin was a quiet thoughtful man without strong leadership characteristics – neither a visionary nor a strategic thinker.[12] His docility encouraged Sam to stay on as effective head of the company, where he continued to take all the key decisions. Unable or unwilling to challenge Sam to let go of power, a leadership vacuum was developing around Mel. The business was starting to drift and lose ground. Sam's inability to retain around himself a loyal and effective team of non-family leaders was now beginning to take its toll. Senior management interpreted the unwritten policy of nepotism as a signal that the top jobs would never be theirs, and the most capable executives started to leave the company.

MUSICAL CHAIRS IN THE BOARDROOM

While still deeply immersed and active in the company, Sam suddenly died of a heart ailment in 1978. Mel Dobrin sensibly stepped aside as president, moving into the chairman's role, and appointing a trusted long serving non-family lieutenant, Jack Levine, to take over as president. But matters were complicated by the presence of Mitzi, who remained a member of the board, operating with considerable force of character and opinions. This was unsettling for the new management team. With Mel Dobrin unable to project strong leadership and emulate the powerhouse that Sam had been, infighting became the order of the day in the conduct of the board. In 1982 Levine announced his retirement, just when the need was greatest for strong leadership to turn the struggling business around.

A second non-family president was appointed by Mel Dobrin and Mitzi to lead the business. Discredited because of a failed marketing campaign at Steinberg's, he lasted a mere 17 months of his five-year contract.[13] The company now decided to come closer to home, turning for help to a former senior executive, Irving Ludmer, who had left Steinberg early in his career to set up his own business. As the new president, he proved to be more decisive than his predecessor and started building momentum towards a turnaround. Foreseeing the possibility of tensions arising with the family, Ludmer had only accepted the job on the condition that he was given the full support of the board to lead the company, and with explicit assurance that the family members would not undermine his authority. However, backstage the family were once again rumbling, and he too fell into disagreement with the owners over key issues.

The new-found success of the business under Ludmer camouflaged deeper disputes, with Mitzi again at the centre. Mitzi was the most forceful of her generation, and now the focal point of conflict was her relationship with Ludmer, which was deteriorating fast. This culminated in a showdown with him, in which he threatened to quit unless Mitzi resigned from management. He won his point, and Mitzi relinquished her executive role in the company, but retained her seat on the board. Steinberg's now had none of the family bloodline involved in a managerial capacity in the business, although Mitzi continued to wield influence through her position.

COMING UNSTUCK

The headline 'togetherness family of the month' had been used by a Canadian magazine in the 1950s to portray the Steinbergs, without a trace of irony. Now, in the absence of the uniting force of their patriarch or a respected leader, the family started to fall apart. One of the touchstone issues was the financial lives and destiny of Sam's three daughters, linked through the trusts that their father had established.

The trusts held their voting shares in the business, and were the vehicle through which they could receive dividends.

As long as Sam was alive he voted the shares, but now his widow Helen took over the role of leading the affairs of the trust. In the early stages there had been non-family trustees whom Sam appointed, but in time they had either left or resigned. The last non-family trustee to depart, Michael Aronovitch, observed the daughters gradually taking over the responsibility for the oversight of their own trust funds. With no outside mediating influence in the trusts, the sisters were now often involved in minor disputes with each other. The casual schooling these women had received at the hands of their parents was a far cry from the concept of responsible ownership. The unified structure that Sam created, where they were each jointly responsible for all their affairs as co-trustees had become a cause of friction. This was an idealistic system. Every parent would love to legislate for the cooperation and amity of their offspring, but this ignores gene politics: the fact that the needs and interests of kinfolk can be divergent and even incompatible.

The event that finally interrupted the status quo was brought on by Mitzi in 1985, when she started discussions with investors to sell the company. It seems that having resigned her position at the firm, after losing her power struggle with Ludmer, she now wanted to exercise power through other means, by either selling the company or gaining control of the family trust. She took her sister Marilyn into her confidence, informing her that she was in discussions with potential buyers of the business, all the while keeping her younger sibling Evelyn in the dark because she felt 'she couldn't trust her to keep a secret'.[14] In the manner of all soap operas, truth will out, and when Evelyn learnt of the move her ire was raised. The bond of trust that Evelyn had until then shared with her elder sister was now becoming dangerously frayed. Tensions spilled over into new areas of disagreement, notably conflict about whom they should engage to run their grouped family investments. Now it was Marilyn who was the frontrunner in the dispute.

Until that time Marilyn had been entrusted by the trustees to manage the administration of the family office and their investment affairs. Now under attack, she resisted the growing pressure for her to relinquish this role. Conflict escalated, drawing their mother Helen into the fight. After trying to make peace, Helen weighed in on Mitzi's side. Marilyn was aggrieved at this, but clung on. The two younger sisters had found common cause – as adversaries of Mitzi – bringing matters to a head in 1987 by succeeding in taking control of the family holding company. News of the family war had started to leak out, and questions arose regarding who was in control and whether the ructions would open up the chance for outside bidders to intervene. In August 1987 a takeover offer was received from rival Canadian retailers Loblaw's, controlled by the respected Weston family.

The glue that had held the Steinberg family together for three generations, from the opening of the first store in Montreal to the flourishing of the supermarket business that Sam had built, had been losing its adhesiveness for some while, and now the structure was falling apart. Sam had created a culture of open and conspicuous nepotism, where the firm existed for the benefit of the family who worked in the ranks of the business. But now the owners had drifted away from the company.

Meantime the war for control of the company was reaching its finale. This was a battle that was not so much about money as about power and who could decide the future. Left in a situation where the three sisters were equals, Marilyn and Evelyn, who had hitherto been the outsiders, were able to win the upper hand in the struggle against Mitzi, their strong-willed sister. There was no mechanism in the governance structure for the disagreement to be resolved.

Now no longer on speaking terms with her sisters, in late December 1987 Mitzi filed a lawsuit against Marilyn and Evelyn. Mitzi, ever the bare-knuckle fighter, fired off the action against her sisters while they were on vacation in Florida. She charged that they were guilty of a conflict of interest. In particular she claimed that they were indulging double standards by blocking the trust from selling Steinberg shares, as Mitzi proposed. At the same time she alleged that they had been disposing of shares they held directly.

With the sisters all speaking to reporters, the fight was capturing the public's attention, with a newspaper cartoonist portraying the sisters in early 1988 fighting furiously like mud wrestlers. The law suit, from which Mitzi eventually withdrew, was the curtain-raiser to the final scene of the Steinberg family drama: the sale of the business in 1989. It was only in this final act that the sisters achieved unity. The Steinberg family had a happy ending of sorts, escaping with their fortunes, while the business continued under other ownership. But it is not a pretty story – leaving a residue of bruised emotions, ruptured relationships and the loss of a great family business name.

COMMENT

This is a classic saga in many respects, repeated again and again, even as we write, where a strong and inspired patriarch departs without a clear succession strategy, which leads to a legacy of unresolved family squabbles. In the Steinberg case there developed a pattern of diffusion and escalation – conflict spreading from topic to topic, fired by the explosive personality tensions among two opposing factions surrounding the sisters, and a mother who was incapable of mediating between them, who ended up herself taking sides. The eldest daughter Mitzi might have possessed the drive and determination of her father, but it seems she lacked the strength of character to bring her energies to bear effectively on the family or the business. A fatal weakness in this situation was the lack of robust governance mechanisms or mediation channels that could have helped diffuse some of the tensions and disagreements that arose within the family.

The hiring policy at Steinberg's, putting the needs of the family first, led to an influx of relatives into the business: descendants both by blood and by marriage. Little attention was given to matching people's abilities with the requirements for the job; family were just expected to work hard and to fit into the role to which they were assigned. There was a conspicuous and fatal failing to incorporate outside non-family talent. The Steinberg family story demonstrates that not only can business success be impacted by misplaced nepotism, family harmony can pay a price too.

THE *LOUISVILLE TIMES* AND THE BINGHAMS – LOSING THE LEGACY[15]

ORIGINS

The story of the Binghams of Louisville's newspaper dynasty throws a spotlight on family dynamics, and how the circumstances of the children's formative years can have a large impact on the development of the family business. In this multi-generation family, the founder's successors enjoyed comfortable upbringings. The parents strove to promote family togetherness and harmony by involving all the family offspring in the business, but the entry of the fourth generation into the business led to highly disruptive tensions.

Robert Worth Bingham was the founder of the *Louisville Times* dynasty. He purchased the business from the proceeds of a $5 million legacy from his second wife Mary Flagler, the widow of one of America's railroad pioneers. The death of Mary through illness caused a minor sensation at the time. In his lifetime Robert, who was known as 'the Judge', also rose to be ambassador to the United Kingdom. He believed that a newspaper should be in the hands of one proprietor, and he chose to pass the business to the youngest of his three sons, (George) Barry Bingham Sr. In effect he cut off his two eldest offspring from the business, providing them with an annual income of $15,000 until their deaths.

Intelligent, wealthy and powerful, Barry Sr and his wife Mary Bingham led vibrant social lives, while they also enjoyed the responsibility of raising their young family. Barry's busy life at the family newspaper meant he had limited amounts of time to spend with his children. Despite the demanding presence of the new-borns, Mary was determined to spend every moment she could with her husband. Mary, who had joined the family business, emerged with growing self-confidence to become a towering influence at the office, helping to shape the direction of the newspapers. Barry always looked to his wife when it came to big calls, and she put the iron in his soul to help him make tougher decisions than he otherwise might have done.

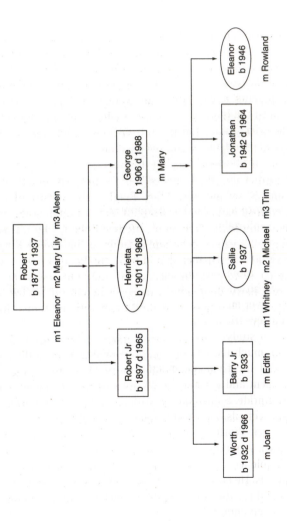

Figure 6.4 The Bingham family

FORMATIVE YEARS

Barry left it to Mary to do the heavy lifting in terms of the children's upbringing. The children experienced their mother as firm and attentive to discipline. Fighting to win their parents' affection, the five Bingham children divided into factions: the older boys Worth and Barry Jr formed an alliance, while the two younger children, Eleanor and Jonathan, formed another. Sallie, the middle child, was left to fend for herself. However, she was the smartest of the children, and earned her parents' approval with her sharp intelligence. Mary ruthlessly punished the boys when they were disobedient or misbehaved. Like the founder, Barry and Mary were determined that their sons would go to Harvard, and sent them to preparatory boarding schools to ready them for their college career.

While Worth enjoyed the independence and athletic possibilities that boarding school afforded, Barry Jr, who had reading difficulties, was enrolled into a remedial programme. A sensitive soul, Barry Jr missed the comfortable security of home, and his longing to be with his father became acute. Sallie meanwhile was securely ensconced within the family, but she was deeply reclusive, keeping to herself, staying in her room reading and writing. Although she missed her brothers, their absence was a blessing for her, especially that of Worth, who would never miss a chance to tease and bully her.

Sallie had few friends and was a delicate girl. Her school did not require her to study maths or other subjects she did not like, and she grew up, much like her father, with few practical skills – unable to understand the financial machinery of everyday life. But with her literary bent and aptitude, Sallie was her father's chief source of pleasure and pride. Sallie considered herself and her father to be the family's intellectuals. They were kindred spirits.

As a teenager, Worth desperately wanted his parents' approval, but was frustrated. A mixture of defiance and lack of ability led him to rebellious indolence, refusing to apply himself academically and failing several subjects. He became laconic, difficult and antisocial. Neither of his parents had the time or the inclination to try to bring him back by supportive intervention. Barry and Mary were not the heart-to-heart types, and their communications with their son were limited.

The other older boy, Barry Jr, fared little better. Besides his reading problems, he was doubly self-conscious on account of his obesity.

But once enrolled at boarding school, things changed dramatically for Barry Jr. He became very self-disciplined, conquered his weight problems, and began to grow in self-confidence. Meanwhile the younger Bingham children, Sallie, Jonathan and Eleanor, all remained at home, growing up in a busy household, although the youngest boy, Jonathan, felt neglected because of his father's long absences. The youngest child Eleanor was a mediocre student but was more independent and self-contained; an effect of growing up under the supervision of a succession of nannies. Overall none of them experienced much contact with their parents. The time and attention of mum and dad were spent elsewhere.

When Worth's foretold entry to Harvard occurred, Barry Sr took care to offer his son counsel against the evils of drinking and bad company. Like generations of college boys before him, Worth listened carefully and respectfully and then set off with gusto to do exactly what his father forbade. Lacking any natural academic gifts to offset his unruly life, Worth barely scraped through. But he grew in confidence that he could work hard whenever he needed to. This he proved during summer jobs at the *Louisville Times*.

NEWCOMERS TO THE FAMILY

Sallie also followed family tradition, going to Radcliffe College in Cambridge, Mass. Unlike her brother she was a bright student. Her inner desire was to emulate her parents' life by developing a good career and having a successful marriage. In her senior year at college, she became involved with and then engaged to Whitney Ellsworth, the editor of the *Harvard Advocate*. Sallie seemed to have achieved what she wanted, and to be headed for a dazzling career as a writer, with a happy marriage, similar to that of her parents.

Meanwhile, Worth had begun dating a woman at Harvard summer school. Her name was Joan Stevens, and aware of Worth's reputation as a young man who never took women seriously, she landed her catch with care. Joan was a well-bred, easygoing and affectionate young woman who shared Worth's sense of humour, and had the gift of bringing out his softer side. Soon they were inseparable, and after a brief engagement they married. After their wedding, Worth began working at the family firm as assistant managing editor of the *Louisville Times*. Their first daughter Clara was born in 1963.

Barry Jr, who followed the family tradition by graduating from Harvard, took up a job as a television researcher at NBC in Washington. Unlike his brother Worth, he had little luck with women but he enjoyed his work. He met a young blonde divorcee, Edith (Edie) Wharton, who lived with her two sons from her first marriage. Edie was beautiful, insightful, intelligent and kind. When Barry Jr was summoned by his father in Louisville to join family business, he reluctantly resigned from NBC and proposed marriage to Edie.

Barry Sr was gradually bringing the next generation into the family businesses and giving them a chance to display their talents. Mark Ethridge, the long-standing publisher of the *Louisville Times*, who had been instrumental in bringing the family newspaper to national prominence, helped to clear the way by retiring in 1963. Barry Sr also worked on plans to pass voting control to his sons, who would be running the business.

FAMILY TRAGEDIES

The youngest son Jonathan was reluctant to follow the family tradition and go to Harvard, but in the end he succumbed to the pressure and expectations, only to drop out at the end of his junior year in 1961 so that he could sign up for courses closer to home at the University of Louisville. He was able to convince his parents that he could do well if he pursued science, which he did, eventually fulfilling his destiny and their wishes by ending up at Harvard Medical School. Alas, that was as far as the road of fate would take him.

One day, while tinkering with an electrical gadget, he took a high-voltage shock and died instantly. Jonathan's premature death shook the family badly, especially Mary who was inconsolable. More was to come. That summer, heading out on vacation, Worth set out to drive his family and their new baby to Nantucket in his hardtop convertible. On the road the car went out of control while avoiding another vehicle, and Worth was struck in the neck by his surfboard and killed.

The loss of the eldest son and the heir to the family business was a blow not just for an emotionally fragile family but for the business. With two of his sons laid to rest Barry Sr made an effort to focus his thoughts on how to perpetuate the family newspaper business. He tried to feel buoyed by the thought that at least he had an heir left in Barry Jr.

THE NEW HEIR AND RESPONSIBILITIES

Barry Jr, the second-born son, was still young, inexperienced and a 'little boy' in the newspaper business, but now he was confronted with the possibility of taking on the responsibilities of editor and publisher. Many of the senior executives at the newspapers felt Barry Jr was a fish out of water and not equipped to do the job. Although Barry Jr acknowledged that he was not ready to take on the burden immediately, he knew that refusing the torch could prompt his father to sell the newspapers. This was unthinkable. In less than a week after Worth's funeral, Barry Jr became the assistant to the publisher. His father retained the titles of editor and publisher with the understanding that as soon as it was feasible, these responsibilities would be transferred to his only surviving son. Barry Jr for his part was ambitious and keen to go full speed ahead.

But the curse of the Bingham boys was not yet played out. Barry Jr was diagnosed with Hodgkin's disease, the cancer that had killed his grandfather. His condition was severe and required extensive radiation therapy and surgery. His parents were convinced that their only surviving son and heir was dying, and so was the rest of the world. The vultures started circling. News of Barry Jr's illness had attracted prospective buyers, and Barry Sr for the first time talked about an eventual sale of the company.

But Barry Jr was a determined character. He had shown this by overcoming the reading disorder as well as fighting his weight problem during his youth. Now he turned these same energies to the task of defeating his illness. This he did through a rigorous and obsessive regimen of exercise and diet. He stuck unswervingly to his plan, and sure enough he found himself miraculously on the road to recovery. We can only speculate whether his self-administered treatment regime worked, whether it was the power of mind over body, or just a lucky gift of the gods, but whatever it was, it worked. Barry Jr returned to his newspaper desk with even more energy and effort, though at the cost of getting a stomach ulcer. All the time these events were unfolding the paper's profits were eroding, and by the mid-1970s the company was barely breaking even.

WOMEN IN THE BUSINESS

Sallie's marriage with Whitney Ellsworth ended in a divorce soon after the birth of their baby son. Soon after she met a young Russian immigrant lawyer, Michael Iovenko, and within less than a year after her divorce they were married. Barry Jr promptly invited his brother-in-law Michael to sit on the Bingham board, an offer he gladly accepted, and he began to forge close bonds with the family. The family took a liking to Michael. But far from making Sallie happy, these developments had the opposite effect.[16] Sallie, who had always stood apart from the family, disliked this creeping incorporation and turned her attentions away from Michael. She had grown bored with him and decided to end the marriage in 1975, returning from New York to Louisville two years later. Meanwhile she also joined the Bingham board but would rarely attend meetings. Barry Sr had been feeling guilty about his relationship with Sallie and what had been happening to her. The bond was still strong between them. He could see how desperate she was, and he yearned to heal her wounds.

Barry Sr had always hoped his daughters would some day become more involved in the business. He felt that all three children would become closer if they functioned as active co-owners of the family business. With his usual optimism, he had never dreamed that his business goals and his family goals could be set on a collision course by putting them in harness together. Like many a parent wishing for peace among their offspring, he gravely underestimated the persistence of the childhood antagonisms that existed among his heirs, particularly between Barry Jr and Sallie. To complete Barry Sr's wish to knit the family together he also appointed to the board his wife Mary, Worth's widow Joan, Barry Jr's wife Edith and his youngest daughter Eleanor.

The youngest of the brood, Eleanor, lacking a profession of her own, depended on her parents for money. The self-sufficient child had grown into an undisciplined adult, with no intellectual pursuits, living for the moment and scarcely thinking about a personal career. Yet she was attracted to the idea of working for the Bingham companies.

So Barry Sr – in accord with his dream of family inclusion – acceded. In the fall of 1978 Eleanor arrived at the newspaper office bearing a grand new job title – director of special services. Colleagues reported that Eleanor did not act as an ordinary employee, and ignored office etiquette. She took long vacations whenever she fancied, and paraded the corridors attired casually in jeans and sweaters.[17]

Both Sallie's and Eleanor's positions with the company were, frankly, little more than sinecures, but they sat on the board. This gave them somewhat grandiose presumptions about their role and contribution. Some board members, not least Barry Jr, felt their comments at meetings were often gauche and embarrassingly lacking in business acumen. Sallie would often pontificate on the responsibilities of ownership and journalistic tradition, and scoffed at Barry Jr's obsession with computerization and cable television. For his part, Barry Jr could not stand it when his authority was challenged. The truth was that none of the Binghams had much business savvy, especially in terms of the company's finances.

A CRISIS OF TRUST

For decades Sallie and Eleanor had been distant from the family enterprise, unlike Barry Jr, who had had the benefit of regular conversations and insights with his father about their shared dream for the family business. Sallie and Eleanor also regarded their dividends as remuneration that they expected to receive independent of the company's performance. They soon felt unwelcome on the board, where they had responsibilities but little influence. The sisters began criticizing Barry Jr in front of employees about his 'anti-women bias'. The emerging split in the family started to become public knowledge when a local magazine headlined an article on the sisters 'The Bingham black sheep'.

In 1980, in order to retain control, the family initiated a share buy-back agreement. The pact stipulated that if a stockholder of the Bingham companies wanted to sell shares to an outsider, the family had to be given 60 days to match the bid. Although Barry Jr was keen to execute this agreement, his sisters demurred. They showed little regard for his leadership, declaring they were not prepared to sign, also demonstrating they retained a vestige of leverage and power. A crisis of trust was developing.

For his part, Barry Jr had failed to grasp that he could not dictate policy in the firm, and that much of his power derived from the confidence that the rest of the family had in him. His disquiet was heightened when Sallie managed to acquire an operational role in the business, as the *Courier-Journal* book editor. This was actually a good role for her. She performed well in the job and began to feel more at home. The position was initially temporary but to Barry Jr's great dismay it was soon made permanent, without his permission. Sallie continued to be liberal in her criticism of his competence, and now she had a platform within the business from which to do this.

Barry Jr, frustrated by his sister's interference, felt he needed external support to guide him through these troubled times, so he brought in family business consultants and reshaped the governance, hiring a professional board of directors. This provided him with the rationale he needed, backed by his experts, to remove his sisters from the company.

But Barry Jr's move to force his sisters to leave the company boards did not go down well with other board members, who felt it was breaking up the ownership group just because he couldn't tolerate his sisters. Trying to bring matters to a head, he presented his parents with three options: to sell all three companies, remove his sisters from the company, or find a new publisher. But he didn't want his father to sell up, and he pressed his parents to get his sisters out of the business. The effect of this manoeuvre on Barry Sr was to puncture his optimism. With the utmost reluctance he concluded the only way to buy peace would be to remove all family members from the board, including himself. Only one member resisted: Sallie. For her, the seat on the board was a family entitlement.

By now in her late 40s, Sallie's relationship with her parents was strained, and she cut herself off from social contact with them. She decided that there was only one choice left to her: to sell her stock in the family firm. She confronted the family with an ultimatum: pay her $42 million for her shares or she would find the highest outside bidder to sell them to. Meanwhile, Eleanor threatened that if she was not given a more active role in the business, she would sell too. Barry Sr and Mary were pressured from all sides by their feuding children, who refused to accept and implement any compromise they suggested. Faced with this logjam Barry Sr decided to sell the family firm, leaving behind him a trail of disappointed children. With this decision the era of the Bingham media dynasty was over. The family's lack of cohesion, shared values and clarity of roles had finally fragmented the firm.

COMMENT

This story of heads in the sand is familiar. Family members become fixated on their antipathies within the family and their demands on each other to the exclusion of all else. In this case the tragic loss of two talented sons robbed the Binghams of succession opportunities, and indirectly soured relationships. Tragedies within families often have the effect of producing a temporary and artificial cohesion, as people cling together at their time of greatest need. But the pain of grief is a lonely experience, and it often ultimately alienates people from each other, and sometimes from themselves.

The family climate of the Binghams was ill-prepared for such shocks. The character flaws of the individuals were uncorrected by good parenting. The family climate that had predominated for so many years made the discipline, vision and purpose that drive a successful family firm elusive.

It is a sad story of people with unfilled needs, personal loss, psychological disconnection and thwarted dreams. Had only a few members of the family come to the realization that they were settling into profoundly dysfunctional patterns, then the outside support and guidance that might have saved them could have been found. That still wouldn't have meant they were fit to run a business, and perhaps the Binghams could have minimized their unhappiness by relinquishing their unfulfilled dreams earlier on. Much of the responsibility here lies in the second generation – with Barry Sr and his wife. The delusions of over-optimistic parenthood kept them on the track that had no promise and no resolution.

SEAGRAM AND THE BRONFMANS – THE RUNAWAY LEADER[18]

ORIGINS

The case of the Bronfmans highlights the difficulty in establishing working leadership models in the next generation. Successively, leadership of the firm was handed over to the male family member with the strongest personality, a formula that will produce action but not necessarily effective results. This is a story of a powerful family who bulldozed all opposition before them. The blind exercise of power is as foolish as any other kind of error, and here, as we shall see, the stakes were progressively raised to the point that the players had to leave the table, defeated.

Sam Bronfman was a legend in his time, who established what was to become the Seagram Corporation, of one of North America's largest business empires. It also turned out to be one of the biggest family financial roller-coasters of recent times. Sam Bronfman arguably became to the alcoholic spirits industry what Henry Ford was to automobiles, J Pierpont Morgan to banking and John D Rockefeller to oil; each a pioneer who shaped their industry and created a model for others to follow. By character Sam was everything one expects in such an entrepreneur: obsessive, egocentric and single-mindedly focused. He was a man of contrasts, soft-spoken at times but with a tongue that could also dispense powerful venom. When his brother Allan returned from fighting the Second World War, Sam was unstinting in his jealous vituperation: 'Christ, they get a few more like him and Hitler's got a chance.'

The Bronfman family emigrated from Moldova to Canada in search of a better life. They quickly proved their ability to earn their living as an entrepreneurial family. Their chosen activity was hotel-keeping, a trade that suited their circumstances, requiring modest capital investment to get established. The main money generator was catering for customers' thirst in the hotel bars. Thus began the family's association with the alcoholic beverage industry.

Sam was the third of four brothers, and by far the most ambitious. The eldest brother Abe suffered from an addiction to gambling. Harry, the second born, was an easygoing individual, and emerged as the leader of the family firm. Later on in his business career Harry was

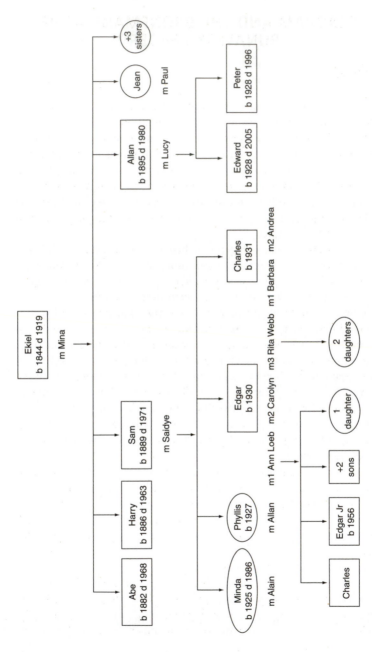

Figure 6.5 The Bronfman family

arrested and accused of bribery and tampering with witnesses. This was a scandal that bruised the family's reputation. Although he was acquitted by the court after two trials, his relationship with Sam suffered in the wake of this incident and a divide emerged between the brothers. Allan, the youngest, was the only family member to acquire professional qualifications, as a lawyer. He came to play a role in the business, but was also sidelined by Sam. Allan's sons Edward and Peter went on to build a very successful business under their own steam.

In 1922 one of the Bronfman in-laws, Paul Matoff, who was married to the brothers' second sister Jean, was gunned down in a shooting. At the time Matoff was running part of the family's liquor operations. The incident came as a shock to Harry, who slipped into depression. Sam saw his chance, and jumped at the opportunity to step up from being number two to become leader of the firm. From this point on he never looked back. So the pattern was set to replicate itself through the generations of Bronfmans, of one powerful family member overbearing the moderate influences of all others.

SAM TAKES OVER

The foundations of the liquor empire that Sam built were laid during the Prohibition years in the 1920s when the sale of alcohol was banned in the United States. Many countries at that time were wrestling with the issue of how to handle the impact of alcohol on their citizens, and prohibition was a futile attempt to stamp out the world's oldest and most popular form of adult beverage. The banning of alcohol sales in the United States, in 1919 under the Volstead Act, provided the Bronfmans with a golden opportunity to develop their business.

The family set about expanding their liquor operations in Canada, establishing themselves as important cogs in a system that kept markets supplied, notwithstanding the ban. Although late starters in the business they quickly caught up with the market leader, Harry Hatch of Hiram Walker.

One of the breakthroughs for the Bronfmans was a partnership they formed with the British Distillers Company, which brought leading brands of Scotch whisky such as Johnnie Walker into their stable, strengthening the Bronfmans' position. After this deal was sealed Sam

Bronfman, by now the acknowledged business leader, snapped up Seagram Distillers, a struggling domestic Canadian distilling business. Adopting this as the new corporate name, Sam now had the means to pursue his vision. This was to offer consumers top-quality products that would earn his company a reputation for reliability.

By the end of Prohibition Seagram's was poised to become North America's leading distilling business. In a very single-minded fashion Sam was reshaping the spirits industry, and bringing to its consumers an aura of respectability that hitherto it had lacked. The brands that he created went on to become market leaders and propelled the company into top spot in the United States. The financial rewards were considerable.

Sam's life centred on the business, though he devoted much effort to his pastoral responsibilities as leader of the Canadian Jewish Congress. Sam and his wife Saidye had four children. Their attitude to their two first-born daughters, Minda and Phyllis, was the traditional one of exclusion from the business. Sadly Minda died of cancer in her early 40s, but her younger sister Phyllis flourished as a strong advocate for the work of architects and as a noted philanthropist. In her lifetime she received no less than 26 honorary degrees.

The two younger boys were Edgar, born in 1929, followed by Charles two years later. There were contrasting personalities. Edgar was something of a rebel, never completing his college education, but going straight on to work in the family business. Charles was a more timid individual, happiest staying close to home in Montreal. The two brothers settled early on what their distinctive roles and goals were, and never felt the need to compete. Charles was happy to play second fiddle. Later in life this would prove costly, as he acquiesced to poor decisions. Perhaps the pact of peace between them owed something to their seeing first hand how destructive and painful sibling conflict can be, having witnessed how their father had sidelined his own siblings to gain supremacy.

THE RISE OF EDGAR

No sooner was Edgar invited into the family company than he began his rise towards to the top, though this was a position that he would not claim until his father died in 1971. In terms of business Sam's final masterstroke in 1963, driven partly by a desire to achieve respectability, was a major investment in an old oil producer, Texas Pacific. The oil industry would soon become one of the major sources of income for Seagram. Sam retained a tenacious grip on the business, and until his dying day the company was run by others with his 'advice and consent'. Edgar was all this time straining at the leash. He struggled to accept the situation, and there was a constant battle of wills between father and son. Notwithstanding the company's financial success, the repeated shouting matches between Sam and Edgar were undermining morale. In the classic imperial folly of many family businesses, the chief overstayed his time.

Liberated by the death of his father, Edgar was able to start pursuing his strategy to reshape the business. In 1981, after a decade under his belt as the sole leader of the firm, he made his biggest contribution to the company. This took the form of accepting a bid by another oil company for Seagram's stake in Texas Pacific. The price of $2.1 billion was many times the value his father had paid for the stock. Now armed with a huge fighting fund, Edgar and the board started to look for ways to invest the cash. His executive group wanted to buy another consumer goods business, but Edgar's advisors pointed him in the direction of another financial investment. This turned out to be a good decision, for Seagram promptly acquired a 20 per cent in Conoco oil and a similar stake in DuPont chemicals. These investments were certainly good for the business from a purely financial perspective, but they also changed the character of the company. Seagram had become a hybrid between an investment company and an international consumer goods business. We can only speculate whether the company would have succumbed to the fate that awaited it had it retained more of a focused identity.

Edgar now presided over a commercial empire that drew the family the accolade of 'the Rothschilds of the New World'. At this stage Edgar's life outside Seagram took on a new dimension when, outdoing his late father, he became leader of the World Jewish Congress in 1981. His absorption with his new political responsibilities was beginning to divert his attention from management of the firm, so sensibly he turned his attention to the issue of leadership succession. Less rationally however, in 1986 without consulting his younger brother Charles, Edgar announced that he was appointing his second son Edgar Jr to be his successor.

JUNIOR'S FOLLY

The decision to appoint a person without obvious experience other than a career in showbusiness, which appeared to be going nowhere fast, to a post of such high responsibility says more about the father than the son. Handing his son of 31 years the baton of leadership could be seen as Edgar Sr's riposte to his late father, who he felt had not loved him and had hung on to power at the firm too late in life. This was a demonstrable act of faith in his son, a boy in whom he could see no faults. It would prove to be an act of serious misjudgment and a near-fatal blow to the business and its shareholders. Neither Charles, who did not approve of the appointment, nor the board of directors were prepared to take a stand in opposition to Edgar Sr, so the young scion duly took over the reins.

In many ways Edgar Jr was in the mould of his father – haughty, with an overweening self-confidence – and he would soon prove to be a poor guide for the family business, judging by how he steered its strategy.[19] Any wrong move could potentially cost billions, and the non-family shareholders, who owned a majority of the stock, would suffer the most.

Edgar Jr, as newly installed head of the business, had carte blanche to set the vision for the future and dispose of the company's assets as he wished, but he was ill-prepared for his new responsibilities at Seagram. As a student he had been undisciplined and he lacked formal intellectual education. His first act was to convince his board that higher growth and returns were to be had in the media and entertainment industry. It was true that the alcoholic drinks market offered comparatively low growth – it was a mature market – but it was a lot less risky than the alternative Edgar Jr was advocating. Nonetheless, Seagram now embarked on a series of investments in the entertainment industry, culminating in the sale of the DuPont investment and the acquisition of MCA/Universal Studios. Again Charles, wanting to avoid conflict, acquiesced with the deal, but he sensed that the company did not have the leadership to make the new investment work.

Edgar Jr was left unchecked by his board to pursue his strategy, and his next and subsequently disastrous move was the sale of Seagram to Vivendi, a French conglomerate. The deal was struck at the height of the dotcom boom in 2000, with the announcement that the merger would create the world's second-largest media and entertainment group. Under the swashbuckling leadership of CEO Jean-Marie Messier, Vivendi had embarked on splurge of acquisitions, using its grossly overpriced shares as currency. Against the advice of their investment bankers and throwing caution to the wind, the Bronfmans in a high-risk move elected to be paid for their stake in Seagram in Vivendi shares. But Vivendi had piled up large debts, and the share price collapsed almost as soon as the ink had dried on the Seagram deal. Indeed Vivendi's finances were precariously balanced.

With the collapse in the value of the shares in the company, the Bronfman family experienced a massive decline in their fortunes. The family put a brave face on the way in which their dynasty had imploded, with Phyllis, the oldest of the three surviving offspring of Sam Bronfman, describing it as 'a Greek tragedy'.

COMMENT

This is a saga with several familiar elements. It is the heady cocktail that comes from powerful family forces and the absence of appropriate restraints and guides for decision making. Interestingly, one of the deficiencies here is conflict. What the Bronfmans needed was a robust debate involving family and non-family. The supine character of the family apart from the designated leaders was counterproductive; any of them could have made a greater attempt at decisive intervention. Worse perhaps was the pliant conduct of the board. This left the family business is at the mercy of whim and personal chemistry.

In the Bronfman case insularity meant hubris – the folly of people who have an exaggerated belief in their destiny. The infatuation with Hollywood was an extension of this delusion. The case also illustrates how public ownership offers limited protection for a business where there is a strong family and weak governance. The case also illustrates how compelling can be tight-knit bonds between a father and his son.[20] Here the ineffectual board allowed the business strategy to turn into a game of roulette with the markets.

7

Schism – the house divided

Remember, blood is not only thicker than water, it's much more difficult to get off the carpet.

(Phyllis Diller)

INTRODUCTION

Conflict is part of life. In our scene-setting for this book in Chapter 2 we outlined the numerous causes and sources of conflict. The causes are often highly rational and objective – as when people dispute over resources and territory. In other cases the roots strike deeper into the emotions and identities of people who feel threatened, diminished or frustrated.

Families are amplifiers of all emotions, positive as well as negative. The roots of conflict also spring from age-old divisions, as we have seen, between parents and children, and between siblings. We shall see these elements recurring here and throughout this book, since they are elemental and universal. But now we look at how structural elements come into play, cause conflicts to become divisions: that is, fights not just between individuals, but between groups or factions.

Let's put this another way. A conflict that looks as if it's about personalities is turned into something much sharper because the individuals in some way represent different groupings.[1] In family business there are many ways in which such divisions can occur – largely because of their unique status, combining the very different and at times challenging worlds of family and business.

In this chapter we shall be seeing three principal varieties of division. They are not independent of each other. You can get all three types of division at the same time!

INSIDERS VERSUS OUTSIDERS

This is one of the most prevalent forms of schism in a family firm – between those who are on the privileged inner circle of running the family business, and those who are external onlookers. This situation arises very naturally in the family firm, when people's career and life choices divide the family into those who see their future in the firm, and those who make their lives outside. The latter group may retain an owning stake in the business – often substantial – yet remain on the periphery of the field of action. This in itself is not a cause of conflict. Problems typically arise over issues of inequity – when the outsiders feel they are treated unfairly, that their interests have not been considered and they have just been taken for granted. But it can also be the insiders who feel unfairly treated – where outsiders receive handsome dividends while the insiders toil away making sacrifices to create the wealth that the rest of the family consumes.[2] Here we shall see mainly the former variety.

DISCONNECTED FAMILY MEMBERS

The connection with the family business is not always a simple division between two camps. There can be layers of association, from an inner circle bathed in the light of the business to an outer layer in dark ignorance. Again this isn't a problem until someone wants something they can't have. From the inner circle's point of view, they see themselves as the accountable and responsible ones – pulling the levers of power for the benefit of the business and all its shareholders. Problems arise when this group does not adequately account for its actions to the non-active family owners, or they draw a veil of secrecy over their activities. Instead, the non-active are treated as bystanders. The outsider group may react in several ways. They may agitate and become dissident when opportunities arise, or they may just switch off, not just from the business but from the family, losing any sense of emotional bond. Thus those running a family firm can end up splitting and alienating a section of the family that otherwise might have maintained some degree of attachment.

FIGHTING OVER THE SPOILS

Perhaps the most obvious cause of division is money. We should pause, though, to reflect that money and emotion are often deeply intertwined, as Freud was the first to recognize. There is plenty of scope for greed in family businesses, where wealth may be created rapidly and just as quickly thrown away. But money, or resources more generally, often symbolizes how much one is valued, belongs to a group or has power and status in a hierarchy.[3] When disputes are expressed in financial terms it rapidly becomes what economists call a zero sum game, where one person's gain is another's loss.

Social psychologists have devoted much attention to the concept of fairness. This is the language in which many financial battles and turf wars are waged. But it is not a simple matter. It is not just about the legitimacy of the division of spoils – 'distributive justice' – it is also about the legitimacy of the way in which the pot was divided – 'procedural justice'. As we noted in Chapter 2, people can get more upset about what they perceive as an unfair process than the inequality of the division in itself.

Once the family enters into rivalry around issues regarding the division of the rewards, it is often well on the road to becoming fractionated. Perhaps this explains why according to research in the United States the owners of just over two-thirds of companies that have entered the second generation agree to split the business, allowing family business owners to go their separate ways.[4]

Successful business families and patriarchs are, however, often opposed to the idea of dividing the assets or the business, seeing this as a backwards step that might destroy the family's unity and their platform for growing wealth. They may also have a strong feeling of passion for whatever has been created and not want to see the family legacy undermined, destroyed or broken up. However, generally family members cannot be kept connected to the family business against their will. In the cases that follow, we shall look at some high-stakes games involving significant resources. We shall highlight not only the causes of the schism but also the process by which they reach the point where a sale or split became the only way out, resigning the legacy and sending family members to go their own separate ways.

PRITZKER – FIGHTING FOR THE SPOILS[5]

FAULT LINES

The Pritzker saga is a case where family fracture lines emerge as the company transitions from being a third-generation sibling partnership to a fourth-generation business of cousins. It starts with the vision of family unity, deeply held by the family patriarch, Jay Pritzker, which steadily unravels following his death. The case is also unhappy proof that business success, however great, offers no guarantee of unity for the family firm. The Pritzker family values put emphasis on hard work and grooming family members to take leadership roles in the business. But this was an unbalanced focus of attention. Little mind was given to helping family members to stay connected with and to retain pride in the family business, irrespective of their individual capabilities and career choices. This culture provided the roots of the schism that emerged between the insiders working in the business and the outsiders who were not involved. A second fault line subsequently developed in one of the branches where a divorce took place, leaving a legacy of perceived inequities and disputed ownership rights among the children of the second marriage. This developed into a veritable canyon of complex splits.

NICOLAS THE GREAT

In 1881, Nicolas Pritzker was just over 10 years old when he and his parents fled the Jewish ghetto near Kiev to arrive at Chicago. Industrious Nicolas supported his family by filling every hour of day and evening with labour, working as a newsboy, tailor's assistant, and on the side as a part-time shoe-shine boy. He soon learnt English and, as an intelligent and resourceful boy, found himself a job as a

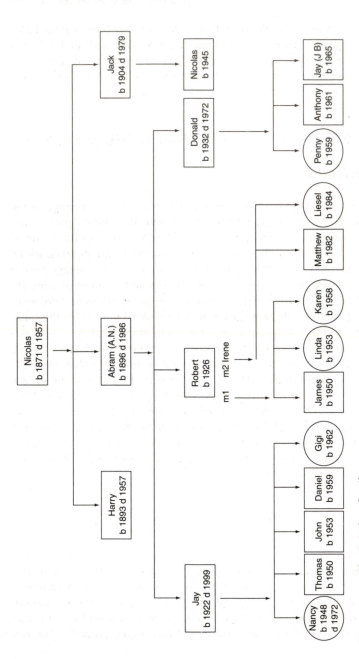

Figure 7.1 The Pritzker family

translator for the *Chicago Tribune*. Before long he was married and sought a steady career to support his family. He started by taking a pharmacy course to become a druggist, which he used to support his enrolment on an evening programme to study for a law degree.

By 1902 this remarkable workaholic had founded his own law firm. He had three sons – Harry, Abram Nicholas and Jack – all of whom followed in his footsteps, taking law degrees and joining the family law firm, Pritzker & Pritzker. After graduating from Harvard Law School, it was the second son, Abram Nicholas, known as A N, who led the move to take the family beyond the practice of law into investment. It was the labours of A N and his younger brother Jack that set down the foundations of the Pritzker business empire, initially by acquiring real estate. By the time A N died in 1986 at the age of 90 he was a billionaire and the family had become a regular feature on the annual Forbes 500 list of the richest people in the United States.

A N had three sons – Jay, Robert and Donald – who were all introduced to the family business as young boys. Soon after Jay finished high school, he attended law school at Northwestern University and joined Pritzker & Pritzker. He made his first acquisition, the Colson Company, in 1953 and brought in his engineer brother Robert to run it. Robert had acquired a reputation as adept in turning around troubled businesses. This became a business model. Jay would buy the companies and Robert would return them to fiscal health. The youngest brother Donald also worked in the family business but died aged 39 of a heart attack. Together Jay and Robert transformed their grandfather's business into a multi-faceted conglomerate with assets in the hospitality, tobacco, credit bureau, container leasing and other miscellaneous industries. Of all these businesses Hyatt Hotels was the best known and the jewel in the family crown.

JAY THE DEAL MAKER

Jay was one of the greatest deal makers of his day. He was an intense listener, curious in all things and totally immersed in the business. People recall him as a very trustworthy, charming, witty and always polite businessman. Jay was always looking for an angle to make a profit and in his career spanning 50 years he bought and sold more than 200 companies. He would acquire them if he thought they were undervalued by the market, or if their tax profiles were such that when combined with other companies in his empire they would help reduce taxes to be paid to the federal government and increase overall returns.

The hotel business was one such purchase: Jay acquired a small hotel called Hyatt Place near Los Angeles airport in 1957 for $2.2 million, and from this relatively modest start grew the prestigious chain piece by piece. The strategy focused on upscale business hotels at airports and city centres, with resorts added later. The corporation now consists of over 200 hotels in more than 40 countries. Other firms that were added to the family's holdings during Jay's tenure included Triton Holdings in marine containers, Conwood chewing tobacco and TransUnion credit bureaus. The Marmon group that was largely managed by Robert consisted of more than 100 companies covering diverse industries with over $6 billion revenues.

Jay had five children: Nancy, Thomas (Tom), John, Daniel (Danny) and Gigi. In 1972 Jay's eldest daughter Nancy, suffering from depression, committed suicide. Jay had intense feelings of guilt over his daughter's death, wondering if he had been too tough and demanding of her. Following her death, Jay transferred his attention and affection to the next child, Tom. Tom, serious and shy by nature, was much less an action man than his father and more contemplative. With a strong interest in Buddhism and Asian art, he published studies on Tibetan cave paintings. Tom joined the family business after gaining business and law degrees. He was closely overseen and trained by Jay himself, who duly became very proud of his son's achievements.

Although Jay brought his two other sons, Danny and John, into the business, neither fitted in happily. Danny, who felt he had a vocation as a musician following his college degree, had leanings to go elsewhere but his father insisted that he join the business. Danny obeyed, briefly, but eventually quit to start his own record company, which the family helped to support.

Meanwhile, John's entrepreneurial ventures were not very successful: for example, one was a failing sporting-goods retail business. Although Jay loved his family, he was by nature blunt and outspoken about such failures. He could appear harsh and dismissive of people who didn't rise to his standards of entrepreneurial success – to be the best, especially in business, which he valued above all other domains of endeavour.

Apart from his own eldest son Tom, Jay was most impressed by his Uncle Jack's son Nick, a cousin who was 20 years his junior. Nick delivered strongly for the family business by aggressively expanding their casino holdings around the world and cutting deals to build new Hyatt hotels. Jay also brought into the family business his niece Penny – Donald's daughter – who spearheaded the growth of the family's commercial real estate empire and Classic Residence by Hyatt, a company building and managing luxury housing for the elderly. So it emerged over time that the new generation of Pritzkers who were leading the business were a triumvirate of Tom, Nick and Penny. Those family members who had no executive roles in the business were largely kept at arm's length from the firm and were expected not to interfere.

Jay's combative nature continued to dominate the business, not least in a series of battles he fought with the Internal Revenue Service (IRS), over the use of offshore trusts and complicated arrangements to limit tax liability. In one case the IRS insisted that the family owed the government over $53.2 million in taxes on the estate of A N Pritzker. In 1994 the family finally reached an agreement with the government, and Jay himself paid the settlement of $9.5 million in order to close the dossier on this issue.

JAY'S COMMANDMENTS

In June 1995 Jay called a family gathering, which was attended by his four surviving offspring, his brother Robert, cousin Nicholas and six of Jay's nieces and nephews. The only two blood relatives who did not attend the meeting were Robert's children from his second marriage, Liesel and Matthew, who were 11 and 13 years old respectively at that time. Jay handed everyone present a copy of a letter, signed by himself and Robert, with instructions about the disposition of the family wealth and their trusts. The letter explained that the majority of the wealth was in corporations controlled by the trusts, which were neither intended for nor were to be viewed as sources of individual wealth. The structure was designed to accumulate capital to invest in the family's business interests and to uphold the family's tradition of giving back through philanthropic donations. The letter enshrined the principle that individuals should not spend more than they themselves earned or contributed to the family and society. Jay and Robert also made clear that the family trusts were not to be broken up, at least for the foreseeable future. What they failed to foresee was how fragile family unity would turn out to be, and the emerging schism that would shatter their rosy vision of the future.

Jay's philosophy harkened back to the family origins – any benefits to individuals should be the direct product of their effort and success, not just because they were in the bloodline. The letter also announced that Jay's chosen successor to lead the family business would be Tom, with Penny and Nicholas also anointed as vice-chairmen on the strength of their proven entrepreneurial and managerial capabilities. The brothers' letter made clear that they expected the children, and all other nieces and nephews, to be morally bound to follow their wishes.

The letter, considering financial benefits for the beneficiaries, outlined a series of lump sum payments and allowances for each family member on a series of milestones, such as graduation from college, reaching the age of 30 and so on. By their 45th birthday, these payments would add up to over $25 million per family member after taxes. The brothers expressed strong hopes that the family's tradition of highly valuing philanthropy would be perpetuated, and that the Pritzkers would continue to be benefactors of important causes in Chicago and elsewhere. Expressing hope for the future the letter, co-signed by Jay and Robert but written by Jay, concluded optimistically, 'I expect our modus operandi will continue harmoniously through this next generation.'

OPEN DISSENSION

The emergence of tensions in the family started before the death of the patriarch Jay Pritzker, even though he continually admonished his successors to respect the family 'system', in which the business was to be run as a single entity for the benefit of all. But it takes more than edicts from the patriarch to instil values and principles in the next generation. Jay made insufficient strides to foster buy-in to a shared vision. Enshrining one's wishes in a weighty document at a time when you command most love and respect might seem like a fail-safe strategy, but time quickly erodes the sentiments and majesty of the occasion.

Only a shared culture can sustain values, and Jay and his brother had focused almost exclusively on creating an environment that valued hard work and business success above all. Thus it was that it did not take long after Jay's death in 1999 for the peace to break down, under two sets of pressures. The first cause was tensions between family members not working in the business and the triumvirate in charge of the firm. The second was an emerging fault line between the two youngest members of the new generation, Michael and Liesel, and their father Robert.

At the time of the letter, a foreboding of the conflict was visible in the open dissension expressed by Danny and John about the succession to leadership of their elder brother Tom. They went to Jay and told him that they wanted to take their money out. Jay refused but threw them an olive branch by increasing their allowances. This did not mollify them. They resented what they saw as Tom's arrogance, for example when he refused to allow them to use the family company's Falcon jet.[6]

Two other factors contributed to the divide. Jay had introduced a system of incentives called 'promotes' in the family jargon, which were a form of financial kicker to reward working family members for the deals they championed. Through these arrangements the trio working in the business earned over $500 million in additional remuneration. While these incentives could be justified because the other family shareholders had made large gains from these investments, a particular transaction, known as the 'turbo promote', involving a casino operation in Elgin, Illinois raised the hackles of the family outsiders.

The structure of this deal was seriously divisive. Tom, Nicholas and Penny shared a 65 per cent stake, with other family members getting as little as 1.5 per cent each. A similarly unbalanced transaction also took place at this time, but was only revealed in 2001. This showed that assets that had become worth $525 million had been transferred in 1979 into a trust – the Marshall Trust – for the sole benefit of Tom and his family, including his mother-in-law, Abigail Marshall. To the family 'outsiders' it looked as if more than $1 billion of the assets belonging to the wider family were now in the hands of the insider trio, who had gained an unfair advantage. To try to appease the younger family members who had not been mollified by their father's letter, Jay reacted once again by reaching for the cheque book, and gave Danny, John and their sister Gigi $30 million each.

A WIDENING GULF

In January 1999 Jay Pritzker died and was laid to rest, but there was no peace for his successors. The fourth-generation heirs were already deeply embroiled in their feuds for wealth and power. By summer 2000, Danny and John had joined forces with Penny's brothers Tony and J B as the 'outsiders'. They confronted Tom, Penny and Nick, demanding that they address their concerns about how the trium-virate were administering the family's wealth. Their complaint was that the insider group were paying themselves excessively and ineq-uitably, and that they were acting in a non-transparent manner. Tom denied the claims, and although he had unlimited power and could have overridden his brothers and cousins, he feared the effects of adverse publicity on the family and on his elderly mother.

The cousins had no such restraint. They had the resolve and were prepared to file claims against the family leaders for 'breaches of fiduciary duties, self-dealing, conflicts of interest and other impro-prieties'. The stage was set for a full-scale battle between the two groups. If one fight was not enough, the family also had to deal with the consequences of Robert's unhappy second marriage with Irene, which ended in 1994 in a bitter divorce. Their separation had led to the couple fighting over custody of their two children, Matthew and Liesel. Irene won the battle and obtained sole custody of the children.

As can happen, the family split and the mother's bond with her children soured relations with their father. Soon afterwards, a dispute blew up over the way in which it was alleged that Robert, who had discretionary powers over his children's affairs, had administered Liesel's and Matthew's trust funds. This culminated in late 2002 with Liesel suing her 76-year-old father, claiming that he had trans-ferred assets held in those funds into trusts benefiting other family members. Liesel, who had a budding career as a Hollywood actress, was not shy about drawing some heavy publicity to her plight, and managed to throw the family and its squabbles even more into the media spotlight. She demanded restitution of $1 billion in actual losses and $5 billion in punitive damages. Her older brother Matthew joined the battle, also filing suit five months later. Robert disputed the claim, insisting that he had acted entirely properly. Three years later, no doubt under intense pressure to sidestep the unwelcome publicity this legal battle was increasingly attracting, serious negotiations ensued to settle Liesel's and Matthew's suit.

SETTLEMENT

For the Pritzkers, whether insiders or outsiders, they were all family, and blood proved thicker than water. These grievances were too serious to ignore. A compromise had to be reached. So it was that that the ruling trio, Tom, Penny and Nick, realized that nothing less than dismantling the group would prevent the fight escalating into a full legal battle. The solution was hardly elegant but it was simple and direct.[7] The entire value of the group was to be divided among them all, insiders and outsiders. Each family member's stake was thought to be worth over $1 billion.

Tom was put in charge of the process, and was given 10 years, until 2011, by which time the entire portfolio of assets should be divested. As part of the agreement the trio kept their 'promotes', and as a quid pro quo Tom agreed to redistribute the value of the companies in the Marshall Trust to other family members. Other key elements in the settlement included putting in place a formal governance structure to properly engage all the owners and keep them informed. To back up the agreement a high-powered arbitrator was appointed to help implement the settlement agreement.

Liesel and Matthew's lawsuit was also settled in 2005 when they relinquished their claim on the family assets in exchange for $450 million each. This cleared the way to allowing the 11 other members of the fourth generation to proceed with the settlement agreement and divide the Pritzker empire among themselves. Each of the 11 cousins had already received $50 million in distributions by late 2004, with an additional $75 million due to be distributed to each member by end of 2005. From being asset rich but cash poor, the outsiders not working in the business were suddenly deluged in money as Jay's legacy started to be dismantled.

Jay Pritzker's view, that the family was best served if the family business was not viewed as individual wealth but as family wealth, was
swept away by this flood of riches. His view of the world could not
withstand the power of the vast wealth that was stored up in the firm.
These events demonstrate the futility of trying to rule from beyond the
grave, especially when competing with the pressure to avoid conflict,
to satisfy strong-willed individuals and to handle the lure of wealth.

COMMENT

This case seems to place money at the root of the conflict. So it was,
in one sense. Economists are right that huge incentives distort behaviour. But they can only do so when there is state of readiness in the
minds of the people affected. Here it was more than mere money but a
feeling of entitlement, and a perception, rightly or wrongly, of having
been unfairly deprived of what is rightly one's own.

Jay's desire for the family to stick together was contradicted, even
when he was alive, by the sharp distinction he created between the
haves on the inside and the have-nots on the outside. The issue of the
'promotes' and the allocation of assets to Tom's family were as much
a problem of perceived procedural as distributive justice – not just a
question of inequality but also of disenfranchisement. In the previous
generation Jay had inadvertently created two classes of citizen, starting from when he wanted Danny to take up law and leave his music
career aside. This divide was exacerbated in the fourth generation,
with the insiders taking charge of the family empire while the others
could only observe as bystanders.

Jealousies were allowed to emerge between the two camps, and
there was no mechanism for the outsiders to vent frustrations,
let alone make any constructive contribution to retaining family
harmony and a sense of common purpose. The trio fell into a defensive posture that made them appear arrogant and self-serving. While
they could justify their actions in terms of good stewardship of the
business, the family leadership model in the Pritzker empire was not
fit for purpose in stewarding the business model, an emerging cousin
consortium, after Jay's death.

There was no one in the fourth generation to pick up the baton from
Jay, with the exception of Tom, whose focus appeared to be limited

to the business. A vacuum emerged in terms of family leadership. Jay had imagined that his letter of wishes, which he read to the family in 1995, would provide the answers and set the mould for years to come. Such is the delusion of many ageing patriarchs – that they can freeze the frame as they leave this world. In this case, Jay had been a great success during his lifetime but he failed with his brother to address properly the challenge of laying the groundwork for an effective generational transition in the family.

Choosing the best business leaders is in itself not sufficient to guarantee that one's wishes will be fulfilled. The family has an equal and vital need for leadership.[8] Leading the business and leading the family are distinct and separate roles often best filled by different people. Any hope of passing on a dynasty and achieving true longevity was handicapped from the outset by a lack of attention to fundamental governance processes. At Pritzker, following Jay's departure, a vacuum emerged where there was an absence of structure and processes for taking orderly decisions that all the family could buy into. Thus emerged the schism that nearly derailed, and certainly diverted, one of America's outstanding business empires.

THE *LA TIMES* GROUP AND THE CHANDLERS – THE CENTRIFUGAL FAMILY[9]

ORIGINS

This is a classic story of serial family entrepreneurship that created a mountain of gold but where in the end the family lost a grip on the business. Otis Chandler was the last in a line of four generations of family publishers at the *LA Times*, and it was his departure that marked the beginning of the end for the family business. One of Otis's reasons for prematurely retiring as business leader was that he felt a lack of appreciation by other family members for his efforts. In the absence of any close ties with the family firm, the glue that had held them together in earlier times dissolved, and with it their ability and motivation to continue as stewards of the family business.

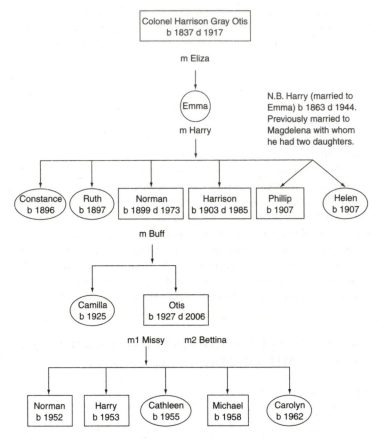

Figure 7.2   The Chandler family

The family became outsiders to their own firm. Similar to the Guinnesses in Chapter 6, the behaviour of some of the family became over time that of detached owners who viewed the firm more as a source of financial return, and less as a legacy to which they owed a day-to-day duty of care. With the family's historic stewardship diminished, the inevitable occurred and the business finally passed out of family control, succumbing to a bid by the Tribune media group.

The *LA Times* dynasty was built on the strong entrepreneurial instincts and drive of successive generations of the Chandler family;

a clan among the earliest settlers in Los Angeles who built a media and business empire that rode on the back of the booming economy of southern California. The founder, Colonel Harrison Gray Otis, with his wife Eliza spotted an opportunity to purchase a share in the *Los Angeles Daily Times*. Working hard to make a success of the business they managed to turn this stake into a majority interest and to take control of the newspaper. By the end of the 19th century the *LA Times* had become a highly successful publication, growing in step with the blossoming fortunes of Los Angeles.

The early growth of the business was also tied closely to the hiring of Harry Chandler, who had left his home on the East coast for health reasons to settle in the warmer climate of California. The dynamic young Chandler rose fast in the company's ranks, and after his first wife died in childbirth went on to become part of the family by marrying the boss's daughter, Emma Marian Otis. He brought to the business an entrepreneurial flair that helped further boost the family fortunes, not just through the growth of the newspaper but also through his talent at spotting promising real estate deals. Harry's energy was unbounded and he set a strong example in terms of his tireless work ethic. His iron grip over the business delivered significant development in the family company. He also made a wider contribution to society, and was credited as one of the main pioneers in the development of the city of Los Angeles.

By the time the third generation took over, inheriting the platform of wealth created by the preceding generations, the family had grown accustomed to a lifestyle of privilege that they could afford as one of the most high-profile families of southern California's business elite. This carried risks – not least for its propensity to split the family between those who were motivated to work in the family company, regardless of their merits to do so, and those who were not, for one reason or another.

The third generation grew up in the shadow of the strong personality that was Harry Chandler. His son and chosen heir Norman followed dutifully in the footsteps of his father to lead the company, and eventually took control of it in 1936 under the title of general manager. But he only truly stepped out from his father's shadow on Harry's death in September 1944. Norman was not a man in the mould of his father – neither a strong leader nor a change agent; he championed the status quo at the firm. His one innovation in terms of strategy was launching a tabloid newspaper named the *Mirror*. The enterprise was misconceived and ended up becoming a large drain on the company's finances. In personality Norman was an understated type, projecting more of a university professor image than that of a business leader. Norman and his wife Buff Chandler raised their children to become prominent members of California's high society, with all the expectations that this brought.

ENTER OTIS

Buff, ever the more powerful and charismatic of the couple, set a strong example as a patron of various good causes. She was a queen of 'cultural politics' in Los Angeles. Buff became the power behind the throne of the *LA Times*, eventually getting her husband to step aside to let her son Otis take over as publisher. Otis, their eldest son, was raised to believe his destiny was tied in with the family firm. On the one hand stood his strong and passionate mother, urging him to succeed; on the other, was the more temperate figure of his father, moralizing about the values of industry and of 'living within one's own means'. By the time he was in his mid-20s his father agreed to Otis joining the business, and launching him on a seven-year bespoke training programme.

Otis was a mere 32 years old when he was thrust, with his mother's encouragement, into the role of publisher of the *LA Times*. Unlike his father, the neophyte publisher harboured ambition and had a vision to take the business forward to become 'one of the world's great newspapers'. To bring the new strategy to fruition he abandoned some of the tenets of conservatism that had long been editorial policy, values that were close to the heart of many family members. This change in direction earned him the disapproval of some family members such as his Uncle Philip, a man of right-wing views, who resigned from the board in protest. Nor did his father Norman approve of all his son's policies, but when the higher standards of journalism started to boost the newspaper's rankings and brought success in the market, he was forced to acknowledge his son's achievement. Meanwhile Buff observed the situation with proud satisfaction that her son had shown much of the drive and passion to succeed she wished for him. A kindred spirit indeed.

LISTING

The family and the company prospered, so much so that they decided to list on the New York Stock Exchange in 1964, offering the prospect of accelerated growth and diversification from the publishing business. Yet the seeds of division were being sown. The decision to float was viewed as controversial by many family members, who disliked the idea of the searchlight of public scrutiny falling upon their private world. The family shareholders, who by now numbered about 20 people, had become accustomed to a steady flow of generous dividends. Flotation took them into a world of uncertainty, and they feared the status quo being overturned.

From a business perspective Otis's strategy brought conspicuous success. Post-flotation he was able to quadruple revenues in the 12 years between 1968 and 1980. But this did not satisfy the family owners outside the gates of the business, who were distinctly short in praise for Otis. At the meetings of the family holding company, Chandis Securities, they continued to agitate and complain. Otis was aggrieved at the lack of gratitude and recognition displayed by his cousins for the job he was doing. Nor did support for him improve as the senior generation of his uncles and aunts faded from the scene. The cousins who took over their shares helped to perpetuate the divisions. In Otis's eyes they were just as hidebound and stuck in the conservative values of their forebears.

Otis himself was not without flaw. He had a habit of spurning criticism and accepting flattery too easily. Tiring of their whingeing, he complained to a friend that 'my cousins are a pain in the ass'. With the business at new heights Otis could take pride in his achievement, but the drive that he normally exuded was starting to recede. With the flame of passion for the business burning less bright, he began to think about when he should quit his role as publisher. In April 1980 four generations of tradition were abandoned when he handed the baton over to the first non-family person to hold the title of publisher since 1882, when Colonel Otis Harrison had assumed the title.

OUT AND DOWN

Once it became clear that Otis was exiting, the family split started to widen. During the 20 years in which Otis had grown profits from $3 million to $100 million, family sentiment and unity had been marching in the opposite direction. The non-active family members, who were in defiance of Otis, continued to become ever more reliant upon their annual dividends, and in some cases dependent on the family's trust funds to support their lifestyles. There was no clamour to join the business. Unlike some fathers who press their eldest son into service, Otis did not demand that his son Norman enter the business with a view to succeeding him when it became clear that Norman was not suited to the profession. After this there were no family candidates to take on leadership roles in such a climate.

While the family continued to retain a stake in the corporation, they no longer held a majority of shares. As often happens in such cases, the company and its strategy by default fell into the hands of management and started to develop a life of its own. Lacking the clarity of vision and strong leadership that Otis had provided, within a decade the fortunes of the business had reversed and the company started to lose money. The corporate governance mechanisms, whose purpose is to protect the owner's interests by holding management accountable, started to become ineffective. In effect, the family had reduced their control over the business and were no longer close enough nor sufficiently well informed to make any meaningful contribution. The owners then decided to capitulate to consolidation and agreed to merge the business into a larger Chicago-based media group, Tribune Co, in 2000, while continuing to retain an equity stake.

COMMENT

This has been a story perhaps less of warfare than disease, where the affliction drains the spirit from the body, leaving it lifeless. The Chandler saga is a tale exemplifying the saying that 'hope makes a good breakfast but a lousy supper'. It is the story of a founder whose charisma and strength laid the foundations for an empire that was never built. The lesson here is that not only ownership, but also vision and a sense of stewardship and attachment, have to be passed between generations. There is nothing wrong in making the decision that the family will not carry on running the family firm, but if they wish to capture and retain what we might call 'family capital' – the culture/performance premium that familiness brings to a business – then the business needs leadership, a vision and strategy. Family do not have to supply all of these, but they do need to take enough of an interest to ensure that these elements are present, rather than relying on a business-as-usual management hierarchy to make all the decisions. Like most minor tragedies, the Chandler case is a might-have-been saga.

FREEDOM COMMUNICATIONS AND THE HOILES – A BATTLE FOR CONTROL[10]

ORIGINS

The Hoiles story brings on stage another media dynasty saga. In this case the origins of their difficulties lay less in family indifference than in caring too much, for here it is ideology that prised open the fissures in the family. The firm is Freedom Communications, a name that became synonymous with conflict among family shareholders over many years. The substantive cause of the schism was in this case a dispute in the second generation about liquidity and the rights of an owner to sell out. This overlaid an unresolved sibling divergence that failed to be resolved and passed, like a poisoned chalice, through to the third generation when they took the reins. As we have seen elsewhere, unresolved conflicts have a way of echoing down through the generations.

Founded in the 1930s by R C Hoiles, the company was in many ways the main rival to the *LA Times*, an important media organization in Southern California, owning the *Orange County Register* plus other media assets including some television stations. R C was a man of deep libertarian beliefs, and the newspapers pursued an editorial agenda defending the rights of the private individual over the government. On his death in 1970 R C was succeeded as publisher by his eldest son Clarence Hoiles, known as C H, who continued the founder's legacy, upholding the family's libertarian values and beliefs.

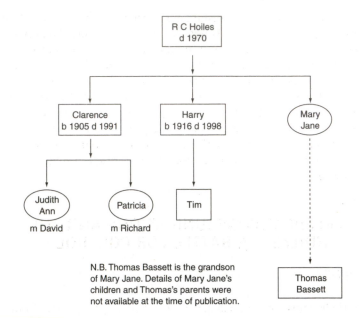

N.B. Thomas Bassett is the grandson of Mary Jane's children and Thomas's parents were not available at the time of publication.

Figure 7.3   The Hoiles family

SPLITS APPEAR

A dispute flared into the open in 1980 when C H's younger brother Harry insisted that he should become the CEO and lead the company. His brother and sister Mary Jane demurred. Blocked in his attempt to take over the reins, Harry threatened to dissolve the company. He made it clear to his siblings that if he was not put in charge he would find a way to unwind the business. When resisted by his siblings, who were committed to carrying on the founder's legacy, Harry decided to force the issue, and filed a lawsuit claiming breach of fiduciary duty by the company and seeking to dissolve the corporation. The suit dragged on and was eventually thrown out by the courts in 1987, leaving deep scars in the family. The following year Harry died and the grievance passed on to his son Tim Hoiles, who continued to champion the cause of family members' right to sell out.

The family were stuck in an impasse, unable to agree upon a vision for the family business that the owners could unite behind, and without a route for disinterested family members to sell out on satis-factory terms. This unhealthy situation persisted until 2003, when matters were brought to a head when the board, after continued persistence by Tim Hoiles, agreed to consider proposals from outside investors to help resolve the situation. Investment bankers were hired, ostensibly to conduct a sale process.

SELLING OUT

It seemed just to be a matter of soliciting the highest bid. That view did not stop a group of the family owners who wanted to retain control and continue the family legacy from preparing their own proposal. This group, led by fourth-generation family member Thomas Bassett, came up with a plan proposing to keep overall control in family hands, but partnered with private equity funding to finance the exit of a number of the family shareholders.

The Bassett-sponsored solution with private equity backing gained consent from the shareholders, unblocking the situation and provid-ing an exit route for the sellers. Perhaps the sale of Freedom has just been postponed for another day. For the time being the schism that divided the family had been resolved, and harmony restored after fighting that had soured relations over two generations.

COMMENT

The lesson here is that schisms have multiple inputs, as we have discussed, and therefore any one solution may be more of a stick-ing plaster than a cure. In this case there seem to have been unre-solved family issues, including many emanating from sibling rivalry. It also shows the importance of ideological issues. Here the basis for dispute was around people's beliefs, a sense of obligation to uphold the mission of the founder, and governance issues around sharehold-ing rules. The prognosis for this to remain a vibrant family firm may be good in the short term but uncertainties remain regarding what the future will hold in terms of ownership. The private equity financiers will seek to crystallize their investment at some point in the future, and the family will have to be prepared for that eventuality.

THE PATHAK FAMILY – SPICE WARS[11]

ORIGINS

Family divisions in business take on the character of their home culture, as we have seen in previous cases. So it does here, where we look at a highly successful British family of South Asian origin, in which there emerged a sharp division in opinion around ownership rights, challenging the cultural mores that bequeath women fewer rights in a business than their male relatives. The subtext here is unpreparedness, for this is a case where lack of clarity and planning combined to create a high-profile public split. This was a battle that pitted a son, supported by his mother together with his wife, who was also his business partner, against his two sisters.

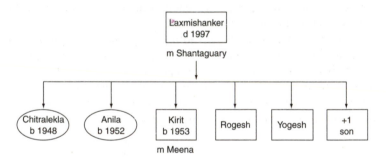

Figure 7.4   The Pathak family

The Patak Foods Company is based in Lancashire, UK, manufacturing an exotic and popular range of Indian sauces, curries, pickles and other foodstuffs. The business was founded in England in 1957 by Laxmishanker Pathak, who had emigrated from Kenya (where there is a large Indian diaspora) to the United Kingdom with his wife and six children. In its second generation the business has become a leader in its market and its products are distributed in over 40 countries. The award-winning food business is headed in the second generation by chairman Kirit and his wife Meena, who together are the driving force behind the success of the brand.

CULTURE CLASH

The dispute was a simple and stark matter of family ownership rights. Back in 1974, when shares were issued, each of the daughters was given a one-eighth share in the company. In 1989 the sisters Chitralekla and Anila gave their shares to their mother Shantaguary to keep in custody on their behalf. Subsequently, in a move that would eventually spark off the family dispute, Shantaguary passed on the shares to her son Kirit. Worth little at the time of issue, through Kirit and Meena's entrepreneurial successes the shares had begun to acquire substantial value, such was the growth and development of the business under their leadership. The two sisters, seeing that their mother had given their shares to their brother, decided to take action to assert their ownership rights.

Thus commenced a clash between an 'old' and a 'new' worldview of south Asian culture. The legal battle that ensued polarized the family on either side of a widening divide. Some maintained the rights of the matriarch Shantaguary, arguing that it was her maternal duty to place the shares in the keeping of her son, so he could be the controlling owner of the business. The matriarch was clear in her views that her daughters were motivated by greed and were trying to get hold of what she believed was not theirs to have.[12] Others insisted upon the ownership rights of the sisters as heirs to the founder Laxmishanker, who had bequeathed shares to them. Eventually the youngest brother Rogesh intervened in support of his sisters, having already disposed of his ownership stake in 1989 by selling to Kirit. He went on public record inviting his older brother Kirit to show leadership and 'do the right thing ... to salvage family unity'. Eventually, and inevitably perhaps, the dispute was settled by recourse to law. In the final outcome an out-of-court cash-settlement compensating the sisters was agreed.

The final chapter of the story was the sale of the business in 2007 to another UK-based family business, the food giants Associated British Foods – a tribute perhaps to Kirit and Meena's entrepreneurial success.

COMMENT

The case highlights the interdependence of distributive and procedural justice – that is, the fairness in terms of ownership, and the fairness of the method by which shares are distributed. But both are culturally dependent. For the sisters, raised almost entirely in the United Kingdom, well immersed in contemporary Western values, this was a double offence. But Kirit saw himself as upholding tradition, claiming the issue was covered by Hindu custom where ownership rights would only pass to male family members.

This case mirrors problems experienced in the other South Asian case we describe, Reliance, where there was also a lack of clarity and specificity in terms of estate planning. Patak's founder, Laxmishanker, had clearly intended control of the business to pass to his son Kirit, but had he intended no shares to fall to his daughters? We shall never know, but the case illustrates how risky it is to rely on tradition and the assumptions embedded in a culture during times of change. It is especially problematic to deal with ownership on the basis of unwritten understandings – the more so the larger the pot of money at stake.

8

Un-civil war

Reason is no match for power and prejudice, armed with guile and cunning.

(William Hazlitt)

INTRODUCTION

Wars are escalators.[1] Picture the scene. Two adjacent groups are living in a state of armed neutrality. One day a representative of one group is roughed up by the other side's border guards after some minor incident. His group's forces make a show of strength in the border area. This is reciprocated. Insults are exchanged. Weapons are brandished. From some unknown source shots are fired. There is a small mêlée and one side takes a couple of the other side's soldiers prisoner. The other side mounts a raid to recapture them. Troops are moved to the flashpoint. The groups are on the brink of war, against a backdrop of public recriminations, blame and accusations of bad faith.

Take away the border and make the two groups rival claimants to the true spirit of a commonwealth, and you have a civil war. In a civil war the boundaries are in the mind, not on the map. In fact, a civil war could be described as the drawing of boundaries where none formerly existed. People start defining themselves as members of this or that faction. Ruptures appear within a territory that was once unified. This is the tragedy of many family wars. A family that once was a growing empire becomes a battleground between groups who define their interests as divided.

We are now at the point in our journey where we observe families at war with themselves, with the conflict diffusing to affect multiple parties. Such conflagrations often have the attributes of a black hole, where negative emotional energy sucks in and devours people who would otherwise have been bystanders. For emotion is the destructively magnetic force in family wars at all their levels, but especially where they attain such a degree of complexity. Once the first shots are fired then controls that normally restrain outbursts start to fall away. As tensions rise, rationality is abandoned.

Conflict can occur safely in healthy communities, but if it recurs continually, hearts become hardened. People draw on negative energy to keep enmity alive, and motives of revenge and reprisal ensure escalation. There is no forgiving and no forgetting. The logic of the vendetta takes the place of rational exchange. People's thresholds for what is acceptable behaviour shift upwards, so that threat, aggression and deception become common currency. In the midst of such mayhem there will always be sensitive souls for whom such conduct is a source of fear and repugnance. They will withdraw, trying to close their minds to the sound of gunfire and everything else. For them, as for everyone, stress exposes character flaws. We may find ourselves amazed to witness behaviour that we would have thought is totally uncharacteristic of a person, even looking at our own behaviour. Thus does civil warfare descend into a kind of collective madness.

U-HAUL AND THE SHOENS – A SHATTERED DYNASTY[2]

ORIGINS

This is the story of the Shoen family who built a unique and new business, U-Haul, from scratch into a billion-dollar American company. Its founder, Leonard Samuel (L S) Shoen, established a nationwide enterprise that became well known throughout the United States, with its distinctive orange rental trailers that were the core of its business proclaiming the success of the firm across the length and breadth of the highways of America.

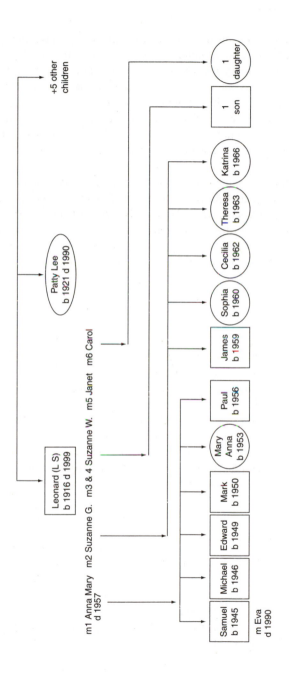

Figure 8.1 The Shoen family

L S Shoen was born in 1916 on leap year's day, the second child to a poor farmer, Samuel Joseph Shoen, and his wife Sophia. Nicknamed 'Stub' by his parents for his stubborn nature, L S, as he became known as an adult, was very ambitious from a young age, working hard during his childhood sweeping floors, washing dishes and doing other menial jobs to earn a living. Through his efforts he managed to save enough to invest in his first business as a barber. By his early 20s he started to demonstrate real ambition, knuckling down to the hard grind of academic study, to a level that gained him entry to medical school. To support himself, he kept his barbershop business going. He believed nothing in life could be gained without sacrifice, and he was prepared to pay the price for success. He felt the difference between him and others, and what brought him success, was his willingness to take risks. Arguably however it was his single-minded clarity of vision and focus that ensured that the entrepreneur in L S was a success.

A FATEFUL ERROR

During his twenties, L S met and fell in love with Anna Mary Carty, a farmer's daughter, a friend of his sister Patty Lee. He was on the point of proposing when he discovered that Anna Mary suffered from a fatal heart condition. He continued the relationship, but held back on making a marriage proposal. Then came a life-changing event – an incident that took him over several fateful thresholds.

The incident that triggered this was when L S, in the spirit of friendly risk-taking, called out present during a roll-call for an absent classmate. His misdemeanour was discovered immediately, and to his total disbelief he found himself summarily expelled from medical school, leaving in ruins his lifetime dream to become a doctor. It also undermined the whole social fabric of his life, as his college friends began to drift away from him. Only Anna Mary continued to regard him with unchanged respect, and in 1944 her loyalty was rewarded with the long-awaited proposal of marriage. The drama did not end here. During the wedding, ceremony to the astonishment of all and sundry, L S's sister Patty Lee jumped up and announced that she objected to her brother marrying Anna Mary. Her protestations were so vocal that the wedding ceremony had to be paused while she was bundled out of the church. Clearly, all was not well under the surface of the Shoen family.

In due course Anna Mary gave birth to their first son Samuel, but shortly afterwards L S, who had enlisted in the navy after his expulsion from college, became seriously ill with rheumatic fever. He was admitted to a naval hospital some 35 miles from home. L S wanted his family members to be nearby and planned to relocate them, but he also wanted to avoid the costly expense of the removal charges. His solution was to find a used trailer, which avoided the need to hire a van. Through such accidents of fate are great business ideas born. The light that ignited in L S's entrepreneurial brain was the vision of a nationwide network of rental locations from which people could rent trailers for one-way moves. He immediately recognized this as a unique business opportunity that could potentially create huge customer demand.

On leaving hospital, L S decided to change his life. To save money and get additional home support while he launched his new venture, he took his family to live with relatives, selling all his barbering equipment and putting the cash into the new business. There was no more thought of going back to medical school. He was now going to dedicate himself single-mindedly to his business venture. Fired with his idea, and with $5,000 in savings, he found a catchy name for it – U-Haul – and started work in 1945 making trailers that would have a simple construction and need little servicing. U-Haul was his obsession, and L S touted his trailers around gas stations to get them to take them and advertise the service, with each trailer cleverly incorporating a built-in billboard. At each stop L S would tell the gas station manager that he was representing a big company, never acknowledging that he was the owner of a two-bit start-up business.

Recognizing meanwhile that he needed to acquire more business-related skills to drive the business forward, L S, always prepared to burn the midnight oil in study, enrolled to get qualifications in law via evening classes at the Northwestern College of Law in Portland. Another breakthrough was about to follow when Anna Mary read about how railroad companies created larger fleets of boxcars through finding fleet owners who could finance them. They realized that using this strategy they could transform their own business and substantially boost the expansion of U-Haul. The Fleet Owner Programme was created in 1952, whereby individuals and small groups invested in trailers while U-Haul assumed all the running costs including insurance, maintenance and distribution. This was the point at which U-Haul started to take off on a national basis. By the end of the 1950s the U-Haul fleet consisted of over 42,000 trailers.

FAMILY LIFE

Yielding nothing to her condition, Anna Mary delivered to the marriage six children: Samuel, Michael, Edward (Joe), Mark, Mary Anna and Paul. In the early days of U-Haul when money was scarce, Anna Mary managed the household on a tight budget – just $200 per month. However, once the business expanded, the Shoens moved to an upper-middle-class neighbourhood in Portland. The four eldest of the Shoen boys were a lively and sometimes aggressive bunch. Among the siblings Joe stood out as the quietest child, with a deeply reserved personality. In sharp contrast, the fourth boy, Mark, was hot-tempered and sensitive. By 1953, after the birth of their first daughter, L S started gifting his shares in the company to his children. Since much of his own childhood had been marked by poverty, he wanted to secure their future. Gifting them shares in U-Haul also had the advantage of giving himself a big tax break. He did this without the benefit of any financial or legal counsel. L S was too frugal to spend money on advice he didn't think he needed.

In 1955 L S, who as usual had set himself the highest goals in terms of achievement, passed the bar exams and graduated from Northwestern College of Law top of his class. In the meantime, the business continued its fierce upward future growth trajectory. L S, now in his early 40s, was becoming ever more aggressive and emotionally headstrong. He ran U-Haul with an iron fist, managing every aspect of the company in detail. His style was increasingly controlling, and he devoted his waking hours to the business, leaving little time for attention to his family and generally ignoring his duties as a father. He had acquired the reputation as an eccentric workaholic, who was inconsistent in his opinions and decisions. Yet he had a warmer side and was considered fair. He was held in affection, loyalty and respect by his workforce.

Meanwhile, family responsibilities were telling on Anna Mary, and there was a recurrence of her heart condition. As the symptoms gradually worsened, Anna Mary masked her pain and adversity under a cheerful and optimistic exterior. But the birth of her last child, Paul, proved to be the breaking point, and in 1957, a year after his arrival, she passed away.

LOSS AND TURMOIL

This turn of events had dire consequences for both the emotional life of the family and the structure of the business. For the family, it meant the loss of its emotional mainstay. The two older boys, Sam and Mike, were more independent, so although they felt the loss acutely, it was not damaging. Not so the younger boys, Joe and Mark, who suffered deeply. L S, steeped with remorse at his neglect of his family, sought to make amends, but there was little he could do to fill the huge void in what had been a strong climate of parental love. Matters were not assisted by a scurrilous rumour being spread that L S had murdered Anna Mary. The business consequences were also weighty. Anna Mary died without a will, and as a result half of her shares went to L S, while the other half was equally divided among her children. With this, L S, now in middle age and riding a still-rising wave of success, became a minority stockholder in his own company.

L S, restless and lonely, started dating within a few weeks of Anna Mary's death. His children were not understanding. This looked like disrespect for the memory of their late mother, especially in view of the little time L S had devoted to home and family while his wife had lived. Could he not have held off for a more respectable period before finding a new partner to share his life with and eventually become a step-mother to his children? Meantime L S hired a succession of housekeepers but was generally not successful in recruiting the right people or retaining them. Lacking parenting and its disciplines the younger boys, Joe and Mark, were becoming increasingly unruly.[3]

L S's first real romance after his wife's death came in the form of his wealthy neighbour's daughter, Suzanne Gilbaugh, a woman almost 20 years his junior who was studying for her Master's degree. Driven to get his way, L S relentlessly pursued Suzanne, and in 1958 at the age of 42 his campaign succeeded, and he wedded his new bride. One of the first decisions they made was to send the two eldest sons to boarding school. This decision was a relief to the couple and it gave the boys a sanctuary away from home. But the immediate side-effect was to raise tensions in the house, forcing closer proximity between the younger boys and their stepmother. Suzanne, for her part, lacked the experience to provide the maternal psychological support they needed. With Sam and Mike in boarding school, Joe was the eldest boy at home, and he took on the role of protector of his siblings against the perceived threat posed by their stepmother. For Sam, the eldest, his father's marriage to his sister's friend and his own direct contemporary in age was disconcerting. Nor was the marriage a smooth ride. The couple soon started to bicker with each other as they struggled to establish a stable relationship.

But life went on and Suzanne gave birth in quick succession to four children, so that by the time L S reached 50 in 1966, he had 10 children from his two marriages. Yet all along L S was unsuccessful in persuading his children with Anna Mary that Suzanne could be trusted as their stepmother. Both Sam and Mike said that they felt unwanted at home since their father had remarried. Joe and Mark were often angered with her way of running the house and their lives, for example, firing a maid that the boys liked.

Mark had become an increasingly troubled presence in the family home since his mother's death, and Suzanne, in her concern, arranged for him to receive treatment by a psychologist. For his part, Joe had developed scoliosis, a spinal condition, and was not growing normally, to the point that periodically he needed to wear a body cast and use a wheelchair. While the older boys Sam and Mike had always been punished severely for any bad behaviour, Joe and Mark were let off the hook and seldom cautioned or disciplined by their father, who felt sorry for them. Children are sensitive to what they perceive to be double standards, even though from a parent's point of view differential treatment will usually be justifiable. Whatever the rights and wrongs, to let such perceptions go unchecked was a recipe for trouble.

Mike was also angered when his father stopped him visiting Anna Mary's mother. On the other hand, the younger boys Joe and Mark seemed to be ceaselessly spoiled by their father. L S even bought them a hydroplane, but conspicuously failed to balance this largesse with much-needed discipline. Their disruptive behaviour went uncautioned. L S was generally uncontrolled in his parenting style, often complaining out loud in front of his children about his marriage, which of course encouraged Joe and Mark to remain in a constant state of rebellion against their stepmother.

In short, the Shoen family dynamic was totally dysfunctional.

FORMATIVE YEARS

While Sam and Mike were fit and hard-working boys, spending school terms at their boarding school, Joe and Mark were an unprepossessing pair, growing up in the munificent lifestyle and comfort of their family house. The youngest two siblings from L S's first marriage, Mary Anna and Paul, also lived at home. As the only girl, Mary Anna, a sensitive child, kept herself to herself. The older children's dislike for their stepmother had tempered by the time they reached adulthood, but Joe and Mark remained locked into a conflictual relationship with Suzanne. Their younger brother Paul also voiced strong negative sentiments towards his stepmother, pleading with his father to remove her from their lives.[4]

Over time Sam had become the family favourite with his warm nature, friendly and intelligent disposition. He retained a clear recollection of his father's struggle to give them all a privileged life. Each of them saw that they were going to have to make their own way in life, except for Joe. Years of special treatment led him to see U-Haul as his birthright. L S had always considered U-Haul as his legacy to his children, and early on had decided to give the company to them. With their stock in U-Haul, each of his children was worth on paper millions of dollars. However, L S's controlling streak held them on a short leash, keeping them cash poor and forcing them as young adults to come to their father for support.

The gap between the siblings' characters and outlooks widened over the years. Joe and Mark had grown to become distant and cool in their behaviour, while Sam and Mike were more tolerant, forgiving and generous. The two older boys found freedom from their father's control through careers in the professions – Sam made his way successfully in medicine, while Mike became a lawyer, taking up a position as deputy county attorney.

But all was not well. Disturbing incidents abounded, such as one time Joe was hospitalized after a collision between his vehicle and a police car. According to one biographer, writing with L S's sanction, this incident and its aftermath started alarm bells ringing for L S. He realized he was becoming over-reliant on the younger boys. Where were his first-born sons? He was especially concerned about his relationship with Mike, and what he feared was his son's alienation from him. L S started to put pressure on Sam and Mike to join U-Haul, despite their clearly expressed desire to stay out of their father's business.

THE SIBLINGS JOIN THE BUSINESS

Meanwhile, with an eye on his future career in the family business, Joe, who already had a law degree, set out to obtain an MBA from Harvard Business School. He made a stormy entrance into U-Haul on graduating with his MBA in 1973. He had high expectations, and overtly set himself in competition with his father. L S had suggested that Joe join him on the road, where he could meet customers and learn how the company operated, but Joe insisted in remaining in the head office at U-Haul Towers where he thought he would have his finger on the company's pulse. Mark on the other hand showed little interest in working for the business but L S still hired him as a member of the management team. Neither seemed to fit in easily. Whenever there were contentious issues, confrontation and hostility filled the air more than reasoned discussion. One source claimed that their demeanour earned them the soubriquet 'the Shoen brats', but L S continued to indulge them.

At the same time in 1973, the two older boys, still reluctant to join the firm, relented to their father's pressure. First Sam arrived, taking up a role as his father's assistant, with Mike following some weeks later, joining the company as its head of legal affairs. Now L S had reason to be content: his four eldest offspring were working in the business, and indeed quickly the talents of the two eldest sons began to pay off. They learnt fast and won their father's favour. Joe on the other hand continued to act in a challenging manner, bombarding all and sundry, but especially his brothers, with his opinions and predictions, including a claim that U-Haul was going bankrupt.

During the early 1970s U-Haul was facing new challenges with the emergence of a competitor trailer hire company, Ryder System Inc, as well as the first international oil crisis in 1973, which profoundly impacted U-Haul's retail and trade customers. Joe saw this as a threat but his brothers thought it alarmism, regarding him to be prone to exaggeration. Sam and Mike concluded that Joe was not to be trusted, pointing to what they judged to be his erratic behaviour. At the same time they responded to the new more hostile market circumstances by launching an expensive investment, U-Haul Centers, company-owned stores that rented a variety of products. The new strategy proved to be unsuccessful, bringing significant losses to the company.

L S, sensing that his sons working in the business could not meld into an effective team, longed for family harmony, and realized they needed outside assistance. In 1975 he asked all his children to attend weekly counselling sessions with a psychologist in an attempt to resolve their differences. Pent-up emotions were vented in the sessions but the counselling failed to resolve any of their deep-seated issues.

Frustrated that the counselling was not working, L S hired a new family psychologist, Dr Jerry Day, who observed that 'cooperative behavior was almost nil' and that the family was split between two competing factions, with Joe and Mark on one side, and L S, Sam, Mike and other siblings on the other.[5] The underlying cause of the emotional maelstrom, he concluded, was severe trauma experienced by Joe and Mark after their mother's death, and that their poor relationship with their stepmother had given them an inferiority complex. This made them both set high goals that they could not achieve, and a supporting set of paranoid beliefs that others would not let them succeed. The doctor described their power struggle in the following way: 'If you really love me you will do as I say. Since you oppose me, you don't love me and therefore I am justified hating you.'

Although L S was now coming to the view that Joe and Mark were projecting their experiences and feelings from their stepmother onto the others, he was unable to modify his ambitions for them. He wanted his sons in the company so badly that he struggled to tell right from wrong and was unable to make rational judgments regarding their performance and capabilities. His controlling personality and ego were helping to stir up conflicts and create an increasingly negative situation. Although he believed that Joe and Mark were creating significant problems for the firm's leadership, L S wasn't prepared to face them down.

Joe continued to challenge L S's and Sam's stewardship of the company, pointing to the failure of the U-Haul Centers, which he argued were having a distracting influence on the core business, unnecessarily draining scarce resources. In October 1979 both Joe and Mark resigned from U-Haul, unable to secure the control and direction for the business that they wanted, especially now that Sam had been appointed CEO. On their leaving U-Haul, L S, unwilling to sever the umbilical cord, appeased them by continuing their salaries, and allowing them to retain their benefits such as company credit cards and free access to use U-Haul cars and planes. All this was too much for Mike, the most reluctant of the U-Haul dynasty. Unable to take the pressure, he also resigned from the family business in 1979.

L S AND WOMEN

L S's personal power and charisma extended into the personal sphere, where his life-long weakness was women. His children had seen it after their mother's death, leading them to wonder whether their father had ever loved their late mother. The truth is probably that he loved his business more, but after Anna Mary's departure he found sustaining other relationships difficult. His marriage to Suzanne deteriorated from the start. In 1997 he started a relationship with a Suzie Whitmore from Cleveland, who became pregnant by him. Despite L S's pleas for her to stay, Suzanne divorced and left him. L S duly married Suzie Whitmore, but that union ended in a divorce within months. Suzie decided that it was impossible to live with a man who was in no emotional state to take on a new commitment. But within months of the divorce, he remarried her in order to legitimize their son Scott.

Continuing his history of philandering, L S had already begun another extramarital relationship with a nurse. This precipitated a second divorce from Suzie, who this time around had found him unchanged: still impossible to live with. In autumn 1978 L S then married his latest amour, Janet Hammer. This relationship also fell rapidly by the wayside, with a divorce coming within months on the grounds that L S found it impossible to live with his new step-daughter from Janet's previous marriage.

So it was that by the age of 62 L S had been married five times to four women and had fathered 12 children. Perhaps beginning to mellow a little, four years later in 1983 he decided to settle down and marry the relatively youthful Carol Copeland, a woman just over half his age. At last he found stability, and the Shoen children immediately developed a bond with Carol. Thus did life become more peaceful for L S after long years of marital turmoil.

In the meantime, Sam had married a young, beautiful and polite Norwegian girl called Eva Berg. L S was particularly happy with this union, and strongly approved of his son's choice of bride. However, when it came to integrating into the wider Shoen family, Eva understandably chose to keep her distance from the emotional cauldron that her in-laws epitomized. Elsewhere among the siblings, Joe dated and then married Heidi Hatsell, a union that was never warmly received by the rest of the family, and which ended up in an acrimonious divorce 12 years later.

POWER STRUGGLE AND DEFEAT

As children, the Shoen offspring had all done U-Haul summer jobs throughout their high school vacations – their only formal training and induction into the business. Those family members who did not end up working in the business naturally had little understanding of the company operations, and as shareholders they were ignorant of most of the issues facing the corporation that they were called upon to vote on.

Another important change had been taking place over the years with the gradual transfer of ownership into the second generation. By the mid-1980s the founder L S had passed on to the next generation almost his entire shareholding, and whereas in the past he had automatically gathered his children's proxies there was no guarantee he would get them now, as Joe now strongly dissented from his father. The crunch came in the autumn of 1982, at the annual shareholders meeting of Amerco (the parent corporation of U-Haul, which stands for American Family Corporation), which Sam was chairing.

Joe and Mark showed up, expressing their determination to take control of the company. Joe, one of the smartest of the clan, had gained considerable business acumen through his experience on the job, and could be very persuasive with other members of the family, presenting himself as a person of high intellect and shrewd judgment.

Joe had been making moves behind the scenes, arguing that the board should exclude his father and Sam, but the proposal was rejected. Notwithstanding this act of mutiny, L S was unhappy that both Joe and Mark were out of the company and thought that the conflict would be eased if he were able to find a way to bring them back into U-Haul management.

Joe, sensing an opportunity to take leadership of the business, made it clear that he would only work at U-Haul if he had real power to run the show. Against the judgment of the management team, L S, persuaded by Joe's vision, duly appointed him chairman of the board, retaining Sam in the role of CEO, in charge of operations. Back in power Joe, assisted by Mark, immediately began to challenge his father and Sam. This developed into frequent heated confrontations with his older brother at the weekly management meetings.

By giving Joe back a seat on the board L S had inadvertently sowed the seeds of his own removal. Joe continued to repeat in the meetings that L S should leave control of the company to his children, and eventually L S, succumbed to Joe's wishes, dispatching a note to employees informing them of his decision to retire. But it was obvious to all that this was no graceful retirement. L S had been forced out by his nemesis, Joe, whose drive for control had proved unstoppable.

SUFFERINGS AND TRAVAILS

This is a story of the blind spots that afflict the charismatic and sow the seeds of their own downfall. L S had always operated with an unshakeable belief in his destiny. Looking at what is illuminated by the glaring headlights of your own ego can make you fail to notice what is going on anywhere else. L S had no notion of educating his offspring to be effective owners, and combined with his controlling instinct, this limited their ability to take the right decisions. He was in thrall to his brilliant but wayward son Joe, whose powerful and erratic emotions he never faced up to. He never imagined that his children would not always back his decisions.

Yet this is exactly what happened in late 1986, when the company had reached an all-time high, leading the market nationally in general equipment hiring, motor home rentals and self-storage. Joe's campaign to take over leadership of the business was coming to a head and he had gathered enough votes to gain control. Mediators were brought in to help achieve a satisfactory outcome to the situation, which was tense for all parties. No sooner was the ink dry on the new board which for the first time ever excluded L S, than Joe, the new chairman, started to challenge Sam's authority as CEO. Sam resigned a few months later, leaving Joe with what he had always wanted: absolute management control.

Joe's vision and ambitions had split the family into two factions. He started to make attempts to buy out other shareholders and consolidate his grip on power. The parties could not agree on reasonable terms. In the absence of any proper governance mechanism to resolve differences and achieve a common view of the business and its family identity, the battles continued, tiring everyone except Joe. In 1988 the turf war in the family reached new heights when Katrina, one of the youngest of the Shoen offspring, whose support Joe had been trying to enlist, decided to back her father's group. After this set-back Joe's camp made a new move to reinforce their position, which subsequently attracted a legal challenge from his opponents.[6] This was in July, when the board of directors issued an additional 8,099 shares to company executives, giving the Joe Shoen camp 50.1 per cent control. The share purchases by the five key executives were funded by $800,000, which Joe Shoen drew from his children's trust account.

With the family now severed into two factions, a shareholders' meeting was held in Reno, Arizona in March 1989. The insider group, now running the business and led by Joe Shoen, arrived at the meeting wearing green lapel stickers to declare their demarcation from their relatives in what became a very rowdy assembly. A complete account of the proceedings was recorded and made public, revealing the extent to which the insiders lavished abusive language on the gathered shareholders. The assembly ended with Mike and Sam, who had both been goaded by what they had heard in the meeting, being drawn into a fight with Joe and Mark. Mike ended up being treated in hospital for bruises on his neck and back. The story was reported in the *Arizona Republic* newspaper, which printed a picture of a bruised Mike Shoen.

The nadir of family fortune was reached when Eva, Sam's wife, was found by her daughter murdered at her mountain lodge on a summer morning in August 1990. In the climate of acrimony that had infected the whole family, even this seemingly random catastrophe was viewed with suspicion. The truth was more mundane. A transient was arrested and found guilty of the murder, but L S continued to harbour the false suspicion that his son Joe was responsible.

It can happen that an unrelated tragic event befalling a troubled family can be the catalyst for sudden movement on other fronts. So it was in this case – an eruption of emotion that found its outlet in the time-honoured arena of family business disputes, the courts. The first move was made by Sam, who issued a legal challenge against Joe, alleging that the sale of shares had been improper and prevented them from gaining control of the company.[7] He won the case and received a financial settlement for damages that even on appeal resulted in an award of $461 million and $7 million for punitive damages. L S had to take sides. He had no hesitation in doing so. He gave Sam his full support and publicly blamed Joe and Mark, on national television, for the problems in the family as well as the murder of his daughter-in-law.[8]

In turn, Joe countersued their father for libel when he heard his father's allegations. However, in spite of the public outcry against him Joe hung on doggedly to the reins of power until he and Mark were able to buy out the rest of the family. Joe and Mark ended up with a 40 per cent minority interest in U-Haul through their holding company Amerco.

The founder L S passed away as a result of a motor accident in 1999 at the age of 85. Even this incident was tainted by rumour – that he had deliberately driven his car into a lamp post in order to end his unhappiness at the denouement to which the firm he gave his life had come. The rest of the Shoen family retreated from the scene, distancing themselves from the business and Joe.

The company was eventually floated onto the stock market in 1993, which was the first year when revenues surpassed $1 billion. Amerco continued however to court drama, being forced to substantially restate its net earnings and value following the discovery of possible accounting irregularities. Subsequently the company filed for Chapter 11 bankruptcy protection in 2003 but re-emerged the following year when new financing became available. At the time of writing Joe Shoen is still serving as chairman and president of Amerco.

COMMENT

U-Haul is a lesson in the darker side of nepotism. It is a Shakespearean drama in which a spiked cocktail of pungent personalities was mixed with terrible decision making. First and at the root stands the monumental flawed character of the founder, whose errors of judgment dogged his life. L S was able to turn to his advantage getting thrown out of medical school, but his other mistakes came back to haunt him. A primary error was his determination to draw his family members into the business regardless of aptitude, competence, motivation or fitness, and to force issues in accord with his will.

Second was a complete insensitivity to the emotions of other members of his family, especially after the dramas and tragedies that followed the death of his first wife, and his failure to recognize the residue of their unhappiness, even into mature adulthood.

Third was his poor reading of character. Joe, a complex and introverted child, needed especially careful parenting. Instead, he was thrust into arenas where his anxieties and frustrations grew into a full-flowering personality laden with contradictory emotions.

Fourth was his inability to manage wealth and income in a way that balanced his family's needs and those of the business. For example he indulged family members who were financially dependent on the business. At the same time he handed over voting control in the company to the next generation who had not been taught the values of stewardship and how to act as responsible owners.

Fifth, his addiction to family sentiment made him prey to every drama that presented itself, without any counterbalances.

Some of these issues would have been resolved by using good advisors, particularly on ownership and tax planning in the earlier days. Good governance, with strong independent voices, could have controlled the power plays and helped to manage the key decisions of ownership and executive control. Without any external support, L S drifted into the world of King Lear – the foolish old king whose offspring wreak mayhem in the family kingdom. The actions of the group stoked up a boiling cauldron in which an internecine family war was brewed and left to simmer.

How much of this can be identified with the complex figure of Joe, who vented his emotions so strongly in his inexorable push to take control of U-Haul, despite the backwash on to family relationships?

It would be easy to scapegoat such a wildcard personality, but Joe's problems were amplified and propagated in the emotional hothouse that his father's empire became. A man like L S cannot be blamed for seeking love and companionship on being widowed, and although this might have been what hurt the children most, especially Joe, there was a more general failure of parenting from L S that was exposed by events. In place of authoritative parenting, where children can grow to independence with the watchful support of parents, the younger siblings became victims of a culture of dependency, while the elder siblings moved to detached alienation.

THE GUCCI FAMILY – A TRAGIC ITALIAN OPERA[9]

ORIGINS

If the U-Haul saga is one of descent into a family hell, the Gucci story is more of a switchback ride, which starts with an inspired founder, grows through the next generation, and ends in the survival of the brand but the loss of the business. This is not quite the paradigm of shirtsleeves to shirtsleeves in three generations, but close to it, as we shall see.

The Gucci name today continues to stand in the public mind as one of the world's most successful and glamorous designer fashion houses; like many such icons it grew from humble origins. The story starts with the founder Guccio Gucci, whose parents scraped a living making straw hats in Florence, Italy. Guccio left home and worked his way to England. He found employment at London's famous Savoy Hotel, and although his wages were low, he worked hard and learnt the skills of his trade. Returning home with his savings four years later he married Aida Calvelli, daughter of a tailor.

On getting married they adopted Aida's illegitimate son Ugo, and soon after their family increased when Aida became pregnant and delivered their first daughter, Grimalda. They went on to have four more children, all boys, one of whom died in infancy. The survivors were Aldo, born in 1905, Vasco in 1907 and Rodolfo in 1912. But it was the adopted boy, Ugo, who was the harbinger of destruction in the family, and who as a man became a local official in Mussolini's fascist party.

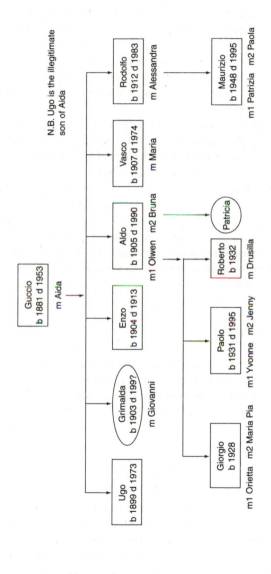

Figure 8.2 The Gucci family

With his modest savings and 25,000 lire from an investor, Guccio opened the first Gucci retail shop in Florence. He bought high-quality leather products from Tuscan manufacturers as well as imports from Germany and England to sell to the tourists who flocked to Florence. He aspired to elegance himself, and was always dressed impeccably in fine shirts and crisply pressed suits. He opened a small workshop behind the store where he made his own leather goods to supplement the imported products, and started a repair business that quickly became profitable. Guccio's hallmark was service combined with first-class workmanship.

As Guccio's children grew, they began to work for the family business, all except Ugo who showed little interest and was always something of an outsider. Aldo had the keenest sense of trade, and stood out from early on as an entrepreneur. Vasco enjoyed spending time on country leisure pursuits, and took on responsibility for production. Rodolfo was less drawn to the business, and as soon as he was old enough to work he set off to pursue his dream of working in films. As a father, Guccio was a strict disciplinarian with a strong personality, and he commanded the respect of his children, whom he parented in a distant and authoritarian manner. He rigorously impressed his thrifty values on his children.

THE GUCCI BROTHERS

Aldo started working in the family business Guccio Gucci in 1925 at the age of 20, delivering packages by horse and cart to customers staying at local hotels. He was also given simple tasks in the shop such as tidying up and rearranging merchandise displays. His knack of mixing work and pleasure was obvious from the start. All the time developing his salesmanship skills, Aldo was able to entice women, knowing they would become his prized customers. In the meantime, he married Olwen, who gave birth to three sons in quick succession: Giorgio, Paolo and Roberto.

Aldo steadily became more involved in the family business, while his brother Rodolfo remained detached and uninterested, something that disturbed his father Guccio. So it was Aldo who possessed the skills to take the business forward, and who proceeded to make Gucci a symbol of status and style in Europe and increasingly in America.

Although Guccio regularly shot down Aldo's ideas, he privately acknowledged his son's flair for business. Rodolfo meanwhile enjoyed his career as an actor, but big roles were not coming his way, so after the end of the war he asked his father if he could join the family business. He had also become a family man, marrying Alessandra, whom he had met when she was a young actress, and who had given birth to their son Maurizio in 1948. Rodolfo's first contribution to the business was to run the Milan store, and later to take the lead in the design of Gucci handbags.

Gradually, Guccio let Aldo take on the mantle of business leader, and by the time of Guccio's death in 1953, Aldo had become the key driving force of the company. Guccio died a millionaire, passing the empire on to his sons, little dreaming of the bitter quarrels that would follow, and for which unwittingly he had laid the groundwork. First, his parenting strategy had always been to play his sons off against each other in the belief that competition among the siblings would stimulate them to perform better. Second, as a traditionalist in his beliefs about gender and labour, he excluded his daughter Grimalda from inheriting shares in the firm.

This was to be the cause of a major rift. Grimalda was incensed on discovering that she was excluded from inheriting any part of Gucci. She had worked tirelessly in the shop while her husband had helped Guccio with funding to see him through the challenging early days of the business. When she realized what had happened she took her claim to court, but lost.

ALDO'S REIGN

Aldo, now the family leader, met his brothers Vasco and Rodolfo every two or three weeks in Florence to discuss business. The younger siblings gave Aldo the freedom to drive the strategic direction of the business, so long as he didn't stray too far from their family's values. His management style was embracing – he treated staff as an extended family and in return benefited from their staunch commitment and loyalty. Aldo now began to encourage his sons to join the business. Like Guccio, Aldo was a tough and domineering father. His sons Giorgio and Roberto both joined the New York office where Aldo was based. However, Giorgio disliked having to live under his father's shadow and soon returned to Italy to take over management of the store in Rome. Meanwhile Paolo established himself in Florence rather than work with his authoritarian father in New York. Paolo was undiplomatic and unrestrained in expression. He let his father know exactly what he thought of his oppressive style. Aldo was coming to realize that he was not going to have an easy time with his children.

Yet as an entrepreneur and leader Aldo was highly successful, continually finding new opportunities and expanding the business to new international markets, including Japan, a crucial market for the firm. By 1974 there were 14 Gucci stores and 46 franchised boutiques around the world. He had also diversified the business into perfumes, which helped provide a vehicle to occupy his sons in business.

In 1974 the middle brother Vasco died of cancer, leaving his one-third stake in the company to his widow, Maria. The couple had no children. The two surviving siblings offered to purchase their sister-in-law's shares in order to keep the ownership of the company in the family, and she agreed. With that, Aldo and Rodolfo became the sole controlling shareholders of the Gucci empire with 50 per cent ownership each. Aldo felt it was time to give his sons a stake in the company, and split a small percentage of his shares between his three sons, giving 3.3 per cent each to Giorgio, Paolo and Roberto. Although he didn't give voice to the sentiment, privately Aldo felt that Rodolfo's 50 per cent stake in the company was out of proportion to his contribution to the business.

Tragedy had struck the family when Rodolfo, at the age of 42, lost his wife Alessandra to a sudden illness. This blow made Rodolfo ever more protective and possessive towards his son and only child, Maurizio, having him followed in a car when the boy went out on bicycle rides and keeping a strict curfew during school term. His strategy for teaching his son the value of money was to withhold the meagre pocket money he allowed him for any infraction. Intimidated by his father, Maurizio became loathe to ask him for anything.

Like many a possessive parent, Rodolfo resented his son's relationships and bitterly disapproved of the young man's marriage to Patrizia Reggiani. He appealed directly to the cardinal of Milan to block the wedding planned for October 1972, threatening to disinherit Maurizio because of his suspicions about his future daughter-in-law's motives. Rodolfo found it hard to believe that she could love his son for himself rather than his fortune. But for Maurizio, Patrizia and her family were a source of strength and protection, and he began to distance himself from his father.

Rodolfo had himself never remarried, and was alone and embittered by what he saw as his son's abandonment of him, and too full of pride to seek reconciliation with Maurizio. So it was that, on Uncle Aldo's advice, Maurizio, who had finished his studies at Milan University, went to work for the family firm in New York.

PAOLO GUCCI

Ebullient by character, creative and at times eccentric, Paolo, the second of Aldo's three boys, did not settle to an easy life. In his private life he married and divorced twice during his lifetime. In the business he always wanted to be his own man, and felt frustrated by his failure to secure a larger role in the family firm. Before long he began to lock horns with his uncle Rodolfo, to whom he reported. Paolo began using his presence at the family board meetings to put his ideas about design, production and marketing on the table. He also started asking uncomfortable questions about company finances, backed up by often quite blunt and critical letters. All this was too much for his uncle to tolerate, and there was an angry confrontation in which Rodolfo suggested that Paulo leave Italy and go to work for his father in New York.

Paulo's response was defiant, but still he took his uncle at his word. Without giving notice or finding a replacement, he packed his bags and left Italy for New York. His nephew's behaviour infuriated Rodolfo. Paolo was now intent on revenge – his burning aim was to destroy uncle Rodolfo's position in the company. But nor was all sweetness and light with his father. Paolo soon found Aldo's hot-tempered ways hard to take.

Throwing caution to the wind, Paolo, now undisputedly the black sheep, decided to launch his own line – the Paolo Gucci (PG) Collection. News of this reached Rodolfo indirectly, from several suppliers whom Paolo had approached. This enraged both brothers, who realized that Paolo could become a threat to the Gucci name and all they had achieved. Aldo had no intention of letting his son compete with the family business while still employed by Gucci. Thus Paolo was fired in September 1980, ending his 28-year career in the family firm.

Meanwhile Rodolfo, who was being treated for prostate cancer, had begun to rekindle his relationship with his son Maurizio, and was encouraging him to become more active in the business. With his nephew Paolo now in open competition with the rest of the family, he wanted Maurizio to help fight off the threat from Paolo by all means possible. Gucci informed all their licensees that if Paolo approached them any attempt to distribute products under the PG name would be blocked.

This conflict was a mere foretaste of the deeper conflicts that were looming. The first major fissure between the second-generation brothers started to develop when Rodolfo realized that Aldo was shifting a significant amount of company revenues into a subsidiary, Gucci Perfumes, in which Rodolfo only had a 20 per cent stake, with the rest of the shares divided equally between Aldo and his three sons. Starting in 1979, the Perfumes division began to take off, fuelled by the launch of a new more mass-market line, Gucci Accessories Collection.

While the family, and especially Aldo's branch, reaped short-term profits from the sales of the new line, the exclusive image of the Gucci brand was being badly dented. Roberto confronted his brother over the issue of ownership inequity. Aldo was not in a mind to back down and give Rodolfo a larger chunk of the new business, and so Roberto approached his lawyers. Aldo was now daggers drawn with his brother, and sought an ally whom he knew shared his feelings: Paulo. Summoning Paolo to his office, he asked him to pledge his allegiance at an upcoming shareholder meeting. He misread his son: Paolo's riposte was sharp and negative. Why, asked Paulo, should I do you any favours when you and Roberto have attacked me and treated me so unfairly? Aldo saw red at this, and picking up a crystal ashtray, hurled it across the room toward his son, smashing it to fragments. It wasn't just the ashtray that was shattered, but any hopes of bringing Paolo back into the family fold. Paulo left determined to bring the house of Gucci to its knees.

PAOLO'S REVENGE

Time passed and Aldo wanted once again to bring the family together and find reconciliation with Paolo. He invited his son for Christmas in 1982 and made him an offer. He proposed to give each of his sons an 11 per cent stake in the firm, while he would retain 17 per cent, and Paolo would be named vice chairman of Guccio Gucci SpA. In addition, he offered Paolo leadership of a new division that would commercialize the products that Paulo had included in his own PG line. This was the role that Paolo had always craved, but he was apprehensive about the proposal. He mistrusted his father's motives. His doubts were confirmed when he attended the next board meeting with a detailed plan for the new division and the directors unanimously rejected his proposals on the grounds that a cheaper product line would damage the Gucci brand. Paulo felt he had been tricked. Matters were coming to a climax.

Paulo came prepared to the next board meeting, in July 1982. He pulled out a sheaf of papers and began to recite his grievances and table what he regarded as critical questions. His intervention was ignored by the other directors. At this point Paulo produced a tape recorder, insisting that his statements were recorded in the minutes. Aldo yelled at him to turn off the recorder. Paulo refused, at which point Aldo ran around the table and smashed the machine. There was a tussle, leaving Paolo's face scratched. Paolo, bloodstained, left the meeting and soon filed lawsuits against the family firm, seeking $30 million in damages. The press was gleeful. The Gucci infighting had become the nation's favourite soap opera.

Paulo had by no means run out of steam. During his years of working at Gucci, he had been quietly collecting and analysing all the financial documents he could get his hands on. He wanted to know the inner workings of the company. In the course of his investigations he discovered that millions of dollars were being siphoned to offshore companies by Aldo under a system of false invoicing. Now he had a nuclear weapon in his arsenal, and he was going to use it to claim his right to market the PG brand.

MAURIZIO GUCCI

Unlike his cousin, Maurizio kept his head down while working with Aldo, whom he admired as an entrepreneur, winning his uncle's trust. Following the death of his father in 1983, Maurizio saw his chance to become the ruler of the empire, especially now that he had inherited his father's 50 per cent stake in business. Maurizio believed that the company needed to be set on a different direction, with major changes to product range and styles. But he didn't yet hold the reins of power or have access to the finances to implement such decisions. Because his father had so cosseted him he lacked experience, if not confidence.

Aldo had not anticipated how much the loss of his brother might disturb his own grip on the business, and he underestimated the forces ranged against him, on three counts. First, he failed to apprehend the scale of Maurizio's ambition to shake up Gucci and reshape the policies that had made the company successful. Second, he was too dismissive of his son Paolo's determination to win the right to do business under his own name. And third, he had put out of mind the very real danger presented to him by the US Internal Revenue Service for his tax evasion. Not only had he illegally transferred millions of dollars to offshore companies, but he had also personally cashed checks worth hundreds of thousands of dollars that had been made out to the company. He had been acting as if Gucci was his own personal kitty bank, with no clear separation made between personal and company affairs.

Maurizio, believing that his uncle could go to jail, decided to seize the initiative and enlist the support of Paolo to create a new company called Gucci Licensing. This would control all licensing under the Gucci brand, in which Maurizio would hold a 51 per cent stake and Paolo the balance. In exchange for this, Maurizio asked Paolo to cast his 3.3 per cent vote with Maurizio's 50 per cent, giving him de facto control of the company. He also made an agreement to buy Paolo's stake for $20 million on condition that all pending legal suits were dropped.

PLOTS AND MANOEUVRES

Thus Maurizio set in motion his plan to oust his uncle Aldo. A board meeting was called at which Domenico de Sole, a sharp legal brain who had been hired by Rodolfo in 1980 and who had been given the controlling proxy by Maurizio, called for the board to be dissolved. Aldo, the mighty leader, was toppled from the empire he had done so much to build up. Maurizio had blossomed into a leader with as much ruthless zeal as his uncle had ever practised.

Before he died Rodolfo had predicted to Patrizia that her husband, his son Maurizio, would change once he had money and power in his hands. In this respect Rodolfo was right. Over the years since Maurizio had become more involved in the family business, his distance from Patrizia and his daughters had grown. He no longer heeded her opinions and advice. She had entered the marriage with an image of herself as a strong woman standing solidly behind a weak man, but now she found the story had changed.

He had become increasingly assertive and neglectful of her. Often he would not come home on weekends, and he was careless of his personal appearance. So it was that in 1985, Maurizio packed a small suitcase and left, never to return to his family. He said that he felt suffocated around Patrizia and wanted freedom. His estranged wife's world was falling apart and she became depressed. Although Patrizia made every effort to bring Maurizio back to her, Maurizio made it clear to the children that he no longer loved their mother. Yet the break-up of his marriage was just one of Maurizio's problems. Aldo's retaliatory move against Maurizio for seizing control of the company was to file a case against him, supported by his sons, alleging that he had forged his father's signature on his share certificates after his death to avoid paying inheritance taxes.

Aldo's forced exit from the firm was the beginning of his end. Paolo's earlier betrayal of his father to the tax authorities had set a legal juggernaut in motion, and in January 1986 Aldo was forced to plead guilty in New York federal court to defrauding the US government of $7 million in back taxes. He also admitted he had taken $11 million out of company for himself and members of his family. For this, Aldo was sentenced to a year and a day in prison. This was the ultimate ignominy; brought low by his son, his nephew and the state.

By 1987 there were a total of 18 law suits pending that involved the Gucci family. At one court meeting an advocate was heard to say, 'Here we have to save Gucci from the Guccis.' In the Gucci world of shifting alliances, Maurizio's plan to ally with Paolo was short lived. Paolo, always quick to spot treachery, concluded that Maurizio was out to cheat him, and determined to teach him a lesson. Again, whistle-blowing was his preferred instrument of revenge: Paolo proceeded to send photocopies of documents to tax authorities showing how Maurizio had diverted funds to evade taxes. The repercussions were immediate, and the authorities came with an arrest warrant. Maurizio was hauled in front of a court in Milan and found guilty of tax fraud, for which he was given a suspended jail sentence. There was also a large bill to pay of millions in taxes and fines.

THE FINAL CURTAIN

Maurizio, facing mounting pressure on his personal finances, dreamed up a plan that would ease his personal situation, secure the ousting of the other branch of the family and create a platform to rebuild the business. His scheme was to find a financial partner to buy out the shares owned by his cousins. Supported by Gucci's new partners, Investcorp, he succeeded in buying the shares of Roberto and Giorgio, leaving Aldo with his 17 per cent stake. To Aldo it became clear that he could no longer exercise any power. He had little option but to follow his son's lead and to sell out. Shortly thereafter in January 1990 Aldo, a spent man, passed away at the age of 84. Paulo, his maverick son, died bankrupt a few years later in 1995 of liver disease.

Meanwhile, under Maurizio's management, the company's strategy had been refocused on luxury products and sales had started to decline, while a profligate approach to expenses led to a slide in profits. Maurizio's plan to buy out his partners, Investcorp, was heading nowhere as his credibility began to crumble. With the company ever more deeply into the red, his financial investors concluded that Maurizio was ineffective as a business manager, and moved to buy out his 50 per cent share. Maurizio, his own finances in poor shape, was forced to concede, thus ending the Gucci family dynasty.

The troubles for the Guccis were not at an end, and there was a dramatic postscript. Maurizio's ex-wife Patrizia was angered to learn that her husband had deprived her children of their heritage by selling his stake. Maurizio, now living with his new partner Paola, moved against Patrizia, serving her with divorce papers, ordering her to stop using the Gucci name and banning her from entering the family estates. Patrizia, who had been diagnosed with suspected cancer, was deeply hurt by Maurizio's hostility. When she had been in hospital, recovering from a successful operation to remove a benign tumour, Maurizio had not even taken the trouble to visit her. At that point Patrizia vowed to destroy her ex-husband, jealous of his self-indulgent lifestyle. She wanted nothing less than his life, and she started looking for a hit-man to terminate his existence. On 27 March 1995, a hired killer shot Maurizio on his way to his office. Patrizia was eventually arrested and tried for the murder of her ex-husband. She was found guilty and sent to prison for a sentence of 29 years.

COMMENT

Thus did the curtain close on the Gucci family dynasty – European in location but pure Hollywood in plot line. It is a story that illustrates several key truths. Number one is the truth about character. The gene lottery means that sometimes it can occur that people with street-fighting instincts are all vying for the same space in a family. If people do not manage their weaknesses they will destroy them. Second, bad blood breeds bad blood. The sins of the parents are inherited by the children if there is no moderating or regulating force within a family, a role often played by spouses.[10] But here two generations were fighting personal and proxy wars simultaneously. Third, they say revenge is a dish best eaten cold. Here it was hot and calculated to burn people at every turn. The only possibility is escalation.

What could have been different? Failings in parenting and leadership abounded here, which could have been curbed or compensated for. The abundance of money only acted as a turbocharger for people's need and greed. Concepts such as love, loyalty, forgiveness and charity were entirely absent, and needlessly so. This was a great business, built with care by a family. It was worth loving and nurturing as a collective project from which all could gain.

Again and again in these sad sagas of family feuds we see people with their eyes fixated on their narrow self-interest, not the commonwealth that could save and support them all.

This is the last of our family war cases, and it seems like a gloomy note to close on. But this, as in all other cases, is also a story of might have been. Many wonderful firms with the same kinds of inputs and characters find redemption and salvation. We shall touch on a few of these in our final chapter, for there is nothing inevitable about wars in family business.

9

The lessons – the price of war and the prize of peace

A family is a place where principles are hammered and honed on the anvil of everyday living.

(Charles Swindoll)

When the smoke has cleared and the armies have left the field, what remains? Do we just shake our heads in sorrow for the casualties of war? Can no good come out of this mayhem?

Let's get things in proportion. First, let us remember that most of these firms survived and remained successful despite their conflicts. In some cases you might even say they did so because of their troubles – you can come out of a fight wiser and perhaps even stronger if it teaches you new disciplines. This final chapter is dedicated to this cause. We shall not just review how conflict can be avoided or resolved, but how it can be made productive. You can have too little conflict as well as too much.

Second, despite all the sad destructiveness of war, it is also true that it has the capacity to cleanse and renew. If it were not for warfare the spread of technology, social innovations and new materials would have been a slow and haphazard process in the march of history. Likewise, without takeovers, corporate failures and strategic errors we would lack the governance systems and management practices that enable firms to serve markets efficiently.

In this chapter, as we draw lessons from the family wars we have described we have three objectives. First, we want to look at the big picture – the deeper insights about human nature, management and family dynamics that are revealed by our analysis, and what lessons can be learnt from this. Second, we provide an inventory of warning signs and practical measures that firms can adopt to immunize themselves against warfare, if not against conflict. Finally, we shall review the question of how people can make conflict productive in family firms.

FROM POISONED ROOTS TO THE FRUITS OF SUCCESS – THE ESSENTIAL LESSONS OF WARFARE

Let us review the major lessons in terms of three stages of inception and possible intervention:

- the root causes of family wars;
- the process or conduct of family wars;
- the aftermath or consequence of family wars.

STAGE 1: AT THE ROOTS

The identity of the leader

Let us start by thinking about founders – or, more strictly speaking, founders as fathers and patriarchs. Many of the problems we have described have their roots in the identity of the founder. We are faced with the paradox that some of the greatest builders of family business empires are also the greatest destroyers. It is the double-sided face of power and personality.[1] Each positive aspect of character has its dark side. We should not just demonize family business leaders here – each one of us has a duality to our identity. If we are hard workers, then we can also be prey to perfectionism or the tendency to drive others unreasonably hard. If we are creative, we can drive people crazy by trying to change things that don't need fixing or by starting fruitless initiatives, just to keep ourselves stimulated. If we are caring and conciliatory we can be weak and ambivalent where we should be tough and direct. Looked at this way, a weakness is just a misplaced strength (and vice versa!).

Three essential steps to personal effectiveness are: first, know yourself; second, read the situation; and third, discipline yourself. These are three tough steps for many entrepreneurs. First, they are often people not much given to introspection, who are much more likely to be motivated to focus on their strengths than on their weaknesses. Second, they are much more at home creating situations rather than merely responding to them. Third, the only discipline they are inclined to believe in is the need to focus their powers on the task in hand. They see no need to apply a mute to their voice.

This is what we have to do. These elements hold the key to success – to know one's fatal flaws, to perceive external threats and to have self-control. Who can help entrepreneurs to go against their instincts? Wives, friends and trusted advisers are the most obvious candidates, but dare these people say what needs to be said? Can they capture the willing attention of the charismatic leader? If they can, then what will they say? There is only one way to get below the defences of powerhouse leaders, and that is to focus on objective reality and the compelling logic of desired outcomes.

Nicolò Machiavelli, the first and one of the greatest writers on leadership, closely studied the leaders of his age – Popes, dukes, diplomats and military leaders. He started out being impressed by many of them, but then turned out to be repeatedly disappointed at their shortcomings.[2] This led him to a single powerful overriding conclusion: leaders fail in their undertakings because of their fatal inflexibility in the face of changing circumstances. The best service people can render to leaders, therefore, is to help them see how the challenges and demands of the situations they confront require flexibility and different remedies from those that instinctively come to the mind. The Bronfmans' risky flight into entertainment in response to slow growth in the liquor market was a case in point.

That is in the business domain. When the leader is the father the problem is compounded. For many family business leaders the one child they care most about is the firm. They spend so much time embroiled in its entrails that they scarcely come up for air to see that their real family exists. When they do, they tend to apply the same blunt instruments that they use to drive the business, with the end result of families flip-flopping between being neglected and being pushed around.

The family may be able to adapt to the intermittent attentions of the leader, and go along with what is demanded without too much visible complaint. But trouble starts when the leader, who is in no position to make an impartial assessment of his children's gifts and interests, then embarks on either thoughtless decisions about their role in the business – such as the rigid application of the rule of male primogeniture, such as we have seen in the Bingham case – or makes a series of role allocations on the basis of superficial presumptions. The family appointments to leadership positions at Steinberg's is a classic example of this error taken to the extreme.

Most parents are unaware of the gene lottery and its implications – the apparent paradox that siblings and parents might share 50 per cent of their genes, but there is a zero correlation between their personality profiles. Instead, they assume that their children are 'just like' them. This is what psychologists called 'projection'. In Chapter 2 we introduced the concepts of the 'script' – the story about who we are and what is our destiny – that may be handed to us by parents, friends and teachers. Sometimes these are the unlived lives of frustrated and regretful parents who want their children to achieve their dreams for them. Many people go through life living a script that is scarcely their own, sometimes waking up in mid-life to reclaim their true identity and throw aside a misfitting identity and bad script that they have been carrying for years. When this happens suddenly to someone in the middle years it is known as the 'mid-life crisis'. We have seen such attempted script enforcement in several cases, most notably in Bata where the parents expected Tom Jr, as the new CEO, to obey their wishes, and when Brent Redstone allegedly rejected his father's request for support on Sumner's divorce. In these situations the parent who will not be gainsaid has cloaked their child's ego with some unsuitable mantle.

Another kind of attempted script enforcement is the leader who seeks immortality by ruling from beyond the grave, through legal mechanisms and verbal edicts. These are supposed to secure his undying vision, regardless of what happens to his earthly frame. Jay Pritzker was a prime example of such wishful thinking. More worrying are those who have become so intoxicated with their own powers that they scarcely feel the need to think about their own mortality. Many of the problems we have reviewed started when a leader died intestate (without leaving a will) – for example with the Ambanis, Pathaks and Batas.

There are two connected reasons. One is that the leader is so fully 'in' himself – aware of his vitality and power – that this is something he doesn't have to think about now.[3] Second, there is another psychological defence mechanism at work here – avoidance. Making a will means having to think about things you don't want to contemplate, not just your own mortality but the thought of others, less qualified than you, taking control of everything you have devoted your life to building up. It also means facing up to the possible shortcomings of successors, and the knotty problem of how to divide the spoils.[4] These are tricky matters, and for sure if they have not been seriously thought about before mum or dad dies, they could prove to be the undoing of the empire.

It is this same impulse, and the fear of death itself, that lead many family business leaders to continue well beyond what is rational in terms of their capabilities, or reasonable in view of the alternatives. We observed in our opening chapter that many leaders quite rationally fear death from disengagement, since all they have ever known in their lives is their role as leaders.

So what can we advise for dealing with leadership and succession?

■ Leaders need to set up mechanisms that will help raise their awareness of the challenges that can emanate from various quarters and how they may be changing. This includes not just the tangible – markets, competition, stakeholders – but also the intangibles – culture, relationships and ideas. Leadership style needs to modulate as a business matures. Bringing in professionals from outside the family is the most obvious step to achieving this, though in our cases routinely it was one of the most neglected strategies.

■ The powerhouse leader cannot be muffled. This is not the answer. Rather they need the tools of insight. Understanding your own psychological profile and its dualities is a prerequisite for self-control, and there are many psychological assessment tools and methods that can be administered quite painlessly by a coach or counsellor.

■ Leaders need help in appraising the talents of other people. They need to accept that their gifts might not include those of character divination. The story of modern good governance in family business is one of recognizing that these decisions are highly complex, and distancing leaders from sole responsibility for them.

- The gentle disengagement of great leaders is hard to achieve. Indeed there is nothing wrong with the powerhouse leader staying as long as they are fit to do so – firms benefit from their wisdom and presence. But this needs to be transitioned into something other than the leadership it was in its prime. As in tribal societies, people can honour and find a role for the ageing chief without expecting him to command to the last detail as he might have done in former times.
- Leaders can do themselves and their families great service by finding a 'third career' path where they can exercise their drive and enthusiasm. Some choose philanthropy as a rewarding area of focus. Whatever the chosen route, great leaders often find fulfilment beyond the workplace, and one of the by-products may be rediscovering their true family.

The art of parenting and family dynamics

We have seen in more than one case leaders who, while not subject to the disorders of despotism, sowed the seeds of destruction through various failures and delusions of parenting, for at the centre of just about every case in this book is a dysfunctional family climate.

Perhaps the most benign, but nonetheless one of the most deadly, is the myth of the undivided family. Indeed in Indian business the 'Hindu undivided family' is recognized as a legal entity for taxation purposes, and perhaps it is no accident that our two South Asian firms, Reliance and Patak, were nearly torn to pieces by this myth. As we observed Chapter 2, it is in our genes as parents for us to wish our children to be united in a common harmonious identity. We all desire our kids to get along, for each to have the opportunity to do well in life, and after our death to continue to pursue our vision of collective happiness. This is dangerous if people try to cast a net over the freedom of young adults. In some cases, like the Steinberg family, the vision acts as powerful magnet, sucking family members into an unsustainable vortex, purely by the force of the leader's unshakeable optimism.

But back comes harsh reality in the form of the gene lottery. The truly random assortment of characters that this delivers to every family makes each family unit a puzzle, with its own set of unique adjusters to make it work. This means that people may go off and do their own thing, form alliances and antipathies, and regulate their interaction to accommodate tensions that arise. Sensible parenting can be an enormously rewarding task of blending a natural diversity of human types into a uniquely effective micro-culture. Many great family firms have benefited from the infusion of this spirit.

There are uglier dynamics on display in our cases, such as brothers fighting each other relentlessly as in the story of the Dasslers, or fathers being both defensive and confrontational with their own offspring, as was visible in the Haft case. What motivates such behaviour? Many leaders – even some of the most powerful – are vulnerable to feelings of insecurity and inadequacy.[5] They know instinctively what the evolutionary theory predicts, that their children do not always want the best for their parents, especially if their parents get in their way.

Fathers are fearful of this truth. Fathers also do not want to be reminded of their failing powers. Many look forward with ambivalence and even fear to the day that this boy, who once looked up to them as all-powerful and all-wise, will be faster, stronger and smarter than they are. It is not that they wish ill of their children, only that they wish themselves not to be diminished by them.[6] The narrower the age gap, the more threatening the challenge becomes. Some fathers can be brutally defensive towards their children, as we saw with Wallace McCain, who was convinced of his son Michael's ability to take high office in the family business.

Failures of parenting abound in our cases. We have seen some where parents were so tough on their kids that all they did was to bequeath the child an inheritance of neurosis. Much of what isn't determined by genes in our character is the product of our early upbringing, and we have seen here numerous cases of what can only be called uncontrolled parenting – especially exemplified by the Shoen saga. It is a direct precursor to a lifetime of poor decisions that the children will make when they grow up.

Such calamitous cases are thankfully rare. More common are simply tough parenting regimes, where excessive control stifles the autonomy and healthy growth of kids.[7] In some cases, such as Gucci, this spills over into attempts to control the children's marriages, relationships, and every last detail of their lives, as if they were their parents' subjects. Tough parenting is not always a disaster, but it does set up a machismo role model that is laden with future risks. Family leaders need to tread on the right side of the subtle but important distinction between authoritarian parenting – do it because I say so – and authoritative parenting – do it because I can show you why it's right.

In the introduction we discussed marriage, usually the only non-genetic bond in the family, as a fault line in the kinship structure. In the Shoen case there were more fault lines than in crazy paving. Even if we would not wish to morally censure a man like L S Schoen for his unrelenting search for lasting love, we can sound the note of warning that the romantic diversion of six marriages plays out ill against a game plan that requires cooperation around the unitary aims of the business.

In many of our cases the role of women has been crucial – either as key protagonists, like Mitzi in the Steinberg case, Eleanor Ford and Sonja Bata, or as vital agents behind the scenes. Sometimes this is for good, as with Laura McCain, where wives are a stabilizing force and a source of wisdom. In other cases women can egg men on to greater extremes of conflict.[8] Generally, however, it is the silence and under-utilization of the talents of women that is most evident here, where they would have been a legitimate force for good sense and moderation.

The other chief source of difficulty is the perpetual risk of sibling conflict. The inputs that make this likely are: same sex (male), narrow age gap, similar drives for success, and mutually exclusive opportunities. Around the world there have been and are many examples of successful sibling teams, such as the Hindujas in India, the Mars brothers in the United States and the Barclay twins in the United Kingdom. Many of the sibling conflicts we have observed were brought about by nepotism and incompetence. We shall have more to say on how these conflicts play out shortly.

Let us conclude this discussion of the roots of conflict with some thoughts on the failure of success. That is when things are too easy so that the first speed-bump people hit overturns the applecart. In several cases wealth came very fast and very early. This can create a form of bad learning. Early success creates the expectation that good fortune is a permanent blessing and will be perpetuated, as in the Gucci case.

Wealth also seems to sharpen rather than cushion conflict. We might imagine that the more there is in the pot, the easier it should be for everyone to be contented with their share. It is curious and paradoxical that the opposite seems to occur – it raises the stakes of envy and amplifies the cost of possible loss. The more there is at stake, the more people seem able to generate negative energy. Patriarchs like Jay Pritzker, raised on principles of thrift, fail to adjust their families to times of plenty, creating an environment where wealth becomes hotly contested. In other cases grandiose ambitions can lead a business off course into strategic swamplands, as they did with the Bronfmans' disastrous Hollywood escapade, even though they made good in the end.

So the lessons here include:

- Everyone in family business should understand the gene lottery and abandon the fiction either that their kids will be just like them and realize their unfulfilled dreams, or that by grooming and coaching they can mould them at will into the people they would like them to be. The reality is that parents need to understand their children as unique individuals, as indeed they themselves are, and do what they can to make the chemistry between them work the best it can.
- The idea of the undivided family also deserves to be treated as an aspiration, not an article of faith. Families should overtly explore the values that they hold in common, and if possible, identify a vision that unites them. When the needs of family members are subordinated to a dream and principles that are not shared, a fiction is created that stifles individuality and can lead to disunity.
- Models of parenting need to be consciously considered, not initiated ad hoc according to the whims and instincts of parents. Both parents need to be aligned around concepts of authority plus support that are clear and consistent for the child, not indulgent, neglectful or oppressive.
- Watch out for fault lines and pay attention to them. The most dangerous are between fathers and sons, between brothers, and between husbands and wives.
- Keep wealth and materiality under control – don't let it raise the stakes of whatever conflicts are incipient. Money is not a cure for all ills. Parents should guard against a culture of dependency and expectation developing among their children.[9]

STAGE 2: THE PLAY'S THE THING – HOW CONFLICT UNFOLDS

Conflict as narrative

Perhaps one of the saddest features of the family wars we have observed is that over and over again bad blood breeds bad blood. By this we mean it is amazing how ancient conflicts can echo down through the generations, like a mutant strain. How little it would have cost in relation to the long-term benefits for someone to attempt a reconciliation of long-past conflicts. It is the tragedy of family wars that too often too few people make too little effort to overturn the tyranny of the past and start afresh. Instead we see people making alliances on the basis of ancient tribalisms, making appointments out of spite and revenge, and only letting cronies from outside act as sources of advice and guidance, as Henry Ford did in giving Bennett full reign after the death of his son Edsel.

It is like a narrative – a story line – that everyone seems to be trapped in, each acting out their roles as from a script. We have seen numerous scripts come into play. Some come from deep in memory and the unhealed scars of previous generations, like the Dassler case, where Adi and Rudi's unresolved battle became entrenched in the warfare between Adidas and Puma. We have already discussed the narrative of the undivided family and brotherly love (as with the Mondavis), and those who strive to overcome some of their children's disinterested orientation to the business (as with the Binghams).

Families are particularly prone to the belief that the future will be like the past, as was Henry Ford. The reality of course is that change affects all parameters of family business decision making. We have seen many family business patriarchs, like fabled King Canute, seated on their thrones by the water's edge trying to command the tides of change. The assumptions of today may not hold tomorrow. Look, for example, at how trusts can be set up with elaborate care for an unreal vision of the future, and then immediately start to unravel following the death of the person who set them up, as happened with the Pritzkers.

The tides of change often lie in the evolving values of the surrounding culture. The next generation comes with a different set of ideas and assumptions about what is normal. Younger and older siblings may inhabit different eras of values and interests, such as split the Gallo brothers. Parenting style has to adjust, not only as children mature and require different kinds of attention and resources, but also with the historically shifting values of the ambient culture. Yet if adaptation turns into inconsistent treatment among siblings over time, as it did in the Shoen story, it can produce a schism in the family.

Schisms are a narrative of a particular kind, as we have seen. Parents can create two classes of citizen, most often between children working in the business and those who are not. Three kinds of split seem to have predominated: insiders versus outsiders, disconnected family members, and turf wars with factions fighting for the spoils. Around them form narratives to do with justice, fairness, inequality and status. There is often also the double whammy of distributive and procedural injustice. Not only is the division grossly unequal, but it is arrived at by a process that aggrieved parties consider to be illegitimate. Sometimes belatedly a family member tries to right a perceived wrong with money, but this will not work if the unfairness is to do with process more than material wealth, as the Pritzkers found.

Change in life circumstances can be organic, a product of personal development. Husbands and wives can grow apart, with serious consequences for many family businesses. The organic change we see most in our cases here, though, is to do with leaders growing into their roles in ways that few would have predicted. Look at the apparent personality transformation of Maurizio in the Gucci case once he acquired the leadership of the business. This transformation is actually an illusion. What happens is that new circumstances reveal dormant aspects of personality rather than creating new ones. We are apt to judge too statically and superficially the personalities of others, and fail to see how disregarded features may flourish under the stimulus of a new role or a new relationship.[10]

Power is one of the greatest transforming forces in this way. People who didn't realize they had a taste for power can suddenly discover that they relish the ability to make decisions, command others and be looked up to. When it becomes intoxicating, this is what people mean when they say power 'goes to someone's head'. Henry Ford, Herbert Haft, Sumner Redstone, Chester Waxman and the Count de Lur-Saluces are just a few instances in our case histories of powerful men who acted with what could be seen as insufficient self-restraint. This could be said to be a failure of the narrative of leadership. Leaders may have a story about themselves and the business that turns out to be destructive because it is based narrowly upon a singular vision and their will to achieve it.

In the introduction and at various points in this book we have invoked what we call the vessel principle – the idea that if you put enough pressure into a container, eventually it will find the structural flaws and split the vessel asunder. At several points in our case reports we have seen stress bending people out of shape. Stress often has the effect of regressing people to a more primitive level. Thus some quite rational and sane adults can be observed to throw tantrums like children when they are put under pressure.[11] Family tragedies also have unpredictable consequences. They may completely reconfigure relationships within a family, as happened in the Shoen case. Tragedies test people. Loss and thwarted dreams can rewrite the narrative in new and dangerous ways if people do not reach a point of acceptance.

So what are the lessons? Here are a few:

- Never surrender to the narrative. Be aware that every family has its sagas and mythologies. Don't let them suck you into a perspective that restricts your freedom of choice and sense of self-determination. Better tear up the script.
- Being an adaptive family does not mean you have to sway with every breeze. On a firm foundation of strong values and principles you can afford to be flexible. The means to achieving this are the practices of open communications and taking a problem-solving approach to difficulties, without expecting too much of yourself and others.
- Treat the past as a place where you had your origins but from which you have migrated to a new land. Find ways of wiping the slate clean – forgiving, if not forgetting. Families need truth and reconciliation processes in order to move forward and not be imprisoned by the wrongs and errors of their ancestors and others.
- Expect the future to be different from the past or the present. Organic and accidental change will happen. You just need to be aware, and mindful of the need to change your style and attitudes to reflect evolving realities.
- All power needs countervailing forces so it can be self-aware and adaptive. Leaders need people who will not only support and forgive them, but also restrain, challenge and advise them.

The poisoned game

One version of the game is two-in-a-box. You get two young people with strong needs for recognition and success. You put them in a situation where only one of them can win. You yoke them together with ties of blood, ownership and duty. Brothers who might otherwise have been the best of buddies end up in blood feuds that are truly MAD – mutually assured destruction. People with sharp elbows should not be forced to sit close together. Look at the Dasslers – they did it to themselves by choosing to inhabit the same house – or the Mondavis, where their father's wishes put the siblings in a box close together.

Closeness in personality – via the gene lottery – is a liability under such circumstances. It's better where brothers can differentiate themselves as types. Even this is not guaranteed success. Consider the case of the younger McCain boys, in the box of joint leadership. Their marked differences in style and personality could have been made to work as a true sibling partnership, but it only takes one or two acts that are judged by one or the other party to be breaches of trust for any partnership to dissolve. A few simple acts of trust building and open communications would have saved them all the grief that ensued, as would a shared belief in the value of listening to external counsel and advice. Likewise the Ambanis, where the structure of ownership failed to disentangle their distinctive gifts. In families enmity seems to be capable of being the equal and opposite quality to love once a bond is broken.

Many family wars seem to be aroused, fuelled and amplified by nothing less than lack of self-restraint – people acting on impulse or wish fulfilment. Even a virtue is dangerous when taken to excess – look at L S Shoen's over-generalized frugality for example, which led him, among other factors, to fail to seek professional advice. His remarkable capacity for loving different women also created several problems for family unity. Hard work can turn into dangerous workaholism if unchecked, as happened in the Adidas case to Horst Dassler, whose untimely death came at the age of 51.

Some of the most poisonous wars are stimulated by more than just self-indulgence: by acts that trip a switch in the circuitry of conflict. Some are deliberate. Some are just thoughtless. Some are ambiguous. Parents can unintentionally start the rot in a family conflict by setting up their children to compete with each other, in the mistaken belief that it will make them more adaptive and strong. We have seen how this can be an unwitting cause of conflict, such as seems to have been the case when Robert Mondavi split the leadership of the company between sons Michael and Tim. Neither is it unknown for children to become victims in their parents' wars, such as the difficulties created for the Pritzker children, Liesel and Matthew, when Robert divorced his wife Irene. More calculated are numerous cases of what we may call acts of exclusion, where one family member is effectively isolated from the others, or denied a right that others have, as occurred in the Redstone case.

In their most extreme manifestations some of these cases look more fictional than real. Every soap opera on television subsists on a diet of lies and concealments by parties. Without them the drama would be empty. In some of our cases there was a good deal of such skulduggery. Look, for example, at the financial manipulations and open accusations of tax avoidance that populate the Gucci story. Consider the amazing saga of the Waxmans, where communications and decision making were decidedly opaque, and motivated by the naked self-interest of one branch against another. More everyday instances abound.

One phenomenon of particular interest is what social scientists studying negotiation call 'ultimatum bargaining'.[12] In this laboratory game one party is given $100 and told to share it with a partner, in whatever proportion they like. The partner with whom they are sharing has no influence over the proportions of the division but can accept or refuse what is offered. The power of the second party is that if they reject the offer, both parties walk away empty handed.

This paradigm is of particular interest to economists and psychologists, whose theories it tests. A purely rational economic perspective says the second party should accept whatever share the first party offers, since something is better than nothing. The psychological perspective says no, people will only tolerate what they consider as fair and will veto on principle a deal they consider to be unjust, even if they lose financially by doing so. The psychologists win the argument in almost every run of the game, and the family wars we have examined illustrate the truth of it. People will play a spoiling game rather than accept a deal they consider to be unfair, as did the count in the Chateau d'Yquem story.

In many cases, we could not say a single act precipitated a family war. More often than not there is a spiral of escalation, as in the

Steinberg case and many others. The most primitive form is tit-for-tat. Reprisals continue, gradually building beyond the point where anyone has the power to stop them.[13] Sometimes the escalation becomes turbocharged by people taking the private into the public domain. The effect of public acts of conflict is to create shame, embarrassment and reputational damage. These are emotions and outcomes that have more power to rouse anger than many others. The Hafts and the Steinbergs are prime examples.

The most common avenue for switching on the spotlight of public scrutiny is of course the law. In fully half our cases, legal battle was joined in the courts, where the families aired their grievances publicly. This is not always a bad thing, for the law can be the catalyst that brings matters to a head, reveals what was concealed and culminates in a clean break, enabling both parties to walk away with something and their pride intact. But more often attorney wars sap the wealth, mental state and energy of the protagonists, as they become entrenched in a protracted conflict. They can be very expensive affairs, dragging on over years, as in the Koch dispute, with few winners in the end – except the lawyers perhaps. In such conflagrations, people who would be impassive or uninvolved bystanders also get sucked into the fire.

In these predominantly male wars we also observe that women play a significant role. In terms of peacemakers, the mother Kokilaben's belated intervention in the Reliance case is an example of where it was key to success. Sonja Bata was an influential force at Bata Shoe, playing an important role on the board, if not always agreeing with her son. In others like the Binghams, women are in the forefront of the action, though often ambiguously – sometimes buffering and sometimes amplifying conflict, as we saw with the Steinbergs. It would be a mistake to assume women do not have an influence in the cases where we have no direct evidence. It is well known in family business that women often occupy a subtle but determining role behind the scenes – sometimes as 'Chief Emotional Officer', over the dining room table or on the conjugal pillow, gently but firmly nudging the minds and moves of the chief actors.[14] Glimpses of this are visible in several cases, such as Dassler and McCain, where, denied any formal role, women are clearly influencing the actions of the principals in quite critical ways.

The lessons here are several:

- Look at the rules of the game – which goals and resources are shared and which are mutually exclusive to parties. Evaluate whether these arrangements increase or decrease the probability of conflict.
- Even close relatives need to engage in trust-building displays and acts. Transparency and openness should be practised in the family, while maintaining confidence. Failure to do so can engender suspicion.
- The colourful qualities of leaders who are not afraid to be themselves in family business are a source of strength and distinctiveness, but they need boundaries and restraints. This means feedback for awareness, and self-discipline as a response to awareness. Family, friends and advisors also have a duty to help with home truths, delivered with support and sympathy, to help family leaders doing a difficult job.
- If you have a grievance, start by airing it privately. Public broadcasting amplifies negative emotion beyond a point of reasonable recall and recovery.
- Don't play the ultimatum bargaining game. It is too unpredictable, and more often than not it will end in tears.
- Give women voice and meaningful partnership, so they can play their individual roles to the fullest and help to mediate conflict.

STAGE 3: WHEN THE SMOKE CLEARS

We have seen how many families stumble blindly and foolishly into conflicts, though in a few cases naked greed and malice are the demons driving the actors. If people have accidentally slid into conflict before, it can happen again. We shall be discussing some specific measures for conflict management in family firms in the next section, but let us here briefly consider some overall principles.

First, business success can be either a great insulator against conflict – people will desist so long as they have something more important to do – or it can be an amplifier, by raising the stakes. Families need to beware of the nature of the times they are living in and their demands. When you are busy it is easy to be blind to unresolved underlying tensions. Families should beware of what look like simple costless options that are in fact only papering over the cracks.

If the root causes of feuds are not addressed, they can fester beneath the skin and later break out and spread with renewed vigour, like an untreated infection.

Second, the family as a concept can be contested territory, with people holding different ideas of what a family is all about. The fact that there is a strong business brand associated with the family does not mean people can take for granted the solid integrity of the family itself. Look at the Guccis. Families can come to grief over names and brand identities, as we saw when the Gallo brothers became so agitated about their younger brother's adopting the family name to promote his cheese business. The bottom line is there is no substitute for a strong, cohesive, self-aware family culture. The most important task of leadership is culture building.[15]

What keeps culture in place? It exists in the head, the body and the legs. The head is the leadership – the messages, the expressed values and communications that come from the top in a business, family or otherwise. The body is the structure – the systems, the rules, rewards and machinery of the firm. The legs are the people – what they think, believe and take for granted. To build a strong culture at the head you need clear leadership with confident messages about the real underlying values of the business. In the body you need goals and rewards that are consistent with the messages from the top. In the legs you need excellent people who are motivated to join, stay and perform because they feel the culture is one that enables them to do their best work.

Family members need to participate in the maintenance of the culture. If any are left as disinterested bystanders they will drift away. Successful business families involve the family in setting the values, ensuring goals are aligned and playing active roles in supporting the culture.

Third, for families to add value and not poison the business, attention needs to be paid to family relationships. More often than not this means mediation. Adaptive families mediate their own conflicts, for every family has its tensions. We have already discussed briefly the special role of women in this area, but it is neither their prerogative nor their bounden duty. Anyone and everyone shares responsibility for the relationships around them. There is wide cultural variation here. Asian families, for example, usually keep their dirty linen well out of public gaze, drawing upon the wise heads of the extended family to mediate where necessary. As we have seen, this is not always reliable, especially where, like the Pathaks, the dispute erupts from an unconventional source – in this case disgruntled sisters seeking to uphold their rights in the courts.

In the West our family resources are often depleted or too compromised to play such a role. In very few of our cases did any of our firms look for external mediation, and when they did (in the McCains case) the family were unwilling to follow the sensible advice they were given. Use of advisors is a matter of timing. Executive coaching is a growing business, but in many firms it is used furtively as if it would be a sign of weakness to admit that you need coaching or counselling. This negative stereotype is disappearing, thankfully, but it persists in many areas, and here we sense that it would offend many a family leader's sense of self-reliance to have recourse to such counsel. Too often the only advisors we have seen here have been legal counsel, coming in at the point of litigation or when preparing an ownership continuity plan. Here lawyers can find themselves in difficult situations, where what may be the right solution for the family as a whole may not be what their client wants. Today, many families have recourse to family business specialist consultants to get advice that best supports the needs of the family as a wider group. Other growing areas in terms of family business support include mentoring, career counselling and interventions that explore personality issues and team dynamics.

Finally, as the smoke clears what every firm needs is governance. Many of the strongest and most admirable firms in the world have got to where they are by enduring, surviving and learning from crises. They have implemented governance systems that make provision for solving problems before they occur. They embody independent voices to counsel against poor or biased decisions. They contain processes for the orderly transition of power and the effective execution of major strategic decisions. They have provisions for transfers of ownership, the extraction of benefits and the protection of the asset base for the next generation. Last but not least, they systematically review risk factors at both the business and the family level, and develop contingency plans in preparation for unplanned occurrences.

WARNING SIGNS AND PRACTICAL MEASURES

WARNING SIGNS

Now let us come down to specifics. What are the warning signs to look for and what practical measures can firms adopt to immunize themselves against warfare and to manage family risk factors?

Here are 20 classic early warnings that should set a bell ringing in any family business. Most of them indicate that an issue has the capacity to arouse strong and potentially negative emotion. They may be visible in structures or processes; but what marks them out is their capacity to arouse conflict.

- **Behaviour change:** any sudden and inexplicable change in the behaviour of a family member. This is likely to indicate some change of heart and mind, and you need to know whether it concerns the family or the business.
- **Perceived unfairness:** complaints about fairness, from whatever quarter. Remember, if something is perceived as real it is real in its consequences.
- **Errors:** frequent errors from any party, however minor. They signify distraction, role overload or some other source of stress.
- **Communication gaps:** failures to connect frequently between people who have a shared responsibility, task or ownership interest.
- **Procrastination:** taking a lengthy time to reach any decisions; putting off making choices that are important.
- **Process disagreement:** failure to agree by whom and how decisions are to be taken in both the family and the business context.
- **No consensus:** inability of the group to reach a consensus even over relatively minor decisions.
- **Unclear goals:** an absence of clarity of vision on the part of the owners about the goals and direction that they want the family firm to pursue.
- **Disconnection:** family members starting to drift away from the business, finding themselves lacking emotional and financial attachment.
- **Privilege:** perceptions that family members are in privileged positions, receiving unfair advantage by virtue of their status.

- **Hanging on:** the senior generation overstaying their normal tenure/agreed retirement age and blocking new leaders from exercising effective authority.
- **Nepotism:** hiring policies that are unfairly biased in favour of family members, leading to a mismatch of skills in the firm and demotivation of non-family employees.
- **Role ambiguity:** family managers unclear regarding their roles and responsibilities.
- **Ivory tower:** an absence of independent voices and individuals on the board, or a lack of any open discussion that holds the management and the owners to account.
- **Inequity:** individuals or groups taking disproportionate benefits in relation to their contribution.
- **Lack of planning:** especially around generational transitions, a reluctance or inability on the part of family and board to agree to succession plans.
- **Absence of open dialogue:** meetings where everyone is in agreement and no fundamental issues of purpose and feeling are ever discussed.
- **Executive instability:** finding non-family managers, particularly those in key roles, hard to attract and harder to retain.
- **Bad gossip:** prevalence of alarmist rumours. Bad gossip suggests a problem culture.
- **Factionalism:** formation of subgroups, especially around family members, where there is little interaction or open exchange among them.

CONFLICT RESOLUTION

Conflict is likely already to be under way by the time a few of the red flags we have just listed are seen. We shall discuss preventative strategies shortly, but what is the family to do that finds itself in a sudden conflagration? We wonder how many of the big conflicts we have seen here could have been nipped in the bud by judicious action early in the day.

What is the first thing you do when you receive an insulting e-mail, when someone slights you at a public gathering, or when someone makes a decision that they must know flies in the face of what is really important to you? Do you immediately call foul and let them know your displeasure? Do you just lower your opinion of the offender, withdraw and make a private vow not to trust them in the future? Or do you dispassionately analyse what must have been going on in their minds to make them act like that, and find out how to understand them better?

Some people more than others find it easy to be cool, rational and detached when confronted by negative energy, but all of us underestimate the degree to which emotions bias our judgement and lead our responses. It is very hard to see the other person's point of view when your head is booming with its own shouting voices. Yet that is precisely what is needed to avoid unnecessary escalation, or worse, where some ill-judged act will put you in the wrong or take you into deeper water.

The ultimate psychological goal in all conflict is what Nicholson calls 'decentring'[16] – where both parties are able to see the partiality of their own perspective and comprehend the very different perceptions, motives, dilemmas and pressures that may be guiding their would-be antagonist. Most skilled mediation strategies aim to do this. Family firms that bring in a psychologically oriented consultant to help them find peace will find them devoting a lot of attention to helping achieve deeper shared understandings of each other's worlds. The kids come to understand what dad is trying to defend, and dad begins to see that the threats he imagined are not real. Brother and sister come to appreciate what the other might feel if they were in each other's position.

This does not solve the problem, but it does quieten the atmosphere, for the first step in all disputes is 'cooling off' – separating the parties until a context for dialogue can be created. Next are the steps that will enable the parties to shed their cardboard cut-out caricatures of each other, and to stop demonizing each other's motives. This means a realistic appraisal of what is really going on. This is what negotiators call 'interest-based' dispute resolution[17] – procedures that bring to the surface parties' real underlying needs, desires and hidden agendas. Then, aided by a mediator, they can trade their interests – each side conceding to the other what is less important to them than it is to their counter-party.

The holy grail is the 'integrative' solution, where differences of interest are sunk in an appreciation of the wider shared values and goals that unite them.[18] This is what solves conflicts in most family firms. The family, its heritage, values and commonwealth is the roof that shelters all, and if the pillars of the family indulge their desire to pull each other down, then all will lose as the house tumbles, as we have seen so often in this book.

But we have also seen that cases where the dispute is more about naked power than interests, and that the game is a high stakes winner-takes-all game. Most of the battles we have seen joined in this manner have ended up in the courts. Here the winner's curse seems often to apply: more damage has been done than the winner ever benefits from. In other cases we have often seen belated out-of-court settlements, as in the Koch, Pathak and Pritzker cases. What these tell us is that the law is a lousy, expensive and uncomprehending instrument of dispute resolution, and had the parties seriously negotiated they could all have come out with something better.

But better still are preventative strategies. Let us now turn to the most common risk factors and what can be done about them.

FAMILY RISK FACTORS AND REMEDIES

The firms we have looked at hardly constitute a random sample. Far from it, they are all high-profile extraordinary sagas. So we cannot pretend they are average or normal in any sense, yet at one time they were. That is why they captured our attention – because they started on the same bright path to success trodden by many new enterprises, but then fell into the various pitfalls we have documented. It is for this reason we need to look at the risk factors and consider how they could be avoided through good practice. The issues listed in Table 9.1 give our assessment of the types of risk factor that predominated in the cases. First, it is striking that every case exhibits several of these issues. So to some extent all the remedies we have listed are appropriate for just about all of these firms, or indeed any maturing family firm. This is perhaps the critical point.

Table 9.1 Risk factors and remedies for them

---

1. **Nepotism**

- Establish a written hiring policy for family members
- Develop career plans for family members
- Institute appraisals, regular feedback on work output and mentoring for family members
- Offer tailored skills development/education for family members
- Complement working family members with highest-calibre non-family talent

---

2. **Intergenerational struggles**

- Create an ownership continuity plan that defines how shares will be passed on to, sold, divided among and owned by the next generation, if at all
- Create a leadership continuity plan that includes a process, with agreed triggers and timetable, for selecting new business and family leaders
- Agree a policy for objective third-party oversight of the leadership selection process by independent directors, trustees and/or close advisors
- Appoint skilled non-family professionals to fill business leadership roles

---

3. **Disagreement over remuneration and rewards**

- Establish a family liquidity policy (for dividends and possible share buybacks) to balance owner and business needs
- Create an exit policy (for sale of shares): to enable family members to access capital and to allow for a natural pruning of the tree (don't assume family shareholders are on board for ever)
- Remunerate working family members at market rates

---

4. **Sibling rivalry**

- Clarify roles of all working family members
- Establish regular communications between the siblings
- Appoint a neutral 'ombudsman' as co-mentor for a sibling team
- Encourage siblings to enjoy time out from the business on occasions for fraternizing

---

Table 9.1 *(continued...)*

5.	Not letting go
▪	Set an enforceable normal retirement age from the board, enshrined in the company by-laws
▪	Keep the retiring senior generation involved when they leave their business role in an honorary capacity as 'wise men'
▪	Assist seniors in planning a third career
▪	Give them a hero's send-off to applaud and recognize all they have achieved

When a firm is in its young entrepreneurial stage it needs little in the way of cumbersome and time-consuming procedures and methods.[19] Family businesses are notoriously light in their use of bureaucracy. It is one of their appealing characteristics, and an aspect of their speed and flexibility in problem solving. Their informality and intimacy makes elaborate decision-making methods unnecessary. However, it is a common failing of all growing businesses that they do not recognize how growth is changing them. They are like a child who stays in short pants even when they're splitting at the seams. Firms of different size and shape require new structures. A degree of formalization – especially around management and decision making – becomes essential. If a firm leaves it too late, it courts the hazards of stress, bad decisions, errors, miscommunication and loss of coherence. These can be triggers for cultural ills, such as mistrust, alienation and conflict.

All this is true for family firms, though in their case there is the vital additional level of complexity – this is the nature of family ties and shared ownership. So in addition to the systems for good corporate governance we could recommend to every maturing business that there is a need for specific mechanisms to allow the family to find its distinctive voice, to 'speak to itself' in an open and constructive manner, and present a coherent unified front to the business and not a squabbling cacophony.

In sum, there is a need for family governance to complement the business governance. Families add tremendous value to a business in terms of spirit, perspective and values. Their underlying energy needs to be captured and tamed, not neutered. Family governance processes and architecture that include the management of family risk will enable the family's contribution to be enhanced. Any emerging frictions and conflict can be detected promptly, and steps taken to resolve issues at an early stage.

So let us list the general remedies and measures that a family firm can deploy to avoid these pitfalls. They fall into a few distinctive categories:

- **Generational transitions:** mechanisms that enable succession to be a smooth process and not damaging to either the departing or the incoming leader.
- **Planning and information:** planning systems that ensure decisions are taken with due process, access to adequate data and enough critical evaluation of their presumptions.
- **Communications:** to bring clarity and purpose to each position or set of interests within the overall framework of defining a common purpose.
- **Family governance:** a forum for the family, to provide an opportunity for multiple voices and perspectives to be heard, and for a common set of values and goals to be forged.
- **Corporate governance:** an independent board that ensures oversight of management and the objective scrutiny of corporate strategy.
- **Education and training:** equipping all family members with the knowledge and skills to perform their roles as responsible owners and stewards.
- **Liquidity and exit mechanisms:** ensuring fair returns to shareholders, whatever their position, and the right to make choices about their own financial futures.
- **Conflict resolution:** provision for open debate and problem solving to deal with exceptional circumstances and changing needs.
- **External benchmarking:** openness to voices from outside the family and the firm, for expert advice, wise counsel and emotional support for the difficult task of managing the family firm.

IN PRAISE OF CONFLICT

Let us conclude with a note of praise for conflict. As we have said, without conflict there would be little progress. Good ideas have to win out against inferior ones. Best practice needs to supplant antiquated methods and outmoded behaviours. We need to learn, and change is often a painful process.

In the study of groups it is recognized that there are three kinds of conflict: task, process and relationship.[20] Task conflict – disagreement about the task – is usually productive, when it is not infected by ego and emotion. Process conflict – disagreement about the rules, norms and procedures the group uses to conduct its tasks – is risky. Sometimes it is productive, sometimes destructive; it depends on the spirit with which it is engaged. Relationship conflict – disagreements about the value of people and their contributions – is almost invariably destructive. Research shows that these three types of conflict are very hard to disentangle. Sometimes families have an advantage here, because they accept their relationship differences more easily than people who are just working together.

In many of the cases we have seen here, there was a thin line that was overstepped in engaging in conflict. Had a better separation been achieved between these elements, many of them could have realized even more greatness than they did. And as we have remarked, it is a sign of the enormous capabilities of these firms that so many continue to thrive today. One could say that our review identifies the main casualties of family wars as the family and its involvement with the firm.

Family firms, to achieve glory, have to trade on features that are unique to them, and not shared with any other firms:[21]

- Co-ownership by a kinship group. This makes family firms close to our ancestral origins, where there was no rigid boundary dividing work and family. It is also what gives family firms such tremendous pride and spirit in their brand, their identity and their values.
- Inter-generational transmission of assets. Family firms have the benefit of long time horizons because they do not regard the firm as a bundle of assets to be simply chopped up, squeezed hard or disposed of, but rather as a legacy for future generations. This gives strength, confidence, range and purpose to all their planning.
- Teamwork between kin and non-kin. This is essential for a firm to grow, so the concept of the family has to be broad and embracing, able to involve and make best use of the talents of non-family.

This requires a confident and pragmatic approach to leadership – comprehensive in scope and skilled in execution. It means recognizing the family's limitations, and having a willingness to partner with people who bring different skills and perspectives.

Everything we have observed in our cases underlines these points. Family conflict will always be with us, but it doesn't have to turn into warfare and pull the house down.

Notes

CHAPTER 1: FAMILY WARS

1   See Andrea Colli, *The History of Family Business, 1850–2000* (Cambridge University Press, Cambridge UK, 2003); also M C Shanker and J H Astrachan, Myths and realities: Family businesses' contribution to the US economy: a framework for assessing family business statistics (*Family Business Review*, **9**, 1996, pp 107–24).

2   R C Anderson and D M Reeb, Founding family ownership and firm performance: evidence from the S&P 500 (*Journal of Finance*, **58**, 2003, pp 1301–26). See also D Sraer and D Thesmar, Performance and behavior of family firms, evidence from the French stock market (Working paper, CREST, Centre for Research in Economics and Statistics, France, 2004); and Panikkos Poutziouris, *The UK Family Business Plc Economy* (Institute for Family Business, London, 2006).

3   See The world's oldest family companies (*Family Business Magazine*, Winter 2003, pp 43–51). Also W T O'Hara and P Mandel, The world's oldest family companies (*Family Business Magazine*, Spring 2002, pp 37–49). (www.familybusinessmagazine.com).

4   See Harry Levinson, Conflicts that plague family businesses (*Harvard Business Review*, **45**, 1971, pp 90–98); also Manfred Kets de Vries, *Family Business: Human dilemmas in family firms* (International Thompson Business Press, London, 1996).

5   For example, Fred Neubauer and Alden G Lank, *The Family Business: Its governance and sustainability* (Macmillan, Basingstoke, 1998); and John L Ward, *Perpetuating the Family Business: 50 lessons learned from long-lasting successful families in business* (Palgrave Macmillan, Basingstoke, 2004).

CHAPTER 2: THE IDEAS – THE ROOTS OF FAMILY WARFARE

1   Also encouraged by both real and false optimism about winning: see Stephen Van Evera, *Causes of War: Power and the roots of conflict* (Cornell University Press, Ithaca, NY, 1999).

2   After one has factored in economic reasons, personalities and dynastic ambitions have played a part in the origins of warfare: see David S Landes, *The Wealth and Poverty of Nations* (W W Norton, New York, 1998).

3   For an account of the great family business dynasties see David S Landes, *Dynasties: Fortunes and misfortunes of the world's great family businesses* (Viking, New York, 2006).

4   'Familiness' is analysed from a resource-based theoretical perspective by T G Habbershon and M L Williams, A resource-based framework for assessing the strategic advantages of family firms (*Family Business Review*, **12**, 1999, pp 1–25); and T G Habbershon, M L Williams and I C MacMillan, A unified systems perspective on family firm performance (*Journal of Business Venturing*, **18**, 2003, pp 451–65).

5   For arguments on the superiority of family firm culture, see R Beckhard and W G Dyer, Managing change in the family firm – issues and strategies (*Sloan Management Review*, **16**, 1983, pp 59–65); and C M Daily and M J Dollinger, Family firms are different (*Review of Business*, **13**, 1991, pp 3–5).

6   See Danny Miller and Isabelle Le Breton-Miller, *Managing for the Long Run: Lessons in competitive advantage from great family businesses* (Harvard Business School Press, Boston, Mass, 2005); and D Denison, C Lief and J L Ward, Culture in family-owned enterprises: recognizing and leveraging unique strengths (*Family Business Review*, **17**, 2004, pp 61–70); also T A Beehr, J A Drexler and S Faulkner, Working in small family businesses: empirical comparisons to non-family businesses (*Journal of Organizational Behavior*, **18**, 1997, pp 297–312).

7   See R Tagiuri and J A Davis, Bivalent attributes of the family firm (*Family Business Review*, **9**, 1996, pp 199–208); also Nigel Nicholson and Åsa Björnberg, Familiness: fatal flaw or inimitable advantage? (*Families in Business*, March 2004, pp 52–54).

8   There has been a debate in the family business literature about the special liabilities, vulnerabilities and risks family firms face. These are highlighted by an agency theory perspective as hazards and temptations to bad decisions by family business owners. See W S Schulze, M H Lubatkin, R N Dino and A K Buchholtz, Agency relationships in family

firms: theory and evidence (*Organization Science*, **12**, 2001, pp 99–116); and W S Schulze, M H Lubatkin and R N Dino, Exploring the consequences of ownership dispersion among the directors of private family firms (*Academy of Management Journal*, **46**, 2003, pp 179–94).

9   However, an unfashionable but well-argued counterpoint in praise of nepotism can be found in Adam Bellow, *In Praise of Nepotism: A natural history* (Doubleday, New York, 2003).

10 See for example James M White and David M Klein, *Family Theories*, 2nd edn (Sage, Thousand Oaks, Calif, 2002).

11 The necessity for disruption and conflict for radical innovation is argued by Clayton Christensen in *The Innovator's Dilemma* (Harper Business Essentials, London, 1998). See also D Tjosfold, Cooperation and competitive goal approaches to conflict: accomplishments and challenges (*Applied Psychology*, **47**, 1998, pp 285–342).

12 For a comprehensive account of conflict in organizations see M Afzalur Rahim, *Managing Conflict in Organizations*, 3rd edn (Greenwood Press, Oxford, 2000).

13 See for example Alice H Eagly, Reuben M Baron and V Lee Hamilton (eds), *The Social Psychology of Group Identity and Social Conflict: Theory, application, and practice* (American Psychological Association, Washington, DC, 2004).

14 See Robert M Milardo and Steve Duck (eds) *Families as Relationships* (Wiley, Chichester, 2000).

15 Ernesto J Poza, *Smart Growth: Critical choices for family business continuity* (Jossey-Bass, Chichester, 1997).

16 See Sudipt Dutta, *Family business in India* (Response Books, New Delhi, 1997).

17 The tendency to over-attribute causes to persons and personality is called in psychology the 'fundamental attribution error': see L Ross, The intuitive psychologist and his shortcomings: distortions in the attribution process, in L Berkowitz (ed), *Advances in Experimental Social Psychology*, Vol 10 (Academic Press, New York, 1977).

18 See Roderick Kramer and Tom Tyler (eds), *Trust in Organizations* (Sage, Thousand Oaks, Calif, 1996).

19 See Dean G Pruitt and Jeffrey Z Rubin, *Social Conflict: Escalation, stalemate, and settlement* (Random House, London, 1996).

20 The ability to avoid conflict and solve problems by understanding other individuals' perspectives has been called 'decentring' by Nicholson (after Piaget). See Nigel Nicholson, How to motivate your problem people (*Harvard Business Review*, **81**, January 2003, pp 56–67).

21 See Jerry Greenberg and Jason A Colquitt, *Handbook of Organizational Justice* (Erlbaum, Mahwah, NJ, 2004).

22 This is a matter of people and their organizations having aligned or congruent expectations, what organizational psychologists call the 'psychological contract'. See Denise M Rousseau, *Psychological Contracts in Organizations: Understanding written and unwritten agreements* (Sage, Thousand Oaks, Calif, 1995).

23 Contract violation is regarded by evolutionary psychologists as a fundamental area of hard-wired human sensitivity. See Leda Cosmides and John Tooby, Cognitive adaptations for social exchange, in J H Barkow, L Cosmides and J Tooby (eds), *The Adapted Mind: Evolutionary psychology and the generation of culture* (Oxford University Press, Oxford, 1992).

24 See Carlfred B Broderick, *Understanding Family Process: Basics of family systems theory* (Sage, Thousand Oaks, Calif, 1993).

25 See Randel S Carlock, Ludo van der Heyden and Christine Blondel, Fair process: striving for justice in family business (*Family Business Review*, **18**, March 2005, pp 1–2).

26 Evolutionists have studied how social groups solve this problem. See Michael Price, John Tooby and Leda Cosmides, Punitive sentiment as an anti-free rider psychological device (*Evolution and Human Behavior*, **23**, 2002, pp 203–31).

27 Free-riding in work teams is called 'social loafing'. See Jayanth Narayanan and Madan M Pillutla, Social loafing, in N Nicholson, P Audia and M Pillutla (eds), *Blackwell Encylopedic Dictionary of Management: Organizational behavior* (Blackwell, Oxford, 2005).

28 See the agency theory research of Schulze *et al*, op cit; also Kelin E Gersick, John A Davis, Marion McCollom Hampton and Ivan Lansberg, *Generation to Generation* (Harvard Business School Press, Boston, Mass, 1997).

29 Attributed to the American pragmatist philosopher C S Peirce, 1839–1914.

30 See Gersick *et al, Generation to Generation* (op cit); and for a fuller exposition of the ideas in this section, Evolutionary psychology and family business: A new synthesis for theory, research and practice (*Family Business Review*, in press).

31 See Nigel Nicholson, Gene politics and the natural selection of leadership (*Leader to Leader*, 20, Spring 2001, pp 46–52).

32 See J N Davis and M Daly, Evolutionary theory and the human family (*Quarterly Review of Biology*, **72**, 1997, pp 407–25); and S T Emlen, An evolutionary theory of the family (*Proceedings of the National Academy of Sciences*, **92**, 1982, pp 8092–99).

33 For an authoritative account of modern Darwinism see Daniel C Dennett, *Darwin's Dangerous Idea: Evolution and the meanings of life* (Simon & Schuster, New York, 1995).

34 For an application of the ideas to business see Nigel Nicholson, *Managing the Human Animal* (Thomson Learning, London 2000).

35 This idea is called sexual selection in Darwinian theory. For an account of its relevance and importance to modern social life see Geoffrey F Miller, *The Mating Mind: How sexual choice shaped the evolution of human nature* (Heinemann, London, 2000).

36 This is a key concept in evolutionary psychology. For a clear non-technical account see Robert Wright, *The Moral Animal: Evolutionary psychology and everyday life* (Little, Brown, New York).

37 Richard Dawkins, *The Selfish Gene* (Oxford University Press, 1989); see also Stephen Pinker, *How the Mind Works* (Norton, New York, 1997).

38 See S J Silk, What humans adopt adaptively and why does it matter? (*Ethology and Sociobiology*, **11**, 1990, pp 425–26). However, stepchildren remain especially at risk, lacking protection of shared genes: for example, see Martin Daly and Margot Wilson, Violence against stepchildren (*Current Directions in Psychological Science*, **5**, 1996, pp 77–81).

39 See Martin Daly and Margot Wilson, The evolutionary psychology of marriage and divorce, in L Waite, M Hindin, E Thompson and W Axinn (eds), *Ties That Bind: Perspectives on marriage and cohabitation* (Aldine de Gruyter, Berlin, 2000).

40 See Diane Ackerman, *A Natural History of Love* (Random House, London, 1990); and two books by David M Buss, *The Evolution of Desire: Strategies for human mating* (Basic Books, New York, 1994), and *The Dangerous Passion: Why jealousy is as necessary as love or sex* (Bloomsbury, London, 2000).

41 See S Foley and G N Powell, Reconceptualizing work–family conflict for business/marriage partners, a theoretical model (*Journal of Small Business Management*, **35**, 1997, pp 36–47).

42 The hazards of copreneurship – husbands and wives working together – have been documented in M A Fitzgerald and G Muske, Copreneurs, An exploration and comparison to other family businesses (*Family Business Review*, **15**, 2002, pp 1–15).

43 See Cameron Anderson, Dacher Keltner and Oliver P John, Emotional convergence in close relationships (*Journal of Personality and Social Psychology*, **84**, 2003, pp 1054–68).

44 See Robert L Trivers, Parent–offspring conflict (*American Zoologist*, **14**, 1874, pp 249–64).

45 There is plentiful evidence for cross-cultural differences in parenting styles: for example, M H Bornstein and L R Cote, Mothers' parenting cognitions in cultures of origin, acculturating cultures, and cultures of destination (*Child Development*, **75**, 2004, pp 221–35).

46 See for example Ivan Lansberg, *Succeeding Generations* (Harvard Business School Press, Boston, Mass, 1999); also M H Morris, R O Williams and D Nel, Factors influencing family business succession

(*International Journal of Entrepreneurial Behavior and Research*, **2**, 1996, pp 68–81); and W C Handler, Succession in family business: a review of the research (*Family Business Review*, **7**, 1994, pp 133–57).

47 For a review of major approaches see Robert Sanders, *Sibling Relationships: Theory and issues for practice* (Palgrave Macmillan, Basingstoke, 2004). See also Stephen P Bank, and Michael D Kahn, *The Sibling Bond* (Basic Books, New York, 1982).

48 See Douglas W Mock, *More than Kin and Less than Kind: The evolution of family conflict* (Belknap Press of Harvard University Press, Cambridge, Mass, 2004).

49 See Sanders (op cit).

50 See Sanders (ibid).

51 See Sylvie McGoldrick and Randy Gerson, *Genograms in Family Assessment* (Norton, New York, 1985).

52 This argument about children adapting to the ecosystem of the family is most associated with the work of Frank Sulloway. See for example *Born to Rebel: Birth order, family dynamics and creative lives* (Pantheon, New York, 1996); Birth order, creativity, and achievement, in M A Runco and S Pritzker (eds), *Encyclopedia of Creativity* (Academic Press, New York, 1999); Birth order, sibling competition, and human behaviour, pp 39–83 in Harmon R Holcomb III (ed), *Conceptual Challenges in Evolutionary Psychology: Innovative research strategies* (Kluwer, Amsterdam, 2001).

53 Empirical evidence that application of the rule impairs the business performance has been found in a very careful and detailed study of a large Danish company database; see M Bennedsen, K M Nielsen, Pérez-González and D Wolfenzon, Inside the family firm: the role of families in succession decisions and performance, working paper 12356 (Cambridge, Mass, National Bureau of Economic Research, 2006).

54 See Frank Sulloway, *Born to Rebel* (op cit).

55 Birth order research is steeped in controversy. Effects are hard to detect in conventional personality instruments. This means that birth order shapes the adaptive strategies children adopt within the family and beyond, rather than personality traits.

56 See McGoldrick and Gerson (op cit). Family size also diffuses conflict. See Bank and Kahn (op cit).

57 See R Hertwig, J N Davis and F J Sulloway, Parental investment: how an equity motive can produce inequality (*Psychological Bulletin*, **128**, 2002, pp 728–45).

58 Derived from E E Maccoby and J A Martin, Socialization in the context of the family: parent–child interaction, pp 1–101 in E M Hetherington (ed), *Handbook of Child Psychology Vol 4, Socialization, Personality and Social Development*, 4th edn (Wiley, Chichester, 1983).

59 See D H Olson and D H Gorall, Circumplex model of marital and family systems, pp 524–48 in F Walsh (ed), *Normal Family Processes*, 3rd edn (Guilford, New York, 2003).

60 See Salvador Minuchin, *Families and Family Therapy* (Tavistock, London, 1974); also Teresa M Cooney, Parent–child relations across adulthood, in R M Milardo and Steve Duck (eds), *Families as Relationships* (Wiley, Chichester, 2000).

61 See Minuchin (ibid).

62 Attributed to the psychoanalyst Carl Gustav Jung.

63 The concept of script is usually associated with transactional analysis, a development of psychoanalytic theory around the adoption of 'parent', 'adult' and 'child' roles in relationships. See Claude M Steiner, *Scripts to Live By: Transactional analysis of life scripts* (Grove Press, New York, 1974). See also Robert P Abelson, Psychological status of the script concept (*American Psychologist*, **36**, 1981, pp 715–29).

64 See Nigel Nicholson and Åsa Björnberg, *Ready, Willing and Able? The next generation in family business* (Institute for Family Business, London, 2007).

65 See Teresa Cooney, Parent–child relations across adulthood (op cit).

66 Developed theoretically and empirically through the development of six scales measuring these dimensions, by Åsa Björnberg and Nigel Nicholson: see The Family Climate Scales: development of a new measure for use in family business research (*Family Business Review*, **20**, pp 229–46).

67 See Olsen *et al* (op cit); also W R Beavers and M N Voeller, Family models: contrasting the Olson circumplex model with the Beavers systems model (*Family Process*, **22**, 1983, pp 85–98).

68 See Pauline Boss, *Family Stress Management: A contextual approach*, 2nd edn (Sage, Thousand Oaks, Calif, 2002).

69 Evolutionists call this process 'assortative mating'. See for example David M Buss, Marital assortment for personality dispositions: assessment with three different data sources (B*ehavior Genetics*, **14**, 1984, pp 111–23). See also Virginia Blankenship, Steven M Hnat, Thomas G Hess and Donald R Brown, Reciprocal interaction and similarity of personality attributes (*Journal of Social and Personal Relationships*, **1**, 1984, pp 415–32).

70 The idea that peers have a major influence over personality development has been advanced by Judith Rich Harris in *The Nurture Assumption: Why children turn out the way they do* (Free Press, New York, 1998).

71 See for example Alan P Fiske, *Structures of Social Life: The four elementary forms of human relations* (Free Press, New York, 1993); and

Emmanuel Todd, *The Explanation of Ideology: Family structures and social systems* (Blackwell, Oxford, 1985).

72 See E W Markson, *Social Gerontology Today: An introduction* (Roxbury, Los Angeles, Calif, 2003).

73 See Robert Hogan, John Johnson and Stephen Briggs, *Handbook of Personality Psychology* (Academic Press, New York, 1997); also Gerald Matthews, Ian J Deary and Martha C Whiteman, *Personality Traits*, 2nd edn (Cambridge University Press, Cambridge UK, 2002).

74 See J M Digman, Personality structure: emergence of the five-factor model (*Annual Review of Psychology*, **41**, 1990, pp 417–40); and Kevin MacDonald, Evolution, the five-factor model, and levels of personality (*Journal of Personality*, **63**, 1994, pp 525–67). See also Matthews *et al*, *Personality Traits* (op cit).

75 See D T Lykken, M McGue, A Tellegen and T J Bouchard, Emergenesis: genetic traits that may not run in families (*American Psychologist*, **47**, 1992, pp 1565–77); and J C Loehlin, R R McCrae, P T Costa and O P John, Heritabilities of common and measure-specific components of the Big Five personality factors (*Journal of Research in Personality*, **32**, 1998, pp 431–53).

76 These are called non-additive genes; see R Ilies, R D Arvey and T J Bouchard, Darwinism, behavioral genetics, and organizational behaviour: a review and agenda for future research (*Journal of Organizational Behavior*, **27**, 2006, 121–41).

77 See Andreas Rauch and Michael Frese, Born to be an entrepreneur? Revisiting the personality approach to entrepreneurship, in R J Baum, M Frese and R Baron, *The Psychology of Entrepreneurship* (Lawrence Erlbaum, Mahwah, NJ, 2007).

CHAPTER 3: BROTHERS AT ARMS

1 Primary sources for this case study were: Koch family foundations, 2004 (available from: http://www.fact-index.com/k/ko/koch_family_foundations.html); CBS News, Blood and oil, 2001 (available from: http://www.cbsnews.com/stories/2000/11/27/60II/ main252545.shtml); *Forbes Magazine*, Forbes faces: the Koch brothers, 2001 (available from: http://www.forbes.com/2001/01/04/0104faces); J Grant, The private empire of Koch Industries (*Financial Times*, 30 January 2004, p 8); Koch Family Foundations, Koch family foundations, 2004 (available from: http://www.fact-index.com/k/ko/koch_family_foundations.html); *Lawrence Journal-World* (2000) Kochs end family feud, 2000, (available

from: http://www.ljworld.com/section/stateregional/storypr/31316);
Brian O'Reilly, The curse of the Koch brothers (*Fortune Magazine*, 17
February 1997, pp 78–84); Robert Tomsho, Blood feud: Koch family
is roiled by sibling squabbling over its oil empire (*Wall Street Journal*,
Eastern edn, 9 August 1989, p 1); B Williams and K Bogardus, Koch's
low profile belies political power (Center for Public Integrity, 2004,
available from: http://www.publicintegrity.org/oil).

2   Readers should note that these genograms are simplified, to map the
main relationships that figure in the narrative. They are not exhaustive
family trees.

3   See Show me the money (*Economist*, 6 May 2006, p 55); Obituary: Anna
Nicole Smith (*Economist*, 17 February 2007, p 93).

4   See Williams Bogardus (op cit).

5   Primary sources for this case study were: The Reliance Group split-
up: what went wrong with the Indian conglomerate? (Case study ref
no 305-394-1; ICFAI Business School Case Development Centre,
2005); Indu and V Gupta, The Reliance Group saga (Case study ref
no 305-474-1, ICFAI Center for Management Research, 2005); A S
Patel and A V Vedpuriswar, The turmoil at Reliance (Case study ref
no 305-582-1, ICFAI Business School 2005); A V Vedpuriswar and
V Pattabhiram, Reliance industries: the dispute between Mukesh and
Anil Ambani (part A) (Case study ref no. 705-003-1, ICFAI Knowledge
Center, 2005).

    Other sources used for this case study were: Primogeniture rules, Ok?
(*Economist*, 27 November 2004, p 87); Hand rocks cradle (*Economist*,
25 June 2005, pp 78–81; The Lex column: Asian family businesses
(*Financial Times*, 18 July 2005); M Kripalani, How to divvy up a \$22.5
billion empire (*Business Week*, 4 July 2005, pp 44–45); E Luce and K
Merchant, Reliance brothers in dispute over group's ownership (*Financial
Times*, 19 November 2002); E Luce, Brothers urged to settle feud over
Reliance (*Financial Times*, 7 January 2005); Tussle over Reliance enters
political sphere (*Financial Times*, 25 February 2005); K Merchant, Indian
group soars despite power struggle (*Financial Times*, 26 November
2004), Anil Ambani quits job at IPCL (*Financial Times*, 4 January 2005,
p 21); Reliance deal means group will be split (*Financial Times*, 20 June
2005); Corporate India keeps power in the family (*Financial Times*, 12
July 2005); Board of Reliance approves peace deal (*Financial Times*,
8 August 2005); A Shukla, Mother to settle feud at Reliance (*Sunday
Times*, 9 January 2005).

6   These details are documented in the ICFAI Business School Case,
Reliance Group saga (op cit).

7   The primary source for this case study was Barbara Smit, *Pitch Invasion: Adidas, Puma and the making of modern sport* (Penguin, London, 2006). Other sources used were: Adi Dassler – the man who gave Adidas its name (Adidas.com 2007, available from: http://www.press.adidas. com/ en/DesktopDefault.aspx/tabid-49–41_read-1203); Sneaker pimps (Easyjetflight.com, 2006, available from: http://easyjetflight.com/ features/2006/aug/saneaker.html); T Hagler, German feud inspires boots town (bbc.co.uk, 2006, available from: http://www.bbc.co.uk/go/pr/fr/ -/1/hi/world/europe/5055542.stm); R Milne, Fancy footwork (*Financial Times*, 6 May 2006).

8   The primary source for this case study was Robert Mondavi, *Harvests of Joy* (Harcourt Brace, San Diego, Calif, 1998). Other sources were: J Ashworth, California wine celebrity seeks friends in Europe (*The Times*, 14 December 2002); N Buckley, Constellation bids for Robert Mondavi (*Financial Times*, 20 October 2004, p 25); T Fish, Mondavi to sell La Famiglia winery, but keep the brand (winespectator.com, 2001, available from: http://www.winespectator.com/Wine/Daily/News/0,1145,1384,00. html;) J Flynn, Grapes of wrath; inside a Napa valley empire (*Wall Street Journal*, Eastern edn, 3 June 2004, p A1); E Hawkes, Mondavi family values (1998, available from: http://www.findarticles.com/p/articles/ mi_m3514/is_12_45/ai_53379158); R F Howe, The fall of the house of Mondavi (*Business 2.0 San Francisco*, **6** (3), April 2005, p 98); Robert Mondavi winery (International Recipes Online, 2004, available from: http://www.internationalrecipesonline.com/recipes/dictionary.pl?5829); J Laube, Mondavi buys Arrowood for $45 million (winespectator.com, 2000, available from: http://www.winespectator.com/Wine/Daily/ News_Print/0,2463,1115,00.html); Robert Mondavi announces major restructuring (winespectator.com, 2003, available from: http://www. winespectator.com/Wine/Daily/News_Print /0,1145,2020,00.html); P-H Mansson, Mondavi gives up on Languedoc project (winespectator.com, 2001, available from: http://www.winespectator.com/Wine/Daily/News_ Print/ 0,2463,432,00. html).

9   The three components of emotional intelligence are a) identifying emotions: the ability to recognize one's own feelings and the feelings of others, b) using emotions: the ability to access an emotion and reason with it, and c) understanding emotions: the ability to identify and comprehend the transition of one emotion to another. See M Zeidner, G. Matthews and R D Roberts, Emotional intelligence in the workplace: a critical review (*Applied Psychology*, **53**, 2004, pp 371–99).

10 The primary source for this case study was Ellen Hawkes, *Blood & Wine: The unauthorized story of the Gallo wine empire* (Simon & Schuster, New York, 1993). Other sources used for this case study were: Family

feud (Bathroomcompanion.com, 2004, available from: http://www. bathroomcompanion.com/gallo.html); R Bradford, It's never easy to change your image in the wine industry (beveragebusiness.com, 1999, available from: http://www.beveragebusiness.com/art-arch/07bradford. html); G Hyman, 2001 achievement awards (jamesbeard.org, 2002, available from: http://www.jamesbeard.org/awards/2001/ achievement. shtml); The curse of the house of Gallo (*Independent*, 3 March 2007); D Rushe, California dream is reality for wine firm (*Sunday Times* (Business), 7 May 2006, pp 3.1 & 3.9); R B Scmitt, Ernest and Julio win family feud over Gallo name (*Wall Street Journal* Eastern edn, 21 June 1989, p 1); L B Zimmerman, Reinventing Gallo (*Market Watch*, November/December, 2004, pp 36–46).

11 Ellen Hawkes (op cit) details a lawsuit filed on 31 July 1986 (p 133).

CHAPTER 4: FIGHTING FOR THE CROWN

1 See Lansberg, *Succeeding Generations* (op cit), and Morris *et al*, 1996 (op cit).

2 David Saltman, Global heavyweight (*Chief Executive*, August–September 2003).

3 See our comments in Chapter 2 about the biological basis for parent-offspring conflict.

4 Wealth heightens agency problems. These are discussed in Chapter 2; see Schulze *et al*, Agency relationships in family firms (op cit).

5 The negative effects of retirement are well known. See for example T L Gall, D R Evans, D R Howard and J Howard, The retirement adjustment process: changes in the well-being of male retirees across time (*Journals of Gerontology*, **52**, 1997, pp 110–17); S V Kasl and B.A. Jones, The impact of job loss and retirement on health, in L Berkman and I Kawachi (eds), *Social Epidemiology* (Oxford University Press, Oxford, 2000).

6 Problems of letting go, and consequences of the different modes of departure of CEOs, are examined in Jeffery Sonnenfeld, *The Hero's Farewell: What happens when CEOs retire* (Oxford University Press, Oxford, 1988).

7 Research at London Business School found little preparation among many leaders at or around retirement age. See Nigel Nicholson, *Leadership, Culture and Change in UK Family Firms* (BDO Stoy Centre for Family Business, London, 2003).

8 See Nigel Nicholson and Åsa Björnberg, Familiness: fatal flaw or inimitable advantage? (op cit).

9 In a study released in July 2006 researchers found that family firms where succession passes to non-family members financially outperform firms where the family takes over management; see Bennedsen *et al*, Inside the family firm (op cit).

10 Henkel was the winner of the IMD-Lombard Odier Darier Hentsch Distinguished Family Business Award in 1999.

11 See Nicole Laporte, Patty digs for Hearst secrets (*Variety*, 26 April 2005).

12 The primary sources for the McCain case study were: Paul Waldie, *A House Divided: The untold story of the McCain family* (Viking, Toronto, 1996); and Michael Woloschuk, *Family Ties: The real story of the McCain feud* (Key Porter, Toronto, 1995). Other sources were: D Berman, Hold the fries (*Canadian Business*, **71** (1), 30 January 1998, p 32); Frozen food, family feud (Cbc.ca, 1998, available from: http://www.tv.cbc.ca/ newsinreview/octpercent2099/Eatons/family.html); McCain business empire has deep roots (CBSNews, 2004, available from: http://www. cbc.ca/stories/print/2004/03/19/ mccainbiz_040319); B Dalglish, Family feud (*Macleans* (Toronto), **106** (36), 6 September 1993, p 32); R Lucie, Obituary: Harrison McCain dies (*Globe and Mail*, 19 March 2004); Letters: Family mistake (*Economist*, 7 June 2003, p 14); P C Newman, Feud of the century: a McCain speaks out (*Macleans* (Toronto), **107** (39), 26 September 1994, p 29); Tales from a mellower Harrison McCain (*Macleans* (Toronto), **111** (3), 19 January 1998, p 50); McCain foods names new chief executive following family feud (*Wall Street Journal*, Eastern edn, 2 March 1995, p B12).

13 Waldie (op cit) interviewed both Harrison and Wallace and found them helpful. He quotes Wallace as recalling, 'All my life Harrison has been telling me "Don't do it. Don't trust your wife or your kids. Don't trust people"' (p 140).

14 Reported by Michael Woloschuk (op cit, p 154).

15 Waldie (op cit) reports Harrison wrote in notes: 'Michael has never made a nickel for us in his life' and that he told Wallace that Michael didn't have enough experience.

16 See *The Raymond Report, 11th edition: Focus on the American family business survey* (Raymond Institute, 17 March 2003). For a more general scholarly discussion of the issue of shared leadership, see José Luis Alvarez and Silviya Svejenova, *Sharing Executive Power* (Cambridge University Press, Cambridge UK, 2005) and Nigel Nicholson and Åsa Björnberg, Critical leader relationships in family firms, in P Poutziouris, K X Smyrnios and S B Klein (eds), *Handbook of Research in Family Business* (Edward Elgar, Chichester, 2006).

17 The primary sources for this case study were: Richard S Tedlow, *The Watson Dynasty* (Harper Business, New York, 2003); Thomas J Watson

Jr and Peter Petre, *Father Son & Co: My life at IBM and beyond* (Bantam, New York, 1990).

18 The primary sources for this case study were: *Bata Shoe Organization (A)* (ECCH, IMD-3-1084, GM1084, International Institute for Management Development, 2002); *Bata Shoe Organization (B)* (Ecch, IMD-3-1085,GM1085, 2002). Other sources were: Thomas Bata: shoemaker to the world (CIC Canada, 2002, available from: http://www.cic.gc.ca/english/department/legacy/chap-4b.html); Thomas Bata (Fact-index.com, 2004, available from: http://www.fact-index.com/t/th/thomas_bata.html); B Wickens, Bata shoe museum opens (*Macleans*, 15 May 1995).

19 See the detailed account to be found in the IMD case report, ECCH (op cit).

CHAPTER 5: THE HOUSE THAT HUBRIS BUILT

1 See Rauch and Frese, Born to be an entrepreneur? (op cit).

2 Business leader failure through unbalanced qualities is termed 'derailment'. See Jean Brittain, Leslie Van Velsor and Ellen Van Velsor, *A Look at Derailment Today: North America and Europe* (Center for Creative Leadership, Greensboro, NC, 1995).

3 Belinda Jane Board and Katarina Fritzon, Disordered personalities at work (*Psychology, Crime and Law*, **11**, 2004, pp 17–35).

4 Definitions of 'personality disorders' as well as the number identified can vary. See Matthews *et al*, Emotional intelligence in the workplace (op cit) for a discussion of them.

5 One of the penalties of success: individuals with high self-esteem, enhanced by prior success, are insensitive to cues that they are failing. See M H Kernis, M Zuckerman, A Cohen, A Spadafora and S Spadafora, Persistence following failure: the interactive role of self-awareness and the attributional basis for negative expectancies (*Journal of Personality and Social Psychology*, **43**, 1982, pp.1184–91); Adam Di Paula and Jennifer D Campbell, Self-esteem and persistence in the face of failure (*Journal of Personality and Social Psychology*, **83**, pp. 711–24).

6 The dark side of charisma is documented in Jay A Conger, *The Charismatic Leader: Behind the mystique of exceptional leadership* (Jossey-Bass, Chichester, 1989). See also Jean Lipman-Blumen, *The Allure of Toxic Leaders: Why we follow destructive bosses and corrupt politicians – and how we can survive them* (Oxford University Press, Oxford, 2006). For a more general treatise on male aggression see Donald G Dutton,

The Abusive Personality: Violence and control in intimate relationships (Guilford, New York, 1998).

7   The primary source for this case study was Peter Collier and David Horowitz, *The Fords: An American epic* (Encounter Books, San Francisco, 2002). Other sources used were: One hell of a birthday, Bill (*Economist*, 14 June 2003, p 75); J Grant, Control traits continue to run in the family (*Financial Times*, 12 June 2003, p 30) ; J Mackintosh and J Grant, Ford approaches 100 with optimism (*Financial Times*, 12 June 2003, p 30); David Magee, *Ford Tough: Bill Ford and the battle to rebuild America's automaker* (Wiley, Chichester, 2005).

8   The case study draws on the following sources: T Agins, Dart group's chief faces another battle as family splinters (*Wall Street Journal*, Eastern edn, 6 July 1993, p B2); Dart chairman takes further steps to distance his son from two businesses (*Wall Street Journal*, Eastern edn, 6 July 1993, p B5); M Baker, Herbert Haft seeks to justify his firing of son from Dart (*Wall Street Journal*, Eastern edn, 12 September 1994, p A11); Rachel L Dodes, Drugstore cowboys (*Washington Business Forward*, 2001, available from: http://www.bizforward.com/wdc/issues/ 2001–05/drugstore); S L Hwang, Herbert Haft fired in ouster led by his son (*Wall Street Journal*, Eastern edn, 6 September 1994, p A3); Son of Dart group's Haft ousted from Crown board (*Wall Street Journal*, Eastern edn, 1 July 1993, p B2).

9   HealthQuick.com ceased trading in 1999 and Vitamins.com in 2000.

10   See Iris Aaltio-Marjosola and Jyri Lehtinen, Male managers as fathers? Contrasting management, fatherhood, and masculinity (*Human Relations*, **51**, 1998, pp 121–35); also John Rowan, Men and women are different – official (*British Journal of Guidance and Counselling*, **25**, 2006, pp 539–43).

11   The case draws on the following sources: M Campbell, Sweet wine turns to sour grapes in Sauternes (*Sunday Times*, 6 February 2005); J C Donnelly Jr, Shareholder disagreements in closely held companies: breaking up is hard to do (*Boston Business Journal*, 7–14 November 1997); W Echikson and P Smith, A vineyard's bitter fruit (*Business Week*, 13 November 2000); J Johnson, Wine dynasty ends its 400-year tenure (*Financial Times*, 27 May 2004, p 12); P-H Mansson, Battle over Chateau d'Yquem ends with LVMH as new owner (winespectator. com, 999, available from: http://www.winespectator.com/Wine/ Archives/ Show_Article_Print/0,2469,2200,00.html); Yquem replaces longtime head with managing director of Cheval-Blanc (winespectator. com, 2004, available from: http://www.winespectator.com/ Wine/ Daily/News/ 0,1145,2474,00.html); J Stimpfig, The white knuckle ride (*Financial Times, How to Spend It* magazine, February 2005, pp 8–10);

Chateau d'Yquem (Winejournal.com, 2004, available from: http://wine-journal.com.yquem.html).

12 This case draws on the following sources: Mel Karmazin (Answers.com, 2007, available from: http://www.answers.com/topic/mel-karmazin); and Sumner Redstone, 2007 (available from: http://www.answers.com/ topic/ sumner-redstone); Redstone's son sues family-run firm (CNNMoney. com, 2006, available from: http://money.cnn.com/ 2006/02/15/news/ newsmakers/redstone); The dog days of Sumner (*Economist*, 9 September 2006, p .76); Redstones are in court over family business (*Family Business Advisor*, 2005, available from: www.efamilybusiness. com); R Siklos, Like father, like son: recipe for a family brawl (*New York Times*, 19 February 2006); M Wolff, Sumner squall, 2001 (available from: http://www.newyorkmetro.com/nymetro/news/media/ columns/ medialife/5696).

13 The primary source for this case study was W Lilley, The scrap of their lives (*Globe and Mail*, 30 January 2004). Other sources were: F Bowman and M L Thomas, Favouring auditor protection (CA magazine, September 2004); J McCann, Court ruling on Waxman family row upheld (*American Metal Market*, 5 May 2004); Scrap saga continues: court freezes Waxman's finances (*American Metal Market*, 16 November 2004); J McInitzer, The Waxman litigation (*Lexpert*, June 2003).

14 This material is drawn from the legal commentary to be found in J McInitzer (op cit).

15 This was recollected and reported in an interview with Michael; see W Lilley (op cit).

CHAPTER 6: HEADS IN THE SAND – THE INSULARITY TRAP

1 See F J Neyer and FR Lang, Blood is thicker than water: kinship orientation across adulthood (*Journal of Personality and Social Psychology*, **84**, 2003, pp 310–21).

2 This is one of the arguments advanced in Adam Bellow's *In Praise of Nepotism* (op cit).

3 See Nigel Nicholson, Evolutionary psychology and family business: a new synthesis for theory, research and practice (*Family Business Review*, op cit)

4 The primary sources for this case study were Jonathan Guinness, *Requiem for a Family Business* (Pan, London, 1998); Derek A Wilson,

Dark and Light: The story of the Guinness family (Orion, London, 1999). Other sources were J Eaglesham, Guinness heir at odds with new meritocracy (*Financial Times*, 30 January 2007); A Neustatter, Relative values – Hugo Guinness (*Sunday Times Magazine*, 16 May 2004); The story of Guinness (Webpages.edu, 2004, available from: http://webpages.marshall.edu/bennett7/guinness/ guinstor.htm).

5   Jonathan Guinness pursued the early part of his career in merchant banking In 1968 he left the City, moving to the countryside where he took up farming, writing, politics and other pursuits. See J Guinness, op cit.

6   See Pino G Audia, Edwin A Locke and Ken G Smith, The paradox of success: an archival and a laboratory study of strategic persistence following radical environmental change (*Academy of Management Journal*, **43**, 2000, pp 837–53).

7   See the discussion of agency problems in Chapter 2, and the work of Schulze and colleagues (op cit).

8   The primary source for this case study was Jane Wolfe, *Blood Rich: When oil billions, high fashion, and royal intimacies are not enough* (Little, Brown, Boston, 1993). Other sources were: Natalie Ornish, *Pioneer Jewish Texans* (Texas Heritage, 1989); E Smith, What ever happened to Robert Sakowitz (*Texas Monthly Biz*, March 1999, p 10).

9   See Jane Wolfe (op cit), p 188.

10 Wolfe (op cit, p 182) recounts how he generated $6 million from these dealings.

11 The primary source for this case study was Ann Gibbon and Peter Hadekel, *Steinberg: The breakup of a family empire* (Macmillan of Canada, Toronto, 1990). Other sources were: Steinbergs (Wikipedia, 2004, available from: http://en.wikipedia.org/wiki/ Steinbergs); Dan Rottenberg, Saul Steinberg and abusive boss syndrome (*Family Business*, Winter 2001, p 9); Michael J Roberts, Sam Steinberg (Harvard Business School, Case 392044, 1992).

12 See also the detailed account of the personalities in this case to be found in Manfred Kets de Vries, *Family Business: Human dilemmas in the family firm* (International Thomson Business Press, New York, 1996).

13 Peter McGoldrick resigned in March 1984, following a deep discount promotion at Steinbergs that did not yield the expected results in terms of market share. It precipitated a fall in annual profits, plunging to $13.4 million in 1983, their lowest since 1975. Unable to project strong leadership, especially in the face of Mitzi, his term of office was short lived, and he served only 17 months. See Gibbon and Hidakel (op cit), p 132.

14 See Gibbon and Hadekel (op cit), p 181.

15 The primary sources for this case study were David Leon Chandler and Mary Voelz Chandler, *The Binghams of Louisville* (Crown, New York, 1987); Susan E Tiffet and Alex S Jones, *The Patriarch: The rise and fall of the Bingham dynasty* (Summit, New York, 1991). Other sources were: Barry Bingham Jr pleads for the return of his daughter (*Courier-Journal*, Louisville, Ky, 1 April 2003); Barry Bingham Jr collapses in Boston (*Courier-Journal*, Louisville, Ky, 6 May 2004); Family feuds: the fall of the house of Bingham, (Courttv.com, 2003, available from: http://www.courttv.com/news/feature/familyfeud/familyfeud_ctv.html); Family business – special family companies (Familybusiness magazine.com, 2004, available from: http://www.familybusinessmagazine.com/hallofshame.html); J C Shifman, Shirt sleeves to shirt sleeves in three generations (tnorthadvisors.com, 2004, available from: http://www.tnorthadvisors.com/pages/ art_shirtsleeves.htm). See also John L Ward, *Perpetuating the Family Business* (op cit).

16 These events are detailed in Tiffet and Jones (op cit, p 359).

17 See Tiffet and Jones, p 330.

18 The primary source for this case study was Nicholas Faith, *The Bronfmans: The rise and fall of the House of Seagram* (St Martins Press, New York, 2006). Other sources were: T Burt, Viacom plays down interest in Vivendi assets (*Financial Times*, 6 June 2003, p 31); Bronfman turns the tables (*The Business*, 30 November /1 December 2003, p 19); Warner music to be sold for $26b (CNN Money, 2003, available from: http://money.cnn.com/2003/11/24/news/companies/warner_music); Better luck this time? (*Economist*, 29 November 2003, p 86); D Jaffe, Dutiful sons: how to succeed as heir to a great entrepreneur (*Families in Business*, November/December 2004, p 47); J Johnson, Family pride is the prize for the Bronfman clan (*Financial Times*, 28 August 2003, p 10); Bronfman pair leave Vivendi (*Financial Times*, 5 December 2003); B Milner, The unmaking of a dynasty (*Cigar Aficionado*, March/April 2003); L Zehr, Outcast nephews of Seagrams founder build new dynasty in Edper investments (*Wall Street Journal*, Eastern edn, 5 November 1984, p 1).

19 This is drawn from the detailed account provided by Faith (op cit, p 232).

20 The father–son relationship, and problems with succession seem to be inversely related to the age gap between them See John A Davis and Renato Tagiuri, The influence of life-stage on father–son work relationship in family companies (*Family Business Review*, **2**, 1989, pp 47–74).

CHAPTER 7: SCHISM – THE HOUSE DIVIDED

1   This is a subset of the more generic phenomenon of the fundamental attribution error, where causes are attributed to persons rather than circumstantial causes. See Ross, The intuitive psychologist and his shortcomings (op cit).

2   This is the free-rider or social loafing problem, discussed in Chapter 2.

3   For a discussion of the symbolic value of money see Mark Oleson, Exploring the relationship between money attitudes and Maslow's hierarchy of needs (*International Journal of Consumer Studies*, **28**, pp 83–92).

4   See Mass Mutual report at http://www.massmutual.com/mmfg/pdf/afbs.pdf.

5   The primary sources for this case study were S Andrews, Shattered dynasty (*Vanity Fair*, May 2003, pp 110–13 and 159–64); S Chandler and K Bergen, Inside the Pritzker family feud (*Chicago Tribune*, 12 June 2005). Other sources were: D Churchill, Family fortunes (*Business Travel World*, November 2005, p 15); P Damian, Court stalls deal to pay Pritzkers (*American Banker*, **170** (6), 2 August 2005, p 3); S Fitch, Pritzker vs Pritzker (*Forbes Global*, **6** (22), 24 November 2003, pp 34–40); Liesel Pritzker suit gets go-ahead (Forbes Global, 2004, available from: http://www.forbes.com/2004/03/05/cz_sf_0305pritzker_print.html); M Garrahan and D Cameron, We could go public, we could merge – Hyatt opens its doors to fresh ideas (*Financial Times*, 10 April 2006, p 15); Hyatt hints at move towards listing (*Financial Times*, 10 April 2006, p 23); J Grant, Youngest cousin puts spotlight on Pritzkers (*Financial Times*, 13 December 2002, p 29); D T Jaffe, The Pritzker problem (*Families in Business*, September/October 2003, pp 78–79); C S N Lewis, Family feuds: the ties that bind – and sue (courttvcom, 2003, available from: http://www.courttv.com/news/feature/familyfeud/familyfeud_ctv.html); M Maremont, Court documents present insight into breakup of Pritzker empire (*Wall Street Journal*, Eastern edn, 11 January 2006, p A3); P Stibbard, Family business succession (*Private Banking Newsletter*, Baker and McKenzie, May 2003, pp 1–5); M Straka, The Princess and the pea-brained lawsuit (foxnewscom, 2002, available from: http://www.foxnews.com/printer_friendly_story/0,3566,72170,00.html; J Weber, The house of Pritzker (*Business Week*, 17 March 2003).

6   S Andrews (op cit) reports that a family friend said that his brothers resented it when Tom would not let them use the Falcon 900 jet, and that they felt that Tom was arrogant.

7   The settlement was supposed to be secret but details were soon leaked, as discussed in S Andrews (op cit, p 163).

8   For a discussion of the unique challenges of family business leadership see Nigel Nicholson and Åsa Björnberg, *Family Business Leadership Inquiry* (Institute for Family Business, London, 2005).

9   The primary source for this case study was Dennis McDougal, *Privileged Son: Otis Chandler and the rise and fall of the L.A. Times dynasty* (Perseus, Cambridge, Mass, 2001). Other sources were: R Andersen, Privileged son (robinandersen.info, 2002, available from: http://www. robinandersen.info/Otis.htm); Obituary: Otis Chandler (*Economist*, 4 March 2006); Paying tribute (*Economist*, 24 June 2006); M Garrahan and A Van Duyn, News corp joins forces with Chandlers in bid for Tribune (*Financial Times*, 24 January 2007, p 17); Chandler family could reclaim *Los Angeles Times* as part of shrewd bid for Tribune Co (*International Herald Tribune*, 19 January 2007); S Meisler, The return of Otis (stanleymeisler.com,1999, available from: http://www. stanleymeisler.com/news–commentary/otis.html); J Rainey and T S Mulligan, Chandlers divided over bid for Tribune (*LA Times*, 13 November 2006); Chandlers, moguls in battle for Tribune (*LA Times*, 18 January 2007); R Rodriguez, Chandlers go the way of all family dynasties in California (Pacific News Service, 14 March 2000).

10   The sources used in this case study were: J Crosby, P J Trotter and J Sonenshine, Hoiles v. superior court 157 CA3d 1192, Civ 30701 (Court of Appeals of California, Fourth Appellate District, Division Three, 1984); Freedom Communications, Hoiles family close deal (*Dow Jones International*, 19 May 2004); J Hirsch, Freedom director quits to protest move to seek bids (*LA Times*, 24 April 2003); Freedom Communications to discuss sale(Mediaweek.com, 2003, available from: http://mediaweek. printthis.clickability.com/pt/cpt?action=cpt&title=Freedom+communic ations); M A Milbourn, Freedom closes $2 billion deal with investors (*Orange County Register*, 19 May 2004); Can the Freedom format settle other family feuds? (*Mergers and Acquisitions*, **38** (12), December 2003, p 12); J Steinberg and A R Sorkin, Freedom communications pulled into a family fight (*New York Times*, 19 August 2003).

11   The sources used in this case study were: Patak family feud is settled (BBC News, 2004, available from: http://newsvote.bbc.co.uk/mpapps/ pagetools/print/news.bbc.co.uk/1/hi/england/lancashire/3645775stm); Family takes food feud to court (CNNcom, 2004, available from: http:// www.cnn.com/2004/WORLD/europe/03/03/britain.foodfeud.ap); J Lawless, Too much heat in a famous family kitchen (*The Advertiser*, Adelaide, 6 March 2004); A Lee, Masala family feud ends in settlement (*Straits Times*, 23 April 2004); Patak's family feud is settled (Rediff.com,

2004, available from: http://www.rediff.com/money/2004/apr/ 21patak. com); L Smith, Spice wars end with £8 million peace treaty (*The Times*, 22 April 2004, p 3); N Tait, Payment likely to end Pathak pickle (*Financial Times*, 22 April 2004, p 3); New lull in legal battle over spices empire (*Financial Times*, 29 July 2005, p 5).

12 As reported in the *Financial Times* (N Tait, op cit).

CHAPTER 8: UN-CIVIL WAR

1 It is well known that people are liable to escalate their commitments, including into conflict, the more so the greater the sunk costs. See Barry M. Staw, Knee-deep in big muddy: a study of escalating commitment to a chosen course of action (*Organizational Behavior and Human Performance*, **16**, 1976, pp 27–44).

2 The primary source for this case study is Ronald J Watkins, *Birthright: Murder, greed, and power in the U-Haul family dynasty* (William Morrow, New York, 1993). Other sources used were: R Tomsho, Dynasty undone: U-Haul's patriarch now battles offspring in bitterest of feuds (*Wall Street Journal*, Eastern edn, 16 July 1990, p A1); U-Haul heir wife slain; inquiry focuses on feud (*Wall Street Journal*, Eastern edn, 8 August 1990, p A4); Five AMERCO directors in judgement make chapter 11 filings (*Wall Street Journal*, Eastern edn, 23 February 1995, p C13).

3 For details of the Shoen family life at this juncture, and elsewhere in the story, we are heavily reliant upon Watkins' account (op cit), which drew upon extensive interview material, but without the cooperation or participation of Joe and Mark. Suzanne also was not interviewed. Since L S was a beneficiary of Watkins' publication, receiving a share of royalties, we must factor in both partiality and incompleteness of the testimonies recorded in Watkins' book. In other words there are probably several possible perspectives on this story, as there are in any conflict scenario.

4 Letters quoted in Watkins (op cit), p 134.

5 The doctor is quoted in Watkins (op cit), p 145.

6 Reported by Paul Rubin, Hit the road, Daddy (*Phoenix New Times*, 29 March 1989).

7 See *Encyclopedia of Company Histories: Amerco* (answers.com, 2007).

8 See Tom Fitzpatrick, Trial and terror (*Phoenix New Times*, 15 December 1994).

9 The primary sources for this case study were Sara G Forden, *The House of Gucci: A sensational story of murder, madness, glamour, and greed*

(Perennial, New York, 2000) and Gerald McKnight, *Gucci: A house divided* (Sidgwick & Jackson, London, 1987). Other sources were History of the Gucci house (Wikipedia, 2007, available from: http://en.wikipedia.com/Gucci); B Catry and A Buff, *Le gouvernement de l'entreprise familiale* (Publi-Union, Geneva, 1996).

10 Empirical evidence for this can be seen in Paul R Amato and Alan Booth, The legacy of parents' marital discord: consequences for children's marital quality (*Journal of Personality and Social Psychology*, **81**, pp 627–38).

CHAPTER 9: THE LESSONS – THE PRICE OF WAR AND THE PRIZE OF PEACE

1 The work on executive derailment analyses this duality. See Brittain and Van Velsor (op cit); also Robert Hogan, Robert Raskin and Dan Fazzini, The dark side of charisma, pp 343–54 in Kenneth E Clark and Mirriam B Clark (eds), *Measures of Leadership* (Center for Creative Leadership, Greensboro, NC, 1990).

2 See Quentin Skinner, *Machiavelli: A very short introduction* (Oxford University Press, Oxford, 2000).

3 Problems of letting go, and consequences of the different modes of departure of CEOs, are examined in Jeffery Sonnenfeld, *The Hero's Farewell* (op cit).

4 See Ivan Lansberg, *Succeeding Generations* (op cit); also John L Ward, *Perpetuating the Family Business* (op cit).

5 This feeling of unreality has been called 'the impostor syndrome'. See Mark R Leary, The impostor phenomenon: self-perceptions, reflective appraisals and interpersonal strategies (*Journal of Personality*, **68**, pp 725–56); also Manfred F R Kets de Vries, The impostor syndrome: developmental and societal issues (*Human Relations* **43**, 1990, pp 667–86).

6 See Taguiri and Davis (op cit). The Freudian perspective pits fathers and sons against each other as rivals: see Luigi Zoga, *The Father* (Brunner-Routledge, 2001). A more identity-based understanding of the conflict is to see it in terms of trying to defend the integrity of one's self-concept and self esteem. See Mark R Leary, *The Curse of the Self* (Oxford University Press, Oxford, 2004).

7 In recent research we have found what we call 'intergenerational authority', ie top-down controlling parenting, to be the strongest negative predictor of favourableness of family climate (cohesive, adaptive and open). See Åsa Björnberg and Nigel Nicholson, The Family Climate

Scales: development of a new measure for use in family business research (*Family Business Review*, op cit).

8   See Sharon M Danes and Patricia M Olson, Women's role involvement in family businesses, business tensions, and business success (*Family Business Review*, **16**, 2003, pp 53–68).

9   See James E Hughes, *Family Wealth: Keeping it in the family* (Bloomberg Press, South Burlington, VT, 2004).

10 See L Ross and Anderson, Shortcomings in the attribution process: on the origins and maintenance of erroneous social assessments, pp 129–52 in D Kahneman, P Slovic and A Tversky, (eds), *Judgment under Uncertainty: Heuristics and biases* (Cambridge University Press, Cambridge UK, 1982).

11 See Earl R Gardner and Richard C W Hall, The professional stress syndrome (*Psychosomatics*, **22**, 1981, pp 672–80).

12 See J Keith Murnighan, *The Dynamics of Bargaining Games* (Prentice-Hall, New York, 1991).

13 See Ronald Fisher, *The Social Psychology of Intergroup and International Conflict* (Springer-Verlag, London, 1990).

14 See Thomas C Dandridge, Entrepreneurial family business: problems of different 'wealth' and different 'currencies', in P Poutziouris (ed), *Tradition or Entrepreneurship in the New Economy* (Academic Research Forum Proceedings of the 11th Annual World Conference of the Family Business Network, London, 2000); Johan Lambrecht, Multigenerational transition in family businesses: a new explanatory model (*Family Business Review*, **18**, 2004, pp 267–82).

15 See Edgar H Schein, *Organizational Culture and Leadership: A dynamic view* (Jossey-Bass, Chichester, 1988).

16 Nigel Nicholson, How to motivate your problem people (*Harvard Business Review*, op cit).

17 See William L Ury, Jeanne M Brett and Stephen B. Goldberg, *Getting Disputes Resolved* (Jossey-Bass, Chichester, 1988).

18 The concept of integrative versus distributive (zero-sum) bargaining was classically analysed by Richard E Walton and Robert B McKersie in *A Behavioral Theory of Labor Negotiations* (McGraw Hill, New York, 1965).

19 See Gersick *et al*, *Generation to Generation* (op cit); and for a more general review of organizational transitions, Howard Aldrich, *Organizations Evolving* (Sage, Thousand Oaks, Calif, 1999).

20 See Karen A Jehn, A quantitative analysis of conflict types and dimensions in organizational groups (*Administrative Science Quarterly*, **42**, 1997, pp 530–58); and for these ideas applied to family business, F W Kellermanns and K A Eddleston, Feuding families: when conflict does a

family firm good (*Entrepreneurship Theory and Practice*, **29**, 2004, pp 209–28).

21 See Nigel Nicholson and Åsa Björnberg, Familiness: fatal flaw or inimitable advantage? (op cit), and Nigel Nicholson, Evolutionary psychology and family business: a new synthesis for theory, research and practice (*Family Business Review*, op cit).

Index